Business for Intermediate GNVQ

John Gardner

STANLEY
THORNES

First published in 1995 by:
Stanley Thornes (Publishers) Ltd
Ellenborough House
Wellington Street
CHELTENHAM
GL50 1YD
United Kingdom

Reprinted 1995

A catalogue record for this book is available from the British Library.
ISBN 0 7487 1883 4

Typeset by Columns Design and Production Services Ltd, Reading, UK
Printed and bound in Great Britain at The Bath Press, Avon

Contents

Unit 2 People in business organisations

Unit 3 Consumers and customers

Unit 4 Financial and administrative support

Core skills

Introduction

The aim of this book is to enable you to produce a complete portfolio of evidence to cover all the mandatory units of the Intermediate Business GNVQ. Each unit, element, and performance criterion set against the range is covered both in the text and in the work which you need to do to compile a portfolio. Your work is more important than this text but this text should help you to do better.

Each piece of work should be examined by an assessor, corrected and then carefully filed by you. You should mark on it which unit performance criteria it covers and keep a separate record of the skills which you have achieved.

I do hope that you enjoy reading this book and find it helpful. I also hope that you will successfully complete the work which is proposed in each chapter and that before long you will have compiled your assessed portfolio of evidence and be awarded your Intermediate Business GNVQ.

As a user you can probably think of ways in which this book can be improved. I should be very pleased to hear from you and will reply quickly and take your comments seriously. Please write to me care of Sarah Wilman, Stanley Thornes Publishers Ltd, Ellenborough House, Wellington Street, Cheltenham, GL50 1YD.

A letter to me, and my reply, could be useful for your evidence file.

What is GNVQ Intermediate Business?

GNVQ Intermediate Business consists of four mandatory units:
• Unit 1 – Business organisations and employment
• Unit 2 – People in business organisations
• Unit 3 – Consumers and customers
• Unit 4 – Financial and administrative support.

The elements of each of these units are specified at the start of each chapter. The book is arranged so that you can start almost anywhere in it and work forwards or backwards from your chosen starting point. If you are on a roll-on-roll-off course this will be particularly helpful. If you need additional material for a portfolio then this book will provide all the opportunities required.

There are also four option units available of which you must do two. The optional units vary depending on which Examining Board you are using.

BTEC Intermediate Optional Units
• Unit 5 – Consumer protection
• Unit 6 – Recording financial information
• Unit 7 – Individuals and the organisation
• Unit 8 – Operating administrative systems

RSA Intermediate Optional Units
- Unit 5 – Business Communication
- Unit 6 – Promotion and Sales
- Unit 7 – Business in the European Union
- Unit 8 – Enterprise Activities

City and Guilds Intermediate Optional Units
- Unit 5 – Business use of the Media
- Unit 6 – Communication within a Business
- Unit 7 – Business and the Environment
- Unit 8 – Organising a Business Venture

All the units consist of a number of elements each of which is subdivided into performance criteria. Each element is set against a range which provides the context.

In addition there is a set of core skills units:
- Mandatory core skills units:
  Communication
  Application of number
  Information technology
- Additional core skills units:
  Personal skills – Working with others
  Personal skills – Improving own learning and performance
- A further core skill unit:
  Problem solving.

Success in mandatory skills is essential in order to gain the GNVQ.

Most of the skills are derived from the work in each of the chapters, but must be recorded separately and show development. In addition to the derived skills there are some opportunities for practising skills given in the Unit tests section at the back of the book. These tests will ensure that your portfolio is complete in every respect.

In each chapter the element specification precedes the information and tasks so that you are able to relate directly the chapter content to what you produce and to the specification in order to build a complete portfolio of evidence of competence and knowledge.

'Please do this' activities and assignments

The 'Please do this' activities and the assignments are directly related to the performance criteria by the numbers quoted. For example, Please do this 1 is directly related to Unit 1: Element 1.2, by the number 1.1.2 which appears to the right of the heading.

All your work should be carefully filed and indexed in order to prove to the assessors and verifiers that you have covered the programme requirements.

Review questions

The review questions have not been field tested and some may be less success-ful than others at determining knowledge. However, they closely resemble test questions currently in use and together with material published by BTEC, CGLI, NCVQ and RSA may be helpful for developing the techniques of answering questions.

To answer some of the questions you may have to do some additional research. Knowing where to go for the required information is one of the skills you will have to develop. Answers are provided at the back of the book.

The case studies

This book is full of case studies about business. All of them concern people I know, although the names have been changed about in some cases. For instance, Peter Goff and Henry Goodman are distinguished members of a nationally respected organisation and, as far as I know, have had no connection with British Rail or the building trade. All the case studies are factually correct so that the evidence is authentic.

I believe that people can recall a story better than a list of 'facts'. I also believe that it is a high-level skill to derive general principles from a single example. The case studies are provided so that you can do just that. Whenever you read about John Stead, for example, the story illustrates a number of things which are relevant to the element with which the chapter is concerned. In one case, I have described John at his market stall in conversation with a customer in order to show all the basic elements of customer services, and I have then analysed the event for you. More usually you will have to read a case study more than once and write notes on what is going on to provide the evidence that you have derived – this you can apply to other situations. The story enables you to derive a formula which you can also apply to all sorts of situations.

I hope the case studies, and John Stead's business progression, are interesting, realistic, clearly illustrative of points in the chapter and the results fairly memorable.

Glossary

At the end of the book is a short glossary of some main terms. In addition to this glossary a few terms relating to information technology are explained in Chapter 15. You will also find that some key terms have been defined within the text throughout the book.

How to get a pass, a merit or a distinction

Getting a pass

Only one grade is given when you have completed your GNVQ. This covers all the units. Individual units are not given a grade. Sometimes teachers will indicate how you are progressing, but if this is done by giving a number which looks as if it might be out of ten, a percentage, or a letter grade, or even a verbal comment like pass, merit or distinction, these cannot automatically be accumulated so that you can firmly predict a final overall grade. It is intended that anyone who covers all the performance criteria set against the range in the mandatory units and the skills units will gain a pass.

Getting a merit

The overall grading of your GNVQ is based on your powers to:
- plan your work,
- seek information,
- decide whether it is reliable and sufficient for your purposes,
- put it together in a meaningful and constructive way, and
- evaluate what you have done.

You should be able to forward plan your activities for a series of tasks. The end of chapter assignments will give you plenty of opportunity for this.

There is likely to be a time schedule for each task so that your planning should indicate what you intend to do first and how much time you think you need to give to each task. This planning is a job which you should be doing on your own, though the word 'independently' which is used in the official publications, does not, apparently, mean that you should not ask for help or guidance if you are stuck. However, getting help should not be a regular feature of your activities if you wish to gain a merit.

Of course, once you have established your plan you must try to make it work. If it is perfect, then you are a lot cleverer than most people! In writing this book I have been backwards and forwards with it from the original plan, carefully monitoring how the plan was going and checking how I was getting on and whether the text could be improved. You must do the same. As you proceed with your work, check how your original plan is going and make sure that you write amendments to the plan as you go along – these are valuable evidence.

You should, in any case, consult your teacher when you adjust your plan. If you have become stuck because of a lack of information again consult your teacher.

You therefore have to identify what information you need and whether it is relevant and accurate. In addition, you must put the information together in a logical and sensible way to cover each of the tasks you are required to do, so that you can demonstrate that you have synthesised knowledge and skills with understanding. This is to be supported by use of the technical language appropriate to business. You would not refer to 'an electronic machine which stores information input from a keyboard and which contains editing devices'; you would just say, 'word-processor'.

Finally, you will need to evaluate what you have done, both in terms of what you have achieved compared with the original intention and how you have achieved it. Whilst working out the 'how' you no doubt considered alternatives. You should say what these were and why you rejected them.

If you successfully manage these strategies in at least a third of your portfolio, as well as completing the units successfully, you should gain a merit.

Getting a distinction

Probably not a lot of distinctions will be awarded, but you should try for one. The principal difference between the merit and the distinction is that the planning stage should be for a set of tasks with built-in complexity. The revisions to the plan should be made independently. (For a definition of 'independently' see 'Getting a merit', above). As far as the information is concerned, it is the complexity of the activities with which it is associated which determines whether you get your distinction – and of course whether you can correctly identify the information which is required and reliably sourced.

To understand what this is all about; take an example. Planning an itinerary from Leeds to London by train would require little more than consulting a timetable or, if journeying onwards, a British Rail information desk. However, organising a rail journey to Leningrad with stops on the way, involving hotel bookings, changing money in different countries, attending meetings with business people during the trip and returning with samples of products by plane at a given time via Rome, would be another matter.

You should be able to sort out information and justify the reasons for your selection. When in doubt, or even when you are not, write down what you have done for your assessor's benefit.

The criteria for establishing the quality of your work referred to in 'Getting a merit' are the same for a distinction, apart from the complexity of the tasks and the added requirement that you should demonstrate a fluent command of the technical language of business.

In evaluating your work you should perform the same level of judgements as for a merit but should be able to provide detailed accounts of the advantages and disadvantages of your approach. You should also indicate how the way you approached and carried out your work might have been improved. This is being clever after the event, but that is generally how we learn to get better at what we are doing.

Do not forget that although rather more than a third of your portfolio must give evidence of your information gathering and utilisation, and your ability to explain why you have done what you have done, the whole of your portfolio must indicate increasing knowledge and skills in both depth and breadth. You can do it. Go to it!

How to write an assignment

Formulate a plan

Look at the text carefully and see exactly what is required. Examine and define any words about which you are unsure. Lay out a plan of how you are going to approach the assignment. This should consider:
* where and from whom or what you are going to collect the information you require,
* how you propose to put it together, and
* how you propose to present it.

You can include the names of other people you intend to consult (or their official positions).

Discuss your plan

Discuss your plan with your assessor indicating why you have decided to proceed in the way that you are proposing. If your assessor points out difficulties and makes suggestions which would improve the presentation take careful notice. If you incorporate the suggestions in your presentation, remember to give credit where it is due.

Collect the information

Sources
Make sure that each source is carefully noted. If it is a book, lay out the references like this:

Smith, J. (The author's name) *European Trade in the 21st Century* (title of the book), Walsingham Press (name of the publisher), 1994 (date of publication) pages 273–4.

You may add the International Standard Book Number (ISBN) which, if it is published in the UK, will start with a 0 followed by a unique set of numbers (e.g. 0 579 12345) and a terminal letter (e.g. X), so giving 0 579 12345 X.

If the source is an article in a magazine the layout is:

Smith, J. 'European Trade in the 21st Century', in the *Economic Review* (name of the magazine), 21 December 1994 (date of publication), Vol. XXIII No. 12 (issue number), pages 27–39.

Brainstorming
If there is a problem which may be solved more easily by more than one person, try brainstorming. For example, someone in the group describes the problem and then asks for as many contributions as possible. The members of the group do not have to look for conventional answers to the problem. Each answer should be written on a blackboard, or on a large sheet of paper. At the end of ten or 15 minutes the ideas should be carefully examined. Where there are overlaps they may be grouped together. The group considers each idea in terms of it being:

- reasonable
- possible, or
- unlikely.

Examine how the 'possible' ideas will fit in closely with the problem, and how the others, however far fetched they might be, may well support the apparently most relevant ideas, and how adaptations and combinations will work towards a novel and constructive solution.

Interviewing
While brainstorming involves a number of people in one place, interviewing is likely to involve dealing with one person at a time in a variety of places. The important first step is to consider exactly what you want to know and write it down in as few words as possible. Then try the questions on a few people who are not going to be involved, to see if what they say in response makes it apparent if your questions work or not. Avoid questions which require only 'yes' or 'no' answers unless you are surveying people's opinions or activities. Supplement the original question if the first answer given to you is not complete or you wish to have additional information. Write down the answers in note form. When you have finished the interview, say so and thank the person you have been interviewing for his or her time and help.

The library
Make use of your school, college or public library. The staff are not obliged to (and should not) do your research for you. However, their advice is often very valuable and should be treated with respect.

Work experience
Your work experience is a valuable source of information, but remember that businesses of whatever sort are very much in competition with one another and need to keep a lot of information confidential. Do ask questions and make observations, but do respect their confidentiality.

Surveys
Survey procedures are covered in the core skills Chapter 14.

Evaluate the evidence

If you are enquiring about how to sell newspapers, you would go to a newsagents or a current street newspaper seller. There is little point in asking someone who was doing the job 20 years ago unless you are interested in history. Your evaluation of a person's evidence referring to the 1970s might well be that is not appropriate for inclusion it in your presentation. Select your evidence carefully and throw away or keep the rest for another time.

Presentation

Use a computer to word process your work, and use the database and spreadsheet facilities where necessary. Arrange the presentation in headlined sections, use appendices where appropriate, and do not forget the bibliography at the end of the document where credit can be given where it is due.

Do not forget that you may have to deliver your presentation orally and perhaps you might even like to make audio or video tapes, slides or overhead projector transparencies.

John Gardner

1 Explain the purposes and types of business organisations

Performance criteria
1. Describe **developments** in **industrial sectors**;
2. Explain the **purposes** of **business organisations**;
3. Explain the **differences** between different **types of business ownership**;
4. Explain the **operation** of one business organisation.

Range
- **Developments:** recent past, present, likely future; growth of the sector, decrease of the sector; typical activities in the sector.
- **Industrial sectors:** primary, secondary, tertiary.
- **Purposes:** profit, market share, customer service, public service, charitable.
- **Business organisations:** private sector, public sector; large, medium, small.
- **Differences:** type of liability (limited, unlimited), use of profit (owners, shareholders, government).
- **Types of business ownership:** sole trader, partnership, private limited company (Ltd.), public limited company (plc), franchise, co-operative, state-owned.
- **Operation:** location; product (goods, services); links with other businesses; purpose; type of ownership.

Please do this 1 ————————————————————————1.1.2

1. Write down reasons why you think businesses are started. (By all means discuss with other people what they think the reasons are.)

2. When you have a number of reasons, try putting them in an order of importance.

3. Will the order be the same for everyone? Explain your answer to this question.

The market trader – introducing John Stead

Holding four tins of Whiskas Prime Cuts, John Stead stands at the back of his stall in Shipton High Street's Wednesday market. He calls out to the passing people that he has a special bargain in high-quality cat food. He intends to give his customers a good deal.

He will make enough to cover his costs and the (very) small profit on each tin contributes to his living expenses. His simple business, conducted on his own,

John Stead at his stall

performs the two essential functions for success in a continuing business:
- making a profit, and
- providing goods or services.

John actually enjoys the job with its contact with fellow market traders and the public, but that is not a bonus available to everyone. Job satisfaction and enjoyment may be affected by an organisation's size and an individual's colleagues.

Please do this 2 ───────────────────────────────────── 1.1.2

Discuss with friends or family what you think businesses do and make a list of these activities and functions, several of which may not appear to be as obvious as others.

Government businesses

Whilst social services is usually part of the local authority, there are central government activities which are affected in exactly the same way. The National Health Service (NHS) finds itself in the same position as the Social Services Department of a local authority. Its employees are affected in the same way. If the service is poor or the budget is cut then a proportion of the employees may well become redundant. The NHS does not make a profit. However, it is required by Parliament to provide certain services and is answerable, through an elaborate hierarchy of managers, to the Secretary of State for Health who in turn answers to Parliament for the good services and any deficiencies.

Government departments are responsible for vast businesses, like the NHS (Department of Health) or Job Centres (Department of Employment), whilst the public corporations, like the Post Office, are all government owned and controlled.

At the start of 1995 central government owns a number of enterprises which are defined as *nationalised industries*. Among these are the railways (shortly to be privatised) and the post office. The government has sold off a large number of state-owned industries, partly in the interests of trying to make them more efficient through competition and partly to use the capital raised to reduce the rate of income tax. Large-scale industries often acquire excessive numbers of employees, hardly noticed owing to other economies of scale or a position akin to a monopoly. *Privatisation*, however, has led to substantial reductions in employment, even in the state monopolies and particularly in the run up to privatisation. Originally, nationalisation was seen as a way of safeguarding essential services and returning the profits made by any state-owned enterprise to the taxpayer.

The public service worker

Jane Cater works for the Kirkdale Metropolitan Borough Council Social Services Department as a care assistant in an old people's home in Greenvale outside Huddersfax. Although subject to all the usual pressures of market force economics the Social Services Department has a variety of sources of funding. These include local authority taxes, central government grants and fees paid for some of the services it provides.

Jane has a job description which lists the tasks she is paid to perform, but like most workers and professionals she provides the old people with much more than the minimum level of care. She is not paid any more for her extra care and service, which is different from John's situation. His care for, and interest in, his customers and their pets, may well be part of the reason for his success and may be rewarded with extra sales and thus increased profits. Therefore, one of the reasons for starting a business is to help other people. Jane is not dependent upon the Social Services Department making a profit, though she may lose her job if the department overspends or has its budget cut. To survive, the department has to provide an increasing range of quality services at an ever-decreasing cost.

Please do this 3 ————————————————————————————— 1.1.1

Peter Goff, like other members of his family, has worked as a shunter with British Rail for 30 years. He is now 50 and is likely to be made redundant along with his brother and brother-in-law in the run up to privatisation. He is currently paid £160 a week gross, of which the government takes £18 in National

Insurance contributions and £22 in income tax. When he becomes unemployed the government will credit his National Insurance contributions and pay him £40 to live on each week. Instead of making an 'income' of £40 a week from Peter (plus VAT on most of his purchases), the government will keep him idle at a cost of £58 per week plus the loss of VAT, say another £12 a week.

1. Provide Peter with an explanation of why it is necessary for him to lose his job.

2. Work out the figures for a miner on £275 a week gross with £47 income tax.

Privatisation

The provision of essential services was, for two centuries, thought to be a matter for central government intervention. However, in the last decade this has been less and less the case, even to the extent that a number of the activities of the police and the prison service have been privatised. Normally, government provided or controlled service or production organisations have been very large in terms of resources employed, turnover and numbers of employees. Many of them have been *monopolies*, a situation which often provokes a 'take it or leave it' attitude.

A charity

Jane Cater's friend, Alys Woodward, works four days a week in the local Oxfam shop. Whilst Oxfam has substantial costs, its sole purpose is charitable and it depends heavily on keeping all its costs low. Alys is not paid for her work and considers that what she does is her contribution to Oxfam's charitable enterprises throughout the world.

Oxfam exists wholly to provide goods, services and essential skills to those who need them – free of charge. Through its shops it sells goods from the Third World, thus providing employment in locations where there are few opportunities. Its major source of income is from charitable donations made by individuals and organisations.

Like other charities, Oxfam cannot live beyond its means, so cost reduction is considered to be the method by which contributions can be most usefully channelled into needy areas.

Thus Oxfam exists to help other people, but like Greenpeace it also puts over some very clear messages. Some of them are about the environment, but many of them are more closely associated with helping people to survive.

Although Alys is not paid a salary, the shop manager is paid – as are many relief workers carrying out the charity's work throughout the world. Then there are the administrators and managers who look after the shops, deal with fund raising and sponsorships, projects abroad, accounting and so on – much in the same way as any other business. At the policy making and planning level there are directors of major parts of the organisation, led by a chief executive. Monitoring and overall control is exercised by a board of trustees who are often eminent people, involved part-time and seldom paid.

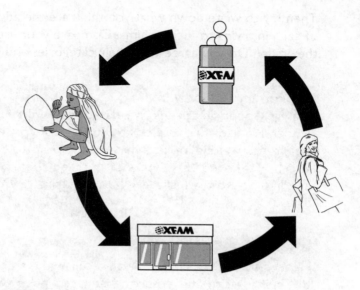

From worker to consumer

Please do this 4 ——————————————————————————————————————1.1.3

There are numerous very large national charities. However, in your neighbour-hood there will be some local charities. Select one of these and do the following.

a Find out what the charity's objectives are and how it sets about achieving them.

b Does it have any paid staff?

c Who are the trustees?

d Does it have any assets in the form of buildings or equipment?

e Where does the funding come from?

f Could the charity be run in a more businesslike way? If so, how can it be improved?

Lobbying

Another reason for starting a business is to put forward a particular cause. Political parties are businesses and they have very powerful causes to promote.

Please do this 5 ——————————————————————————————————————1.1.1, 1.1.3

Take a sheet of A4 paper. Make a list of the types of business on the left-hand side of the page, leaving a couple of lines between each type. Start with 'sole trader' and finish with 'multi-national'. Aim to insert at least four other types. To the right of each type give two examples that can be identified in your area.

Then try to write down what you think are the advantages and disadvantages of each in trying to fulfil its aims. Compare your list with others' and see how they differ. Do you agree with their categories and examples?

A primary industry

Henry Goodman spends five days a week driving a huge Volvo articulated loader. He uses this to pick up 3 tonnes of crushed sandstone at a time and tips it into waiting lorries which transport it to building sites. The quarry in which Henry works is in what is called the 'extractive industry grouping' and like all those which deal with acquiring raw materials is a *primary sector industry*.

A secondary industry

Henry's friend, Gurdip Dhaliwal, receives the truck loads of crushed stone at the building site and ensures that it is tipped where it is needed. He is a builder and works in what is described as a *secondary sector industry*; that is one which makes use of raw materials to create new artefacts.

Tertiary industries

Davinda Patel is an estate agent. Her brother is a solicitor, his wife is a teacher, his nephew sells cars. They all work in *tertiary sector industries* selling goods which someone else has made, or providing services in respect of goods or services.

Please do this 6 ————————————————————— 1.1.1, 1.1.3

For each of the three industrial sectors described above, make a list of three or four businesses in your area or region. Describe what goods and/or services each provides and what type of business it is in terms of sole trader to multi-national. (You may not be able to find examples of every type of business.)

High street chain stores

Walking down the road by the market, John looks at the buildings. He sees Boots the Chemist, Marks and Spencer, Woolworths, Dixons, Next, C&A – all of them present in most towns. Each shop is part of a chain and belongs to a major company whose shares are quoted on the Stock Exchange. The companies have plc after their names. This stands for *public limited company* and means that shares are owned by members of the public.

Other companies, however, are smaller, or have found a way to raise capital which does not involve dealings on the Stock Exchange. These are *private limited companies* and have 'Ltd' (short for Limited) in their titles. 'Limited' refers to the liability of the owners of the company to be responsible for its debts in relation to any legal or other action taken against it.

In John's case, if he drops a case of cat food on a customer's foot he is wholly responsible for the damages which may be demanded, although he is sensible enough to have public liability insurance. In the case of a limited company, if the company cannot pay its way the shareholders are individually liable only to the extent of their individual share holdings. Likewise, their individual benefits (what they get out of the company) are apportioned in the same way.

The partnership

The multi-nationals are at the opposite end of the business spectrum from John. The management of his business is entirely in his own hands. He has all the responsibility, but all the profits and losses are his. If he is not careful, all his existing possessions can be used to defray costs and expenses if he fails to make a profit or pay his creditors. This can leave him without a home if things go seriously wrong.

Fortunately, this is not the case and John prospers. After a while he realises that he is unable to expand his business without help. He considers hiring an assistant, but soon realises that until the business has developed he is likely to work at a loss if he has to pay wages, employer's National Insurance contributions and possibly other benefits such as sick pay. What he needs is someone like himself who combines integrity with the ability to do a lot of hard work.

Over a cup of coffee with a friend John realises that he knows the ideal person. In the past, he had worked with her for years, knows she is honest and hard working, and possesses a good deal of flair for making personal contacts.

John and Sonia Shah talk about the possibilities and decide to go into a *partnership*. John knows that his local veterinary surgeon and the architect who designed the nearby block of flats work in partnerships. It is often the case that professionals providing highly technical services work in this way. However, the corner shop is also run as a partnership between the married couple who own the shop and live over it.

John and Sonia decide to approach John's friendly solicitor to draw up a *partnership agreement*. Sonia agrees to put some money into the business and to run the new market trading stalls in Rossington and Blackley. She can draw on John's expertise and manufacturer contacts whilst being a handy back-up if John falls ill, wants to take a holiday or needs to visit his suppliers.

Whilst a partnership run by two or more people who respect and like one another may have a lot going for it, it also has some disadvantages:
- The partners have total liability for all losses and, unless the agreement says otherwise, are liable in equal amounts.
- It is almost as difficult for a partnership to raise capital as it is for a sole trader.
- Despite any mutual respect and liking, partners may just fall out. Typical areas for dispute are:
  - the allocation and extent of profits,
  - the amount of work put in by each partner, and
  - the beginnings of bureaucracy, in so far as every business decision has to be agreed by all the partners.

John and Sonia do not fall out and both partners prosper. Eventually, John wants to move into a new area of work and the partnership is amicably dissolved. Sonia carries on as a sole trader with a new employee, James Purkiss, who is noted for his honesty rather than for any flair in making money.

Getting bigger and getting on

There may be a few businesses who are completely ruthless and money grabbing but, in general, a very high standard of customer care and service will count a lot towards success and survival. Businesses cannot afford to ignore their customers, but some look after them better than others.

John bought a good car. However something went wrong with it within a month so he returned to the dealer where he bought the car. He stood in a queue at the reception desk behind people paying their bills for car services and eventually reached the receptionist. She phoned for the service foreman and asked John to take a seat. Minutes ticked by towards closing time. The foreman eventually arrived and asked John what his trouble was. John told him. 'Oh dear, that's the third one this week. Sorry, can't do anything about it tonight. Book it in for tomorrow morning.' And he was off, back into the barricaded workshop into which no customer could ever penetrate.

The opposite of a high standard of customer care and service

Next time John bought a car from another dealer, having first carefully tested the service department's policy. As a result of the first dealer's careless customer care the second dealer increased its market share.

Please do this 7 ———————————————————————————— 1.1.4

In Ramstown 1500 new cars were bought last year. One-third were bought from dealers outside the town; the remaining two-thirds were bought from the four dealers in town. A supplied 230, B 175, C 225 and the remainder came from dealer D. This year things were better for the car dealers and 1800 cars were bought. Again one-third were bought from outside the town. The remaining 1200 cars were apportioned as follows: A supplied 280, B 250, D 400 whilst the remainder were supplied by C.

Dealer D congratulated her sales force on an increase in sales of cars, but a closer look reveals that whilst she still sold more cars than any of the other three, she had lost part of her market share.

1. Calculate the market share, in terms of percentages, of each of the four Ramstown dealers for this year and last. (Ignore the out of town purchases.)

2. Point out who has had the biggest increase in market share. The increase in market share may be associated with a trend in favour of the dealer who has increased it the most. This could be because the product:
   • is at the leading edge of technology,
   • is recognised for its value for money, or
   • the after-sales service is considered to be really excellent.

Whatever the reason, and it may be a combination of any or all of these factors, the business looks as if it will develop, and the market could change significantly.

The percentage increase in sales between this year and last year is maintained for each of the dealers and 1600 cars are sold between them.

3. Add another line to your market share and number of sales data and calculate:

   a which is now the biggest dealer

   b the market shares of each of the dealers

   c the number of cars sold.

Use graphical means, preferably computer generated, to make your conclusions clearer.

A retail shop

Meanwhile, John has searched his home town for somebody who will sell him an electric drill, since he has to engage in some urgent DIY. Ramstown does not possess an ironmonger/hardware shop. What it does have is a recently defunct Mexican restaurant close to the busiest part of the shopping centre with extensive free parking only 30 metres away. The nearest large store providing for DIY-inclined people is the B&Q at Accrington, 18 miles away. John has an idea – he will set up a DIY shop in the town.

B&Q, Wickes, Texas, Smith's Do-it-all and Sainsbury's Homebase all seem to exist in places with a population of at least 50,000 and easy access to double that number or more. The overheads of these stores are high. John expects to keep his low whilst giving a personal service. He has a number of advantages:

- he is well known in the town for his absolute integrity;
- he is a chartered engineer with a great many practical skills and is very computer literate;
- he is a sensible, agreeable person with good inter-personal skills.

But this is a gamble.

Setting up the store

John has decided to use part of the money he got when the partnership with Sonia was dissolved to buy stock and convert the restaurant to a shop. He needs to raise more money than he is willing to risk himself so a visit to the bank, equipped with his business plan is a top priority. He also needs to approach the local authority, in this case Ramstown District Council, for planning permission to change the use of the premises from a restaurant to a hardware shop. He will have to think carefully about getting a government Business Start-up Grant to provide him with some much needed basic income during the initial stages of his venture. Finally, he will have to advertise his shop in the local paper to attract customers

Whatever the large retailers offer, John will have to offer too. He does have the great asset of being personally interested in his customers, not something that any superstore can offer. He will not only be a retail outlet but a place where you can reasonably expect to get advice and even help when you need it.

John also needs to take on an assistant because running a shop takes a lot time and he needs to remain open throughout the lunch break. Opening at 8.30 a.m. has its advantages as you can catch people on their way to work. Late night shopping is also a profitable period.

John decides that he needs to have an assistant from the moment he starts. Because he has a close link with the local college he decides that he will get someone from a GNVQ business course who can help by relating John's problems to what is being learned at college.

Needs and wants

You have already learned that businesses come into existence in order to make a profit from the provision of goods and/or services. However, that is not the end of it. The goods and services which are provided must be what people need or want. It is important to know the difference between needs and wants. *Needs* are concerned with the essentials of existence: food, water, clothing, heat and light, shelter and security. *Wants* are concerned with things that people desire as possessions in order to enhance, as they see it, their standard of living. Thus a person who goes jogging could well manage with shorts, a vest and a pair of plimsolls. It is much more likely, however, that he or she will have stylish trainers, designer shorts and T-shirt. This is to do with 'image' and the gaining of satisfactions which are only remotely connected with the need to stay alive and well.

Franchising

The Body Shop is a company manufacturing cosmetics. These are retailed from shops which sell nothing other than Body Shop products but which are run by people who are not employed by Body Shop. Instead they pay Body Shop for the products and the right to use the name and the national advertising.

Please do this 8 ———————————————————————— 1.1.3

Franchising is becoming more and more popular.

1. Make a list of businesses which are franchises, indicating their products or services.

2. Think of the advantages and disadvantages of franchising for:

   a the *franchisor* (the company whose name is over the door, on the product and in the advertising and promotion),

   b the *franchisee* (the person who makes a payment for the right to franchise and runs the 'branch'),

   c the consumer.

The co-operative

There are two sorts of co-operative: the retail co-operative and the producer co-operative.

The retail co-operative

Originally, a number of people got together to buy in bulk and then distribute the purchases. Bulk buying was cheaper than small unit purchases because of the discounts offered for volume. The slight profit gave the group some working capital and a buffer against sales which were unsuccessful. In addition, it could distribute a 'dividend' to members. The original retail co-operative in the UK was the Rochdale Pioneers. It was anxious to provide a better service than the shops owned by the mill owners where excessive profits were made at the expense of the people employed.

Retail co-operatives have the following features:
• they are open to anyone;
• policy-making votes are one per person, not one per share;
• they are owned by the members;
• they are concerned not only with retailing but with social and educational issues;
• they may even put aside some of their income to further such issues.

The producer co-operative

The producer co-operative is owned by the 'workers'. These may range from smallholders to large-scale farmers. Usually their aim is to continue production and provide employment for the members. The classic co-operative of this sort was the Triumph Motorcycle Co-operative. The owners of Triumph could neither run the company nor find anyone to buy it. However the workforce clubbed together and ran it on an equal pay for all basis for some years after the collapse of the original company.

A Triumph motorcycle

Management buyouts

Management buyouts occur when senior managers of a company club together to buy the company from the shareholders. They are common in cases where subsidiary companies are sold off by the main company in a group. Often these subsidiaries have been neglected by the main company and flourish quite remarkably once they become independent. Whilst some management buyouts may be co-operatives, most rely on returning to a typical management/workers set-up as quickly as possible.

Please do this 9 ———————————————————————— 1.1.1, 1.1.3

Without being unduly intrusive, find out what members of your family or close friends have bought in the last week. Make a list, attributing purchases to the purchaser. Where were the purchases made? Why did the purchaser choose that place to buy from? Were there any not very obvious reasons for going to a particular place to buy a specific product? How many of the places which were bought from were local businesses, how many regional, and how many national? Which were the companies in each category? What did each sell? Can you draw any general conclusions about the reasons for going to particular sorts of businesses?

By now you will have gained quite a lot of information on a variety of businesses. We have categorised them according to their ownership, and according to where they belong in the primary, secondary and tertiary hierarchy.

The service industries

Manufacturing – making anything by hand, by machine or by growing – is the process of taking raw materials and creating something useable (even if not always saleable). The manufacturers have to get their products to market and that involves transport, usually by road or rail, but sometimes also by ship or aeroplane. There is often a storage period in warehouses. Wholesalers may buy large quantities of the product and split it up into smaller units. These are distributed to retailers so that they can be sold on to the public, or sometimes to other manufacturers or repairers. The *service industries* support the manufacturers.

We should consider the service industries in more detail. Think of what John has to do:

- He buys from a wholesaler and is himself a retailer.
- He advertises his shop in the local paper.
- He needs to have a secure base for his money and uses a bank and building society.
- He has various insurance policies (public liability, fire and theft, etc.) and a pension plan.
- He uses the telephone and the post to communicate with his suppliers and his customers.

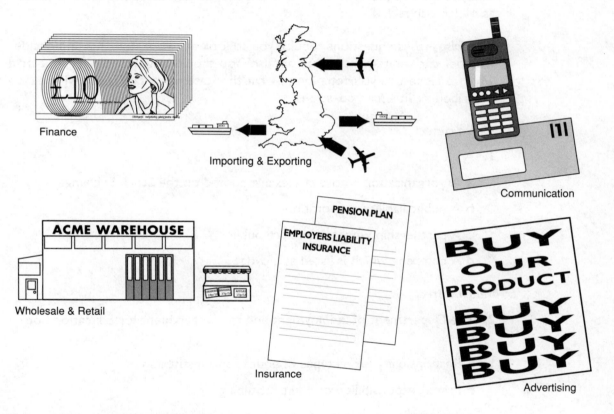

Finance

Importing & Exporting

Communication

Wholesale & Retail

Insurance

Advertising

Elements of the service industries

So, the service industries involve, for example:

- wholesaling and retailing
- advertising
- finance
- insurance
- communications.

In addition, there is importing and exporting which John is not big enough to get into as yet.

Please do this 10 ─────────────────────────────────────1.1.4

Take a local manufacturer.

1. Describe the product and its market.

2. Find out, and describe in detail, the role of each of the service industries in its sales (and production).

Review questions ─────────────────────────────────────

Match correct or Match incorrect – these questions require you to match the first statement against the one correct answer in a, b, c and d. This sort of question will be described as *Match correct*. In some questions you may find that you have to pick out the only incorrect answer; these will be referred to as *Match incorrect.*

True/false – these questions require you to look at two statements and decide whether each statement is true or false. You should ring the pair in a, b, c or d which is closest to your opinion of what the statements say. These will be described as *True/false* questions.

Match correct

1. A plc is:

   a An organisation whose shares are quoted on the Stock Exchange

   b A public liability corporation

   c A partnership whose affairs are public

   d A company which is listed at Lloyd's.

Match correct

2. The Department of Employment and the Department for Education both have:

   a Responsibility for all types of educational institution

   b Prime responsibility for adult retraining

   c An interest in vocational education

   d Responsibility for ensuring that qualified people who are unemployed are placed in jobs.

Match correct

3. Coal mining is:

   a A primary sector industry

   b A secondary sector industry

    c A tertiary sector industry

    d A service industry.

Match correct

4. A public sector organisation exists to:

    a Make a profit to ensure its continuation

    b Provide a service, not necessarily at a profit

    c Make a loss

    d Provide employment for workers in it.

Match correct

5. Which of the following works in the tertiary sector of industry:

    a A wig maker

    b A bus driver

    c A solicitor

    d A printer.

Match correct

6. Council tax:

    a Provides money for local services

    b Is collected by central government to be distributed to local authorities

    c Pays for opted-out schools

    d Is based solely on the value of property.

Match correct

7. A sole trader:

    a Does not employ anyone

    b Issues shares to finance his or her operations

    c Is always a retailer

    d Uses his or her own capital to run the business.

True/false

8. **i** A partnership relieves the sole trader of all responsibility for the operation of the business and can strengthen it by introducing new expertise and/or additional capital

    ii Partners in a business always agree about policy and procedures and enjoy happy working relationships

a i True ii True

b i True ii False

c i False ii False

d i False ii True.

Match correct

9. Transport is:

   a A primary sector industry

   b Always required for all products and services

   c A secondary sector industry

   d A tertiary sector industry.

True/false

10. **i** A limited company is called that because the number of investors is limited by being invited to invest

    ii The investors in a limited company have limited liability for its debts

    a i True ii True

    b i True ii False

    c i False ii False

    d i False ii True.

Assignment 1.1
Locating a new branch   1.1.4

Complete responses to the 'Please do this' activities, plus this assignment, should give you enough evidence to claim competence in this element. Do not forget to file all your paperwork carefully in your evidence portfolio. Be prepared to consult other people, and books and journals for help.

John is thinking of moving into the shopping centre of your town with a new branch of Steady DIY.

Your tasks

1. Look for a suitable street, drawing a map showing its location in relation to car parks, bus and rail station and major national retailers.

2. In the street you have selected, list 30 premises in the immediate area of

the premises you have chosen for the shop. Say what each is used for and give its number in the street, its name and whether it is a sole trader, partnership, limited company, plc, a co-operative, a franchise, a charity, central or local government owned, or a nationalised industry. (You may not find examples of all of these.)

3. Examine the passing trade and consider if a DIY shop would prosper in the place you have chosen. Say exactly what the criteria are that you have used to judge the premises that you have chosen and indicate the extent to which the premises satisfy the criteria. Draft a letter to John saying that you have seen suitable premises (they do not have to be empty at present, though it would help) and include as much of the information above as you feel is relevant. Also indicate the size of the town and the likely competition which he faces.

Skills achieved

The following are the skills which may be derived from this element. The extent to which each performance criterion is achieved within the range will depend upon the depth, breadth and success of your work.

Communication 2.1; 2.2; 2.3; 2.4

Information technology 2.2; 2.3; 2.5

Application of number 2.2; 2.3

Working with others 2.1; 2.2

Improving own learning and performance 2.2

Problem solving 2.1; 2.2

2 Examine business location, environment, markets and products

Performance criteria
1. Explain the **reasons for location** of businesses;
2. Explain **influences of the business environment** on business organisations;
3. Describe **markets** for businesses' products based on demand;
4. Identify **products provided** by business organisations;
5. Explain **activities undertaken by businesses** to improve their market position;
6. **Propose products** which would meet market demand.

Range
- **Reasons for location:** labour supply, natural resources, proximity of other businesses, access to customers, transport services, incentives (local government, national government, European Union).
- **Influences on the business environment:** competition, legal, environmental, public.
- **Markets:** domestic market, international market; value of total market, market share of businesses' products.
- **Demand:** needs, wants; wish to buy, ability to buy; created by consumers, created by customers.
- **Products:** consumable, durable; goods, services.
- **Provided:** to individual consumers, to governments, to other businesses.
- **Activities undertaken by businesses:** marketing research, design, production, marketing communications (advertising, promotion, sponsorship, sales literature), sales, after-sales service.
- **Propose products:** new, developed from existing products.

Location of industry

Toyota
The Toyota car manufacturers decided to set up a huge new factory on the A38 (which had recently been upgraded to a dual carriageway) south of Derby. In discussions reported in the local newspapers the Japanese management gave a number of reasons for choosing the UK, in particular the Midlands, to establish an EU located factory:
- There was a long tradition of high-quality engineering work in the area with many available skilled people suitable for employment in a high-technology industry.
- Both national and local government provided substantial financial incentives for building and the UK tax system favoured large-scale business.

- Labour costs were substantially lower than the other highly-industrialised nations in the EU and lower than all but one of the non-industrialised nations.
- There was a history of good industrial relations, i.e. relatively few strikes or disputes.
- The Nissan plant in Tyneside had been such a success that Toyota was hoping to follow the example.
- The Channel Tunnel would make access to European markets and materials providers easier.
- The motorway network and the improved A38 gave ready access to ports and other centres of population within the UK.
- The new works was within the drive to work area of over 400,000 people.
- The site itself was flat and close to sources of raw materials and bought-in parts.

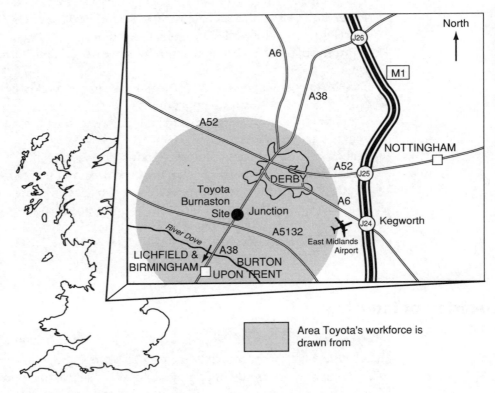

Toyota's UK location

Please do this 11 ──────────────────────────────── 1.2.1, 1.2.2

The list above is specific to Toyota but it contains many of the reasons why a business or an industry chooses a particular location. Using the list as a starting point, itemise the reasons why, and where, a multi-national in the oil industry would site its production works and its headquarters in the UK.

One company, diverse interests

Toyota is one of the largest international companies in the world. Its scale of operations is enormous; tens of thousands of people are employed world-wide. Its scope of operations, that is to say the range of places where it trades, is also world-wide. John has a small business with a very small scope – Shipton on market days. Which is the more successful business in terms of capital employed as an element to determine the ratio of profit? Which business owner derives more satisfaction from ownership? These are quite different, and probably rather irrelevant, considerations.

Toyota's decisions about entering the EU are on a major strategic scale. Most companies have a less dramatic impact on the area in which they choose to do business. Some appear to operate owing to a chance opportunity.

In the 1950s, as plain Mr Hanson, Lord Hanson owned a couple of coaches and two or three removal vans, in the then high-quality wool textile town of Huddersfield in West Yorkshire. In 30 years he became one of the richest and most influential business entrepreneurs in the world. He did not set up many businesses, and it is difficult to find any record of an original invention or product with his name on it, but he provided a remarkable service. He had a flair for taking over businesses which were in the doldrums and transforming them into highly-profitable enterprises before selling them on and buying yet bigger and more diverse companies. Lord Hanson did not depend upon any of the factors which Toyota thought contributed to, or were even essential for, success. Instead, he conducted his affairs from London, New York and other world financial centres because in each of these cities there was a heavy concentration of financial dealers and speculators, a stock exchange and many contacts who could provide new opportunities.

Motivation to relocate

Location may be governed by some wholly emotional factors. Lord Hanson started in Huddersfield because that is where his family lived. He moved out to move on, as his motivation was to get into big business. John centred his activities in Ramstown because that is where he lived and his motivation was only partly tied up with his business, which he saw as a means of ensuring a reasonable living and a way of enabling him to do those things in the community from which he derived most satisfaction.

A hundred years ago Mr Marks and Mr Spencer had a market stall in Leeds. Their business developed to be one of the most successful retailing organisations in the world.

In official terms a *monopoly* is defined as more than a 25 per cent share of any market. Marks and Spencer plc supplies underwear to one in three UK women. Its headquarters are in London although its shops are to be found in every reasonably sized town in the UK and abroad. A headquarters' location indicates the need to be close to financial, political and business power in the country, whilst the location of shops is an indication of where the directors think that they will be commercially successful.

Curiously, there is a non-business and distinctly emotional reason for the location of many Marks and Spencer's branches. In the 1920s, Marks and Spencer was in direct competition with Woolworths. Woolworths retailed very affordable ranges of goods costing 3d and 6d. What it sold was cheap, good value and sufficed. Marks and Spencer was somewhat further up-market and certainly did not try to fix an item's ceiling price in the same way as Woolworths attempted to do.

However, the Marks and Spencer's management publicly declared that it would have a store next to, or as close as possible to, every Woolworths store. There was a bit of jingoism in this decision because Woolworths was a US company and Marks and Spencer was proud of being British. There was also some very good judgement. The customers of the two shops were not that dissimilar and Woolworths did a great deal of expensive market research to establish where their shops should be located. Their competitors just followed an already well-tried recipe in a well-prepared market.

Retail locations

Retailers tend to have town centre locations. Some super- or hypermarkets are located on the outskirts of town within a short car journey to take advantage of cheap or free parking and one-stop shopping habits. Some village shops have retained their places because of the services they supply, for example Post Office branches in the local newsagents, butchers or chemists. One specialised retailer could not survive but *diversification* permits continued success.

Raw materials and location

Access to raw materials is very important to a manufacturing business. Brick and ceramic pipe works are situated close to large clay deposits so that they combine primary industry (clay extraction) with a secondary activity, brick manufacture. They need to be close to supplies of fuel –fairly easy if electricity is required but more difficult if gas, oil, coke or coal are needed.

Government planned location

After the Second World War a positive decision was made by the government and the London County Council (subsequently the Greater London Council) to move manufacturing companies out of London. This was intended to:
- reverse the rural to city migration which had been going on for 150 years,
- disperse industry to areas where there was unemployment,
- cut the size of the population using transport into and around London which was becoming overburdened with the daily tides of workers, and
- reduce pollution caused by industry in a very heavily populated area.

Substantial numbers were moved out to new towns, like Milton Keynes, and some new businesses were created and located specifically for them.

Please do this 12 ——————————————————————— 1.2.1, 1.2.2

Consider Milton Keynes and its businesses under the following headings:
- population and industries/businesses in 1945 and today,
- transport links at present,
- origins of the population,

- differences between Milton Keynes and, say, Buckingham in appearance, size, layout, facilities and diversity of business.

(If there is a new town closer to you which it would be more convenient to study, substitute this for Milton Keynes. In any event try to visit the new town which you are describing. If you live in a new town, make sure that you have another, and much older town in the region, to compare it with.)

Milton Keynes new town

Milton Keynes is a good example of the planners at work. Before it was established as a town, the North Buckinghamshire plain had a remarkably small population and relatively poor roads. Railway trains tended to travel through the area rather than stopping at stations. The area was almost entirely agricultural; now things have changed.

Milton Keynes' town symbol

The single product company

Some companies produce a single product – Rover cars, Triumph motorcycles, K shoes, Parker pens – but each may belong to a group with diverse interests. Triumph Motorcycles is the property of a successful builder, John Bloor, who wanted to produce UK motorcycles which were better than the Japanese or Italians, using a very well-known and respected industry name; and he succeeded.

Please do this 13 ———————————————————————— 1.2.1, 1.2.2

1. Explain why the following types of businesses locate where they do:
   - florists
   - solicitors
   - chemical works
   - boutique
   - estate agents
   - steel makers
   - car sales showroom
   - solid fuel merchants
   - builders merchants.

2. Give details of the names and products/services provided by three com-

panies in each type which you have been able to observe. (It is not sufficient to say, for instance, 'coal' in considering a mine.)

Diverse product companies

Other companies are well-known by one set of consumers for one product and by others for another. Yamaha is a major motorcycle manufacturer but pianos and electronic organs feature in its widely diversified range.

There are some businesses which go in for *vertical integration*, from raw materials to retail sales. A glass of cider may come from a company which owns:
- apple orchards,
- the transport used for moving apples to the works where the cider is made,
- a bottle manufacturer whose products are used in bottling,
- the transport to move the bottled cider to distributors, and
- the maintenance works where machinery and transport are looked after.

Going one stage further, many brewers also own large numbers of retail outlets (pubs).

Other businesses go in for *horizontal integration* and buy up their competitors, often shutting them down in the process.

Some businesses are not in the business they think they are. Before the Second World War it dawned on the management of the Cunard shipping line that it was not in the steam ship business, despite owning the Queen Mary, the Queen Elizabeth and many other sea going palaces, but in the hotel business.

Please do this 14 ── 1.2.4

1. Compare Boots the Chemist with the local chemist's shop.

 a How big is Boots in financial terms?

 b Who are its competitors?

 c What are its products.

2. Boots is obviously a nationwide organisation.

 a How many shops does it own?

 b Where is its headquarters?

 c What functions are performed by headquarters?

To make a comparison you will need to know what Boots' turnover was last year, how much profit it made and how much capital it employed. Look in the *Financial Times* or a quality daily newspaper to find out what Boots shares are worth today, and the highest and lowest quotations over the last year.

The comparison with the local chemist is easiest done by observation of the shop's stock, the number of people employed, and the number of customers over a certain period.

Comparing businesses

The old cliche – comparisons are odious – is never more true than when making comparisons between businesses. Think of the ways in which businesses can be compared:
- by number of employees
- by turnover
- by profit
- by capital employed
- by scope of operations
- by market share
- by products.

Please do this 15 ——————————————————————————1.2.5

Woolworths and Marks and Spencer are both public limited companies (plcs), so they have to publish annual reports which make publicly available a great deal of information about them.

1. Using the information contained in their annual reports compare the two companies and see what conclusions you come to.

2. What traps might you fall into when making the comparisons? (This is a piece of work which would be suitable for word processing and presentation.)

You can compare any two companies in any industries or businesses but the results are often of no value. Do *not* make enquiries about sole traders, partnerships or private limited companies; all these have a right to privacy and other than observations which any individual can make, you have no right to enquire further, and may give considerable offence if you do so.

Trends in production

Whilst it is obvious that there are some very large multi-nationals which have a substantial hold on world production and influence everyone else in the market, the idea that by the year 2000 half the world's goods will be produced by fewer than 250 multi-nationals may not be true. Not all these multi-nationals are as healthy as they might appear to be on the surface.

Please do this 16 ——————————————————————————1.2.5

1. Imperial Chemical Industries (ICI) has divided and now has an undertaking called Zeneca plc. Find out what you can about the history of ICI and the reasons why it should have split.

2. International Business Machines (IBM) has had a very unhappy history since the beginning of the 1990s. Find out what you can about IBM's problems and the solutions which have been, and are being, put into place to make the company healthy.

Dominating the market

A big company, as we have seen from Toyota, may have a substantial world market share. Almost all such companies have built on first being successful in their domestic markets. The Japanese, particularly, have ensured the success of the home-based industries by what is called *protectionism*. This mostly involves putting heavy import duties or taxes on imported goods, which drives people to buy from the domestic producers. Protectionism is the opposite of *free trade*. It limits consumer choice but makes the country practising it richer, if the rest of the world is trying to reduce trade barriers. Free trade is what the General Agreement on Tariffs and Trades (GATT) is all about. The UK has a catastrophic imbalance of trade with the rest of the world. It could be reduced by protectionism. However, the UK cannot practice protectionism because it is a member of the European Union (EU) and cannot keep out any imports from other member countries.

Please do this 17 ———————————————————————— 1.2.2, 1.2.4, 1.2.5

Investigate the UK chocolate market. There are three major players who have 75 per cent of the market between them; the remaining 25 per cent is split between numerous small and specialist producers.

1. Show, graphically, how the market is split up.

The UK chocolate market

26

2. Consider what any of the three majors could do to increase its market share, or its turnover.

3. Find out if the three majors are the same now as they were ten years ago. If this is not the case, how did the change come about and is there a lesson to be learned for the two other major participants?

4. How is it that small producers manage to survive when the giants dominate the market? Take one example company in the chocolate industry and see how it manages to keep going.

Remember that there are no health warnings on chocolate and the market is worth more than £3000 million a year in the UK.

Getting together

Building societies do not build houses, they lend money to those who want to buy or improve property or who just want a loan. Most of them are called after the places where they originated – The Halifax, The Leeds, The Yorkshire, The Cheltenham and Gloucester, The Skipton, The Woolwich and so on – although most of them have a country-wide operation, through branches, by post, electronically or a mixture of these. Over the years the building societies have reduced in number because of mergers. Mr Bradford and Mr Bingley got together to form the Bradford and Bingley; the Abbey and the National became Abbey National.

Please do this 18 ———————————————————————— 1.2.5

1. Have a look in your local *Yellow Pages* and see how many different building societies there are operating in the area it covers.

2. By consulting earlier years' editions, see if this number has increased (owing to more people wanting to buy houses), or decreased (owing to more mergers).

3. What are the advantages of mergers of this sort?

4. How far do you think they can go before other problems, which you should specify, arise?

Getting bigger to survive at all

It is a world market. Buyers who used to come to a company because it was the only supplier now study the market carefully to get the best value for money. Large companies have large marketing and advertising budgets. These are used to shout their wares, and influence you to buy from them.

Please do this 19 ———————————————————————— 1.2.4

Form a small group to consider all the advantages that a very large company has in the market place, and what it can do compared with smaller rivals. Think of John in his one-man enterprise compared with, say, B&Q.

Please do this 20 ——————————————————————1.2.5

Pharmaceutical companies spend vast sums on research and development. They also spend vast sums on promoting their products. The top ten companies in the world pharmaceutical industry are: American Home, Bristol Myers Squib, Ciba-Geigy, Glaxo, Hoechst, Johnson and Johnson, Lilly, Merck, Pfizer, Smithkline Beecham.

1. Find out the sales of each of these pharmaceutical companies for their last financial year.

2. Given that between them they have two-thirds of the world pharmaceutical market, work out how much market share each one has.

3. Now look at their profits over the same year. If you divide sales by profits do you come up with the same figure each time? If not, what conclusion can you draw?

Present the information you are asked for in graphical form wherever possible.

This country has more very big and big companies compared with its population than any other country in Europe. What the UK lacks is sufficient successful medium-sized and small companies. Even with government help to set up companies, the after-effects of the 1988 budget meant that nearly half the small companies in the UK and a quarter of the medium-sized ones went out of business between 1989 and 1993 – a result of the recession.

The UK recession was brought about by unsound economic policies, fuelled by instabilities in the economic and social fabrics of some other countries, the 'collapse' of communism, and the reunification of the two parts of Germany. Despite the vast numbers of company closures between 1989 and 1993, there still remain many small and medium-sized companies. Consumers like diversity, so there are several small motor car manufacturers. There are even people producing motorcycles to special order. For the most part, hairdressers, architects, florists, solicitors, plumbers, painters and decorators, chiropodists and electricians tend to operate as small companies, providing specifically designed services to individuals.

Please do this 21 ——————————————————————1.2.4

1. Make a list of ten firms in your area which fall into the category of small specialist providers of products or services.

2. Indicate whether you found it easy or difficult to compile the list and why.

3. Can you can draw any conclusions from your comments?

New products and services

If there is one thing which has categorised the last 30 years it is the rapidity of technological and scientific change. In the field of children's games the introduction of computerchip-based games has changed children's leisure habits. Banking used to be a matter of going into your nearest branch and presenting a cheque in order to get cash. In the last 20 years hole-in-the-wall (automatic teller) machines, which function by using a plastic card and a PIN number, have appeared in every high street.

Automatic banking

Innovation may be the result of fashion – short or long skirts, wide or narrow trouser ends – or may impose its own fashion. This text was typed on a keyboard which operated a personal computer capable of doing more than a 20 tonne mainframe computer 20 years ago. It is, therefore, possible for the ordinary person to buy and operate such a machine, enjoying its advantages. Thirty years ago, acquiring the same power and advantages would have been a matter of very serious financial concern for a major university or a local authority and the machine would have been expected to remain 'state of the art' for at least a decade.

Review questions

Match correct or *Match incorrect* – these questions require you to match the first statement against the one correct answer in a, b, c and d. This sort of question will be described as *Match correct*. In some questions you may find that you have to pick out the only incorrect answer; these will be referred to as *Match incorrect*.

True/false – these questions require you to look at two statements and decide whether each statement is true or false. You should ring the pair in a, b, c or d which is closest to your opinion of what the statements say. These will be described as *True/false* questions.

Match correct

1. A large business enjoys the benefits of:

a A monopoly of the market

b Economies of scale

c Being fast-moving in making decisions

d Division of labour so that everyone has exactly the right job.

True/false

2. **i** All small businesses need to grow larger to survive.

ii Large scale is always more effective than small-scale.

a i True ii True

b i True ii False

c i False ii False

d i False ii True

Match correct

3. The following products have had a major effect on expenditure in almost the whole 16–19 age group in the last two years:

a Skateboards

b Bicycles

c Computer games

d Motorcycles.

True/false

4. **i** It was government policy in 1994 to subsidise companies to keep businesses going in order to limit unemployment.

ii The manufacturing base in this country is bigger than it was in 1978.

a i True ii True

b i True ii False

c i False ii False

d i False ii True

Match correct

5. The ideal site for a major manufacturing business is:

a In a green field 20 miles from the nearest town

b Close to raw materials and skilled workers

c Russia

d London.

Match correct

6. Large-scale organisations provide the majority of:

    a Legal services

    b Dentistry

    c Farming

    d Electricity.

Match correct

7. A consumer durable is:

    a Jeans

    b Curtaining

    c Refrigerator

    d Tinned cat food.

Match correct

8. The scale of an organisation can always be determined by:

    a Calculating the number of employees

    b Looking at the market share

    c Seeing if the company responds rapidly to demand changes

    d Looking at the turnover figures.

Match correct

9. A plc has to:

    a Employ many people

    b Make very large profits

    c Publish its annual report and accounts

    d Be in the primary sector of industry.

True/false

10. i Most women who are at work have full-time permanent jobs with pensionable salaries:

    ii Sunday trading is not now subject to any regulations.

    a i True ii True

    b i True ii False

    c ii False ii False

    d ii False ii True

Assignment 2.1
New product ideas

1.2.6

John has had a couple of good ideas for new products in the DIY range. He has arranged for these to be produced by manufacturers who pay him royalties for the ideas. He suggests to you that you might be able to think of a product which satisfies an un-recognised need. Your immediate reaction is to doubt that you could think up any such idea, but you get together with a couple of friends and some ideas come to you.

Your tasks

1. Report to John, in writing, on two or three product ideas. You should:

    a indicate what they are for,

    b draw a design,

    c describe the manufacturing process (including the materials required),

    d indicate a selling price per item,

    e describe the potential market.

2. Consider which companies in your area could manufacture your products in quantity. Try the Chamber of Commerce or your local authority Economic Development Department. If in real difficulty the local Training and Enterprise Council may help, although it may not be inclined to help unless you have a genuine prospect of producing a viable product.

Note: The 'quality' daily papers have already been quoted as a source of information on companies. Most particularly, the *Financial Times* provides an unrivalled international service. It is well worthwhile investing, either as an individual or a group, in a daily copy since the *Financial Times* provides authoritative, well-written and up-to-date information on business affairs in the UK and world-wide.

From time to time the *Financial Times* offers specific services, like mailing out the annual reports of major companies. This can be immensely helpful, even if it does no more than alert you to the existence of specific company reports. These reports indicate the financial situation of companies, and their positions in the general market. Product place in the market and development are also dealt with, together with views and action on employment. Finally, there is always a view of what the future is likely to bring.

Company reports are one of the most valuable sources of information you can obtain, but like everything else that is written, you must look at them objectively.

Skills achieved

You will have been able to practise skills in the areas of:

Communication 2.1, 2.2, 2.3, 2.4;

Application of number 2.1, 2.2, 2.3;

Information technology 2.1, 2.2, 2.3.

The last in particular if you have word processed your answers to the 'Please do this' activities and used a CD-ROM to access information.

You will certainly have developed skills in *Working with others* and *Improving own learning and performance*. There are several problems to solve so that creative *Problem solving* should figure in your claim for skills.

3 Present results of investigation into employment

Performance criteria

1. Describe and give examples of **types of employment;**
2. Collect, **analyse** and explain **information** about employment in different regions;
3. **Compare working conditions** for employees in different organisations;
4. Present results of investigation into employment or comparison of working conditions.

Range

- **Types of employment:** full-time, part-time, permanent, temporary, skilled, unskilled, self-employed.
- **Analyse:** in terms of factors contributing to numbers of people employed, growth and decline of manufacturing and service sectors.
- **Information:** percentage employed (male, female, by age), percentage employed in manufacturing sectors and service sectors, local, national, E.U.
- **Compare working conditions:** in terms of travel to work (time, cost), physical conditions, hours of work, pay (wages, extra payments), safety, job security, career opportunities, training opportunities, use of new technology.

The importance of work

'The truth is that we tend to define ourselves in terms of the work which we do. It gives us an identity and an opportunity to compare ourselves with other people both within and outside the group to which we belong. Working on our own, or with others, gives us the dignity of being productive human beings, adding value to products or the life of the community.'

Like most things we read, there is just enough truth in this statement for it to feel convincing. There is no doubt that miners and their families look at the work that they do as constituting a way of life. It is hard, dirty, dangerous and not particularly well paid. In times of danger and disaster it is also heroic and self-sacrificing. Miners know one another and form a vital part of the local community. The community might not be to everyone's taste, but it often has more strength in mutual support than many urban or suburban communities where the ethos of looking after one's self is sometimes the prevailing one. So at this extreme the opening quotation is abundantly true.

We are what we do

To test this statement further we have to look at what interests people about one another when they first meet. One of the very early questions often asked is 'What do you do?' The answer to this is rarely 'I am a member of the parochial church council,' or, 'I belong to the Castleford and District British Motorcycle club,' or even 'I am a member of the Women's Institute and I go to aerobics three times a week'. The answer is often given in terms of what someone does to make a living. So one may be defined as a solicitor, a sales assistant, a motor mechanic, a teacher, a clerk, or a bus driver. Each prompts a whole range of attitudes and beliefs, and you are 'placed' according to where people think you ought to be. It is sometimes not you and your worth as a human being that interests people, but where you fit into the occupational scheme of things.

The hierarchy of employment

Several years ago the Registrar General invented a scale of occupational characteristics. It was hierarchical and it told you much about the basic philosophy of how people were regarded, in terms of occupation. The scale looked like this:

I	Major professional, senior managerial
II	Minor professional, junior managers
IIIi	Clerical, supervisory
IIIii	Skilled manual
IV	Semi-skilled manual
V	Unskilled manual.

This scale had a substantial effect on thinking for many years and continues to do so even after it has become obsolete. There is no category for the unemployed. Primary school teachers were in category IIIi. Secondary teachers in II, with heads of primary schools; whilst heads of secondary schools were in I alongside brain surgeons and the managing directors of major companies. Clearly, social prejudices as well as convenient allocations entered the picture but you will still find similar scales used for even less reputable purposes. For example, magazines tout for advertising by indicating that their readership is 80 per cent A1 and A2. These are the people who are alleged to occupy the highest status in society and have the highest disposable income.

Please do this 22 ——————————————————————————————**I.3.I**

Give examples of employment, detailing if you can, the company and the occupation within it for each of the employment types: self-employed and employed; full and part-time; permanent and temporary.

Changes in employment patterns

Look at the Registrar General's scale above. Over the years there has been a substantial redistribution of people out of the bottom three groups in particular. Mechanisation has meant that relatively few people are required for whom no training is necessary, since almost everyone is associated with working some sort of machine, often a keyboard linked to a computer. Another substantial

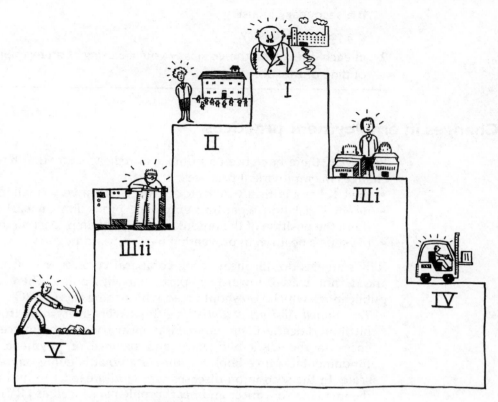

The Registrar General's hierarchy of employment

change relates to the skilled and professional classes. Here 'a job for life' is a thing of the past. Instead, short or fixed-term contracts are much more common. The virtue of this system is that it enables employers to dispense more easily with employees, for whatever reasons. Furthermore, the insecurity which is engendered, particularly in times of high unemployment, ensures that people try to over-achieve and will take on more work and therefore more stress.

Because the skills and knowledge required for a particular job may date very quickly and the job itself may disappear, employers are looking more to short-term contracts. This trend has to be seen against a drive towards a property owning democracy resulting in a high level of people having mortgages. Mortgages last an entire generation, jobs do not. Failure to keep up with mortgage repayments means losing one's home. The home is viewed by many as the basis of a stable society. So, whatever else is important, the possession of a job with prospects, if not for advancement, at least for continuity, is seen by many as an essential.

Please do this 23 ———————————————————————————— 1.3.2

1. Describe the working conditions of a productive worker in:

   a a primary industry

b a secondary industry

c a tertiary industry.

2. In each one, name the company you are using as an example and give an outline of the job.

Changes in employment practices

In the UK there have been a number of major factors that have contributed to changes in employment practices:

- the UK has a critically delicate economy with a very small industrial base,
- recent legislation regarding employee protection (in particular EU legislation), the position of the unions, etc. has had an impact on the UK,
- the state's position in preventing hardship and poverty.

Raw statistics do not mean a lot; comparative ones are useful if they are balanced, not biased towards a particular viewpoint. There are some useful publications which you should read while doing this GNVQ:

- *The Annual Abstract of Statistics* – this covers everything from the number of births and deaths to employment in industry and commerce, by way of references to the UK's budgetary and balance of payments deficits. It is a fundamental source book for knowing what is going on, on a country-wide scale. In the section on diseases you would expect to find an overall rise in the incidence of cancer and heart problems, as well as HIV/AIDS, but might be more surprised to find the recurrence of tuberculosis, a disease of poverty and malnutrition.
- It is dangerous to draw conclusions from single sets of unsupported statistics, which is why the annual publication *Social Trends* is also of interest.
- Department of Employment publications on employment and unemployment.

Of course things have changed. At present, jobs are being geared more and more towards machine minding at one end of the scale, and the invention of machines at the other; nearly all of which are designed to save labour. Unemployment on a world scale exercised the so-called G7 nations (a group of nations including the UK) at the Tokyo summit in 1993. It was then proposed that an international think tank should be formed to consider this problem.

On the one hand, scientific and technological effort is directed to the production of reliable and efficient machinery to ensure that goods and services are available to everyone. On the other hand, the resultant number of unemployed means that there is an enormous burden on the social security budgets of countries, a widening of the gap between the richest and the poorest, and too few people able to afford the goods and services which are on offer.

Self-employment and other changes

Another change is the rise in the numbers of self-employed or those working as part of a partnership. John Stead has found that this does not kill you but it does mean that you are entirely dependent upon your own efforts to secure your living. The UK has always had vast numbers of self-employed workers. Now, workers made redundant may often use their 'pay-offs' to start up in self-employment.

There is now far more opportunity for women to be employed in the 'new-style' jobs where there is much less emphasis on physical strength and much more emphasis on unit labour cost reduction. Women, despite equal opportunities legislation, earn on average only 65 per cent of men's wages. Women are also attracted to part-time work or jobshares because of family or other commitments. Employment is, therefore, likely to be temporary, may not be full-time, and could well make use of high-quality, but very narrow, and possibly not transferable skills.

Getting a job

To be employed means entering a system which is carefully controlled by a variety of laws and regulations. Everyone who is employed by another has to have a contract of employment (see below). Before this is issued it is likely that the candidate has seen an advertisement which names the job and indicates the salary, invites applications or the opportunity of obtaining more details or an application form. The employer is likely to conduct an interview of short-listed candidates whose experience, qualifications and age most nearly fits the job specification which has been drawn up. Finally, the chosen candidate is offered the job, often 'subject to references'.

The contract of employment

The contract of employment between employer and employee is subject to legal definitions. It must contain:
* a job title;
* the starting date;
* the hours of work per week, or over a given period if there is variable working;
* the rate of pay per hour, per week or month and how it will be paid;
* the arrangements for holidays;
* the period of notice of termination that must be given by either side;
* whether there are any arrangements with regard to pensions;
* the status of rights with regard to membership and recognition of trade unions;
* the organisation's rules with regard to discipline.

This is fairly straightforward. What is less clear is the interpretation and the implications of each part of the contract.

Please do this 24 ————————————————————————————————I.3.2

Write an employment contract for:

a a school secretary,

b an assistant at a garden centre.

The job description

In addition to a contract of employment each employee should have a *job description*. This is often part of the package used at the recruitment stage.

Train to drive on one of Europe's largest networks.

LONDON/ORPINGTON/DARTFORD AREAS

Network SouthEast is one of eight British Rail businesses serving Britain's 10,000 miles of railway. Getting millions of passengers to their destinations is a responsible job - so we look to recruit friendly, helpful and hard-working people who can offer our customers a first-class service.

As long as you're enthusiastic, and we're convinced you're the right person for this responsible job, you won't need formal qualifications. You'll spend two months learning the basic technical and practical skills before accompanying a Train Driver as part of the crew. Then, in about 12 - 18 months, when you've completed the rest of your training, opportunities exist for progressing to driver.

Being a highly safety related job, you'll need to reach our medical standard for which you need to be aged 18-45, and 5'4" - 6'4" tall with weight in proportion. You should also have good hearing and eyesight plus normal colour vision, and although you might still be able to join us if you wear glasses (contact lenses cannot be worn), we'll test your eyesight without them to make sure it's up to the standard we're looking for.

In fact, you'll be required to attend assessment days, so that we can carry out a specially designed programme of psychometric tests - we're extremely selective, and we'll have to make sure you've got the aptitude and potential to become a good Train Driver.

And if you have, you'll enjoy a great package. As well as pay of £153.10 a week, plus London Allowance, we'll offer you generous holidays, free and reduced rate rail travel, an excellent contributory pension scheme and real chances for promotion. After initial training you will be required to work shifts and at weekends.

As women are currently under-represented in this area, they are especially encouraged to apply.

For an application form, phone 071-928 5151 and quote referenceLB18. A limited number of applications will be accepted.

British Rail - working towards equal opportunities.

 Network SouthEast

How a job advert might look

Whilst some jobs are very straightforward, others change or become more complicated as the employee stays with the company – hence the job description may be redefined.

Most people manage to find some parts of their jobs which they enjoy or which develop whilst they are working for a company. The balance of activities in a changing environment is a subject for fairly frequent negotiation between an employee and his or her line manager. The job description should include:
- the employee's name and person number;
- the salary or grading for the post;
- the purpose of the job;
- the working relationships:
  – who is the employee's line manager
  – who does the employee in turn supervise
  – other relationships, such as team membership;

- the responsibilities of the post including not only what the employee does but what he or she is responsible for making sure is done in order to fulfil the aims of the job;
- the job tasks which are crucial to the fulfilment of the aims of the job;
- the job context, indicating where the job fits into the business and how it is important to the achievement of the aims of the business.

Both responsibilities and tasks should be limited and realistic in nature – no more than eight if possible. For example, opening and distributing the incoming post would be a task description. How it is done should not be included in the task description.

Please do this 25 ──────────────────────────── I.3.2

Write a job description for:

a a data processor working at a large builders merchants

b a nurse in a large hospital.

What you get for what you do

The reward for working is mainly the receipt of benefit in the form of money. The money is described either as:
- wages – usually money received by the week for hourly work; the more hours worked, the more money in the weekly wages packet, or
- salaries – these tend to be paid monthly, and whilst basic hours may be indicated, the question of overtime does not normally arise.

The surgeon who operates throughout the night after a coach crash will be paid no more; the nurses may get time off in lieu for working through their normal rest periods; the person who cleans up the operating theatre is likely to get paid extra for the additional hours worked.

There are additional payments, for example:
- bonuses for extra effort at busy times,
- rewards related to productivity or company profits, or
- commission which is normally reserved for sales staff in order to reflect sales success.

Some salespeople get no salary or wages and rely entirely on commission. Some companies, and notably the John Lewis Partnership, operate profit sharing schemes; the rewards are larger in good years, smaller in lean years. However, what is available is shared and the workers have a positive stake in the success of the business.

Legal deductions and other matters

Not only are there laws about health, safety and welfare, how and when you must be paid, trade union membership and conditions of service, there are also laws about taxes. Employers are required to deduct income tax from their employees 'at source' and send it to the Inland Revenue regularly. This means that what the employee receives, weekly or monthly, is an amount 'net of tax' (the tax has already been deducted by the employer). The amount an individual has to pay in tax depends on how much he or she earns, whether he or she is married, has children or other dependants, has a mortgage, etc.

Income tax for the self-employed is calculated annually and is payable, generally, twice a year. The assessment is based on predicted earnings, calculated on last years' figures, and can be re-adjusted if necessary.

The Inland Revenue publishes some useful booklets which include:
- PAYE (Pay As You Earn) IR34,
- Income Tax for Students IR60,
- Independent Taxation – a Guide to Tax Allowances and Reliefs IR 90,
- Tax and your business – starting in business IR28, and
- Tax and your business – how your profits are taxed IR 105.

There is also an excellent student pack which contains examples of all the principal documents. This can be obtained from The Inland Revenue Education Service, PO Box 10, WETHERBY, West Yorkshire LS23 7EH. You should make sure you understand all the basic income tax processes and these booklets and pack will help.

Pension fund and National Insurance contributions

If it is a condition of employment that you contribute to a pension fund, then contributions are also deducted, although the advantage is that your income tax is calculated after contributions have been deducted.

Both the employed and the self-employed have to pay National Insurance (NI) at rates related to their rate of pay. There are employees' NI contributions and employers' NI contributions. Both types of contribution go into the Social Fund to cover statutory sick pay, unemployment benefit, the retirement pension and other benefits.

At present the Social Fund is drying up owing to:
- the very high proportion of the employable population who are unemployed and in receipt of benefit,
- the substantial numbers who claim invalidity benefit, and
- the increase in the number of pensioners as a proportion of the working population.

The whole matter of state funded benefits is at present being reviewed as those in receipt of benefits or pensions are viewed by some as a drag on the entire economy and a cause of the vast public spending/borrowing deficit which the government has incurred. The opposite argument is that what little such people receive is all spent on goods and services which keeps other people employed and some people making a profit – otherwise there would be even more people unemployed.

There is another argument that says that a productive nation with enormous riches in natural resources and a reasonable climate, should express its civilised nature by looking after the least advantaged in its community. No one should go short of food and drink, clothing, shelter and personal security. Such provisions are in the Social Chapter of the Maastricht Treaty, but the UK is the only one of the EU countries which has been allowed to opt out of this part of the treaty.

New technology

Some activities are less affected by new technology than others. A solicitor may have clients' files set up on disc, the staff may use word processors with virtually standard letters to cover a variety of situations, and mobile phones, portable miniature dictating machines and fax machines may also be used. On the whole, however, solicitors are happier with the security which locked fireproof filing cabinets containing their confidential materials give them. In contrast, a car manufacturer may have designed the latest model using computer aided design (CAD) and fed the results into the manufacturing process. This in turn involves very large numbers of computer controlled machines and robots – computer aided manufacture (CAM). The effect of these processes on car manufacture can be imagined.

Who does what?

If you want to know how many people are employed and what their occupations are in the UK, you need look no further than the Department of Employment statistics. The local Training and Enterprise Council (TEC) will tell you more about your local community. You may also discover what the rate of unemployment is but be careful – unemployment is calculated very oddly. For instance, the people without jobs are only counted as unemployed if they are claiming unemployment benefit (the so-called 'dole'). But even if they are, no one over 60 counts as unemployed, even though the official retirement age is 65 for men and women, and no one under 18 is counted. There are large numbers of people who have been in work and have taken time out for various reasons who cannot or choose not to claim unemployment benefit. Therefore, these are not counted as unemployed, even if they are searching for paid work.

You also have to take into account the weighting for seasonal adjustment. There are usually more jobs available in the summer than in the winter so the published adjusted seasonal figure in the summer is less than the real number of the unemployed and that for winter is more. So look at published statistics very carefully and bear in mind the basis on which they are presented.

The fact is that there are fewer people in work now than there were last year, and this has been true every year since 1988. Yet there has been, between 1993 and 1995, 17 months of declining numbers of unemployed.

There are no universal rules on presenting statistics for the European Union (EU) countries so that a region of the UK with 10 million inhabitants may have 4 million employed, 3 million who could be employed, but 350,000 who are registered unemployed. The official rate is, therefore, 8.75 per cent, but might in reality be over 35 per cent.

Please do this 26 ─────────────────────────────── 1.3.3, 1.3.4

1. On the understanding that there are no universally applicable recording mechanisms, have a look at the employment and unemployment rates for each EU country (or region in some cases) and then look at the principal employments in those areas. Where may there be a shortage of skilled people?

2. In a market driven economy there will always be skilled people whose skills are no longer needed, or cannot be afforded. Conversely, because of changes in procedures and technology there will always be shortages of some essential skills. See if you can find areas in which skills are needed and regions in which employment levels are high. Have the latter any similarities? If so, what are they? If not, is it pure chance that some areas present opportunities for unemployment whilst others seem to have a surplus of labour. Is this something to do with the extent to which technological change has affected businesses and industries?

Health and safety at work

Employment is also governed by the Health and Safety at Work Act 1974 (HASAWA) which indicates that no unsafe practices are permissible by the management or the employees. A safe machine which has a guard that prevents it from being used at the maximum speed or efficiency must *not* have the guard removed by either management or employees in the interests of improving its performance and therefore company profits or employees' wages. Training in safety must be provided for all employees. In hazardous occupations failure to provide and abide by this training is subject to vigorous prosecution in the event of any sort of accident or notified infringement. The enforcers of the Act are the Inspectors of the Health and Safety Executive.

A business with more than a very small number of employees must have a Health and Safety Officer who should be well-informed not only about the conditions of the Act but also about specific regulations and codes of practice for the industry in which the company operates.

Most stringent of these is the COSHH (Control of Substances Hazardous to Health) Regulations. These deal with substances which affect the health of users or others in and around the premises. Whilst you may not think there are any such substances in an office environment, this is not necessarily the case, since some kinds of office duplicators use an agent which is a solvent.

HASWA is related to the Offices, Shops and Railway Premises Act 1957 which lays down minimum environmental standards for working, temperature, purity of air, toilets and washing areas, lighting and a minimum of 12 square metres of working space. The Factories Act 1961 covers elements similar to the 1957 Act but also specifies that walkways must be defined and free from clutter, that floors must be non-slip, that machines should be fenced and that fire exits must never be obstructed whilst there are workers on the premises.

Unemployment

Whilst employment is a desired state, it is all too often the case that unemployment is a likely fate for many people. Almost everyone at some stage or another in their careers may be unemployed.

Different areas of the UK have different problems. Some, mainly in the North, have endured unemployment off and on for most of the century. Others, like the London area and the South East, have only in the last five years really

Blitz hinted at size of problem

In 1986 the Health and Safety Commission decided to take firm action in reducing the number of major accidents and fatalities in the construction industry. About half the fatalities were known to occur on small sites (less than ten workmen) so an eighteen month programme of enforcedment-led activity ("blitzes") was set up, aimed principally at smaller sites.

In total, 8,272 visits were made, predominantly to "small" sites, and over 10,000 contractors were seen between May 1987 and September 1988. Overall the standard of health and safety found was reported to be "poor" and it was neccessary to issue 2,046 Prohibition Notices (approximately one in four, although some sites were given more than one) and 96 Improvement Notices.

A variety of problems required enforcement notices as shown in Table 1.

The majority of action taken did indeed involve smaller sites; however, this reflects the greater number of small sites visited. In fact, only a quarter to a third of small sites warranted action as opposed to over half of larger sites. There is therefore no justification in targeting a certain size of site in future, says HSE.

Nature of problem	% of Total
Defective scaffold (inc cradles)	28
Roofwork (poor or no edge protection)	18
Ladders (poor use/defective)	10
Fragile roof/rooflights	2
Other unsafe place of work	10
Unsafe access (excl ladders)	4
Excavations (poor support)	2
Dangerous electrics (excl underground cables)	5
Dangerous lifting plant	3
Other dangerous plant	2
Non-use of protective equipment	3
Other	13
Total	100

Table 1. Matters on site requiring enforcement action

Health and safety awareness

Inspectors looked at the knowledge of agents, foremen and supervisors in charge of sites. One third were found to have an inadequate level of knowledge about "basic health and safety requirements" (where the person in charge could be found that is – on 19 per cent of sites the agent or supervisor was unavailable or non-existent!). Not surprisingly, half the sites where knowledge was "poor or very poor" also had matters of serious concern.

HSE found that publicity about the campaign had been effective (over one third of the sites had heard of the campaign) but it is doubtful if awareness of the campaign led to much, if any, improvement on site. It thus seems that publicity must be combined with action to raise awareness of health and safety (and the HSE's role) to a level where companies make the effort to improve health and safety.

The future of the blitz

It is unlikely that blitzes on such a large scale will be organised again as they are very costly. However, "mini" blitzes carried out in certain areas aimed at certain types of contractors, for example roofing specialists, are a real possibility.

Although the blitz had some immediate effects it is doubtful whether there will be any long term improvements in safety standards. However, it will certainly have raised awreness of health and safety matters and is thus one step on the long road to safer working practices.

Campaigning for health and safety

found out what unemployment means. You may be aware in a general sense of the current unemployment situation in your area and its effects. Yet another area may be completely unknown to you except by brief references in the media. One thing is for sure: unemployment hurts. Long-term unemployment is very destructive of hopes and aspirations, the maintenance of skills and knowledge, and the upkeep of a home, good relations within it and the sense of security which goes with it.

Lord Beloff was quoted, in July 1993, as saying that he was brought up in a decade of hope and has just endured a decade of despair. It is not quite as bad as that, but it is certainly true that those who are employed are constantly looking over their shoulders at the likelihood of further job losses and that everyone is working a lot harder in order to maintain a decent standard of living.

Industries in the UK

Some industries are related to specific regions of the country, whilst others are evenly distributed. This distribution is often the result of easy access to raw materials, railways, roads, airports or seaports, or a pool of skilled and employable people.

Coal mining, quarrying, oil, steel and gas all depend upon raw materials which are geographically related, as are pottery and china. Glass is mainly produced in St Helens, Merseyside. Other major industries include computer manufacture, mechanical machinery, aerospace, tobacco, textiles, food processing and beverages, hosiery, clothing, knitwear, printing, publishing, chemicals. Tourism does not quite cover the country, even though banking, telecommunications, insurance and transportation may do.

On the whole, the financial services industries are concentrated in London and Edinburgh, although Giro is in Bootle and Access operates from Southend. Agriculture and forestry is well distributed, although different sorts of farming are undertaken in various parts of the country. Retailing is everywhere and wholesaling tends to find itself regionally located near motorway intersections.

Training and education

It is always an advantage to have qualifications, particularly qualifications which match the sort of job which you might like to get, or can get in the future, or perhaps one which you already have. Nowadays, the qualified person who can show certification of his or her abilities is often preferred to the person who is qualified by experience. To be educated means:
- to have a mind which is capable of working,
- to have wide interests, and
- to have a degree of flexibility in one's approach to problems and to jobs.

To be trained indicates a level of expertise which may be as great, or greater than the job requires. A dentist may be very highly-skilled but may spend a lot of his or her time doing routine inspections and filling cavities. However, none of us would be very happy going to a dentist who could only do that because our teeth may reveal some signs of irregularity or difficulty which only a highly-qualified dentist could recognise and treat. Good qualifications are at least a helpful key to unlock the door on the way to employment. This is probably why you are doing this course.

Deskilling, upskilling and multiskilling

Qualifications are related to skills and knowledge. However, there are changes afoot based on the three concepts of deskilling, multiskilling and upskilling:
- *Deskilling* is based on the intervention of technology in the areas of traditional craft skills.
- *Multiskilling* is best illustrated by the engineering industry where there used to be a clear distinction between mechanical and electrical engineers. Now there is a strong demand for people with the multiskills of mechanical, electrical and electronic engineering.
- *Upskilling* is typically illustrated by the efficient typist who becomes an even more efficient word processing operator.

Please do this 27 ─────────────────────────────────1.3.2

Describe in outline the national system of vocational qualifications and show how it applies to the world of business.

This chapter has raised a number of very serious issues. It is now up to you to put some flesh on the bones of the material here by doing the two assignments at the end of the chapter.

Review questions

Match correct or Match incorrect – these questions require you to match the first statement against the one correct answer in a, b, c and d. This sort of question will be described as *Match correct*. In some questions you may find that you have to pick out the only incorrect answer; these will be referred to as *Match incorrect*.

True/false – these questions require you to look at two statements and decide whether each statement is true or false. You should ring the pair in a, b, c or d which is closest to your opinion of what the statements say. These will be described as *True/false* questions.

Match correct

1. The government can reduce unemployment by:

   a Privatising state industries

   b Increasing taxes

   c Providing training and education for those who need it

   d Removing the powers of local government.

Match correct

2. The working conditions in a mine are often better than those in:

   a A horticultural greenhouse in June

   b A solicitor's office

   c A foundry

   d A hospital.

Match correct

3. A self-employed person might have the following job:

   a A railway train conductor

   b An assistant at Dixons

   c A market trader

   d A bank manager.

True/false

4. **i** More people are now employed on a temporary or part-time basis than in 1979

   ii There are far fewer people unemployed than there were in 1979

   a i True ii True

   b i True ii False

c i False ii False

d i False ii True.

Match correct

5. A deduction from pay which is associated with claims for benefits is called:

a PAYE

b National Insurance

c Council tax

d VAT.

Match correct

6. The Rural Development Commission works closely with:

a City Challenge

b Project Trident

c Rural Training and Enterprise Councils

d Urban Priority areas.

Match correct

7. Training and Enterprise Councils:

a Are based in Scotland

b Start up retail businesses

c Try to promote effective training

d Investigate pay and conditions of workers.

True/false

8. **i** The UK is the only member of the European Union not to have signed the Social Chapter of the Treaty of Maastricht, which is designed to guarantee minimum conditions of employment for workers

ii It is illegal to work more than 48 hours a week in England and Wales

a i True ii True

b i True ii False

c i False ii False

d i False ii True

Match incorrect

9. Which of the following is *not* true about being an employee:

a An employee must do the job for which he or she is employed

b Can claim benefit if unemployed

c Must use the employer's equipment and/or work on the employer's premises

d Cannot claim statutory sick pay.

Match correct

10. Being employed full time means:

a Working 9.00 a.m. to 5.00 p.m. each day

b Being guaranteed permanent employment

c After two years being able to claim for unfair dismissal

d Having to work overtime at short notice.

Assignment 3.1
The local package
1.3.1, 1.3.2, 1.3.4

1. a Indicate how your area (which you must define geographically) is influenced by the natural resources, labour supply and inward investment to determine the sort of industry which exists there.

b What are the problems with regard to changes and closures of industry and commerce?

c What is the level of unemployment among adults and those under 18? (Give separate figures for males and females.)

2. a Look for an area at least 50 miles from where you are, which contrasts with your locality. (For example, if your area is agricultural look for a highly-industrialised area; if your area is a new technology area, look for a first industrial revolution area.)

b Define it and examine it in terms of the criteria you have used to look at your own area.

3. Compare and contrast the two areas in 1 and 2.

4. Describe the extent to which industrial and commercial practices have been influenced by high technology in three contrasting businesses in your area. (For the purposes of this question regard any sort of undertaking as a business.)

Assignment 3.2
Staffing the shop

1.3.4

John has got his planning permission, he has almost completed the refurbishment of the premises, and he has ordered stock which will be delivered in the week before he is ready to open. The matter of an assistant is now pressing, especially as John has converted the original kitchen into a small workshop in which he is able to do welding, metal turning and cutting, plastic moulding and a variety of other activities. These are beyond the skill of the run-of-the-mill DIY person but are very helpful to those who want to complete a job without having to call in an expert to do the whole thing.

Make sure that all the items below are word processed and, where possible, desk-top published, in order to present the most professional image.

Your tasks

1. Write an advertisement for an assistant.

2. Produce a form for an applicant to complete.

3. Provide a set of additional information for candidates.

4. Write a letter inviting a candidate to an interview with John Stead.

5. Write a letter confirming that the candidate has been appointed.

6. Write out a contract of employment.

7. Make up a job description.

'But I only applied for a part-time clerical assistant's post.'

8. Tell John Stead, in writing, what the total cost of employing the assistant for a week will be.

9. Tell John Stead, in writing, how the appointment will be affected by legislation concerning the health and welfare of employees.

Skills achieved

You should be able to claim skills in all the elements of *Communication*, and in elements 2.1 and 2.2 at least of *Information technology*. Dependent upon how you have answered some of the 'Please do this' work you may have reinforced some *Application of number* skills.

4 Examine and compare structures and working arrangements in organisations

Performance criteria
1. Describe organisational structures;
2. Produce organisational charts showing departments;
3. Describe the work and explain the interdependence of departments within business organisations;
4. Identify and explain differences in working arrangements;
5. Explain and give examples of reasons for change in working arrangements in one business organisation.

Range
- **Organisational structures:** hierarchical, flat, matrix.
- **Departments:** research & development, production, purchasing, accounting, human resources (personnel), marketing, sales, administration, computer (IT) services, customer services, distribution (logistics).
- **Differences in working arrangements:** in terms of: team working, centralised, de-centralised, flexible (shifts, flexi-hours), contracts (fixed-term, permanent), workbase (office, factory, shop, outdoors, home, mobile).
- **Reasons for change:** productivity, quality assurance, competition, technology.

The reasons for structures

There is an enormous difference between the business structure that John Stead starts out with and that of the National Health Service (NHS), British Petroleum (BP), British Gas plc or the BBC. The latter are all major organisations with thousands of employees. In John's case he has all the advantages but also all the disadvantages of the sole trader.

There is nothing that John is not involved in, relating to his business, except auditing his accounts. (See Chapter 12 for an explanation of auditing.) If there is a decision to be made, John makes it. When he had a market stall no one else had to be consulted before he changed his wholesale supplier, he dealt direct with the market superintendent over all matters concerning his stall and the days that he used it. He supplied his own transport and kept his own books. A personnel department was unnecessary since he was the only person involved. He arranged his own insurance and pension. In summary, being a sole trader, and the only person involved in the business, meant that John had to do everything and that left him with little spare time. Because of the variety of jobs there were to do, there was an increased opportunity for getting things wrong.

When John got a partner the various jobs were shared. John now had time to get in touch with his suppliers, aimed to get his paperwork up-to-date, made some necessary repairs to his transport, dealt with the market superintendent, helped out with selling at busy times – or even had a quiet cup of tea and a toasted teacake in the cafe.

Differentiation and communication

In Chapter 1 we saw that John went into partnership with Sonia Shah. Unless there is a specific statement to the contrary, partners are just that and share all the advantages and disadvantages of the enterprise. Even so, they may have quite different jobs to do in the partnership. Sonia was particularly good at keeping the books and paperwork in order, whilst John was exceptional at selling and dealing with suppliers. It is sensible that people are asked to do jobs which they are good at and enjoy, so it is easy to guess who did what.

However, John could not go off to Supercats Ltd and order a year's supply of cat food to store in his garage without a word to Sonia. Consultation was essential. For example, John and Sonia would have to decide how to balance the saving on the very large quantity from a single supplier – giving more profit per tin and an opportunity to undercut the competition – against the expenditure of a substantial quantity of capital which would be tied up in this single order. Not necessarily an easy decision, but it had to be made.

What this illustrates is the increasing diversification of activity from the days of the sole trader. Taking the two extremes, a sole trader deals with everything to do with the business while the specialisation in a very large organisation means that an employee may have a very precisely and narrowly defined role.

Lines of authority and communication hierarchies

When a company grows in size it needs to be constantly reassessed in order to establish:
- how it is organised,
- what its lines of authority and communication are, and
- whether there is anything that could be done to make it more efficient.

This fits in neatly with the internal functions of a company:
- planning,
- organising,
- co-ordinating,
- controlling, and
- doing.

We will come back to these again later.

When John expands his DIY business from one shop into two he goes from:

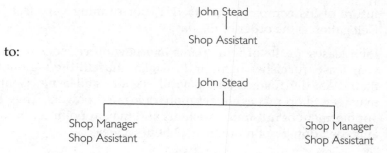

to:

He still controls most functions: stock buying, control, payment of accounts, upkeep of premises, employment of staff and so on. The day-to-day running of the salespoints (shops) is in the hands of the shop managers who may also be responsible for the cleaning of the shops, small repairs and dealing with any minor emergencies.

As John develops his business further, he finds himself with shops throughout the North West of England, and Yorkshire. Instead of two shops close at hand he now has 40 spread over a wider geographical area. He can no longer visit each of his shops daily, or even weekly. He employs well over 100 people and has had to take on additional specialist staff. One of his shops may well look like this:

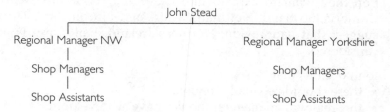

However, a shop manager left entirely to his or her own devices will often lose morale because of lack of contact and support from the owner (management) and may misinterpret policies or procedures. So not only supervision but also encouragement is required. Therefore, with 40 shops John appoints two regional managers, each responsible for 20 shops, and his organisation now looks like this:

Of course, that is not the end of the structure. With more than 100 employees who have to be paid and substantial flows of purchases and expenditure on salaries and shop upkeep, John needs a finance and payroll section. He is well on the way to having a head office which will also include a personal assistant (PA) for him. A PA is also required for each of the regional managers since they each need someone to do their paperwork and keep their diaries up-to-date as well as being a point of communication when they are out of their offices.

For a time John controls the head office, advertises for and appoints all staff, approves all expenditure, deals with leases, shop fitters, cleaners, rates of pay and many other details. One day, he realises that he is no longer thinking of the future of his company, Steady DIY, but running very fast just to keep going. Delegation is the order of the day.

John leases a suite of four rooms in a new office block in Ramstown on a two-year lease, furnishes them and installs himself, the regional managers (RMs), their PAs, the finance and payroll section, and a newly appointed contracts manager. Shop managers get more delegated powers. They have a hand in the appointment of full-time assistants and may appoint up to two part-time assistants each doing not more than 12 hours a week.

John calls a meeting of all the shop managers and the regional managers and suggests a new pay scale for shop managers and their staff which includes an element of performance related pay. He also installs a new computer-based stock and receipts system connected to each of the shops so that every transaction is recorded, checked against stock and restocking is automatically arranged. His organisation now looks like this:

```
                              John Stead
                                      \ PA
        ┌───────────────┬─────────────────────────────────┐
   RM (NW)           RM (Y)                          Head Office
        \ PA              \ PA                            │
   Shop Managers     Shop Managers           Managers: Finance Computing Contracts
        │                 │
   Shop Assistants   Shop Assistants
```

More complex hierarchies

At their weekly meeting, the regional managers make the point to John, that their regions are too large for them to cope with effectively. They suggest that smaller regions, and an opportunity to look for more good locations within their regions might be a means towards development of the company. In addition they want to expand into Cleveland, Tyne and Wear, Northumberland, Cumbria, Scotland, Nottinghamshire and Lincolnshire. The more adventurous suggest that nationwide, Northern Ireland, Wales and France should also be considered.

John decides that:
- there should be smaller regions,
- the regional managers should have a developmental function within the regions, and
- there should also be an overall development manager.

The organisation now looks like this:

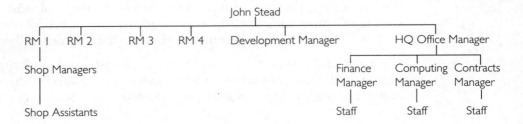

John is a great believer in *flat management structures* – that is the least number of layers of employees between him and the customers.

John now visits his shops once a quarter. His visit is intended to improve morale and show interest rather than monitor progress, which he can do with regional manager reports and computer returns. John is fast becoming a very successful manager.

Hierarchies and functions

Companies, or at least their managements, like to see themselves as hierarchical structures, though it is important to note that structures have to fit functions, not the other way round. A typical hierarchy looks rather like that shown below.

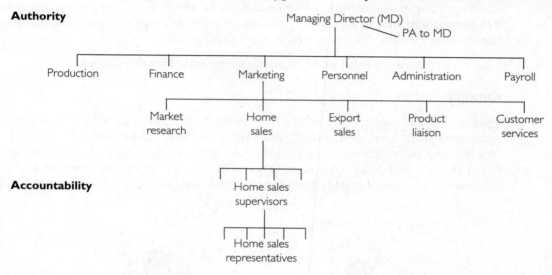

A typical hierarchy

This is a partial organisation chart which shows only some of the major functions. This sort of structure is very like that employed by the Army, Navy, and Air Force. It has the advantage of clearly defined ranks and responsibilities, of clear lines of authority and straightforward lines of communication, as well as relatively short spans of control (that is, the number of people supervised by one person). Everyone in a hierarchy should know exactly:
- what he or she is doing,
- whom to report to, and
- who reports to him or her.

However, it is often hard to show initiative in such structures, as stepping outside the elaborate and comprehensive set of rules may result in disciplinary action rather than appreciation.

Lines of authority and communication: matrices

An alternative is the use of *functional groups* in a relatively flat structure. These may be relatively small and closely task focused. They may also have a limited life, so that when the task is complete they may be dismantled and the members turned to other tasks. This appears to be a brilliant system but it is reliant on a really communicative and supportive management. In addition, employees may feel that the company's need for them to be flexible is rather unsettling:

- 'You never know what is going to happen next.'
- 'If this job finishes, will I still be employed with the firm?'

Lack of continuity has to be matched with a high level of management involvement and communication to reassure employees.

From the management's point of view, jobs will certainly get done, but it will have to keep eternally vigilant to ensure that the next task is dovetailed into the programme just as the present one finishes. The span of control is very wide and reporting relationships may not always be clear. Therefore, management has to motivate employees by explaining clearly the corporate goals, which in turn means that it will have to understand them as well.

This system is very useful when it comes to the use of quality circles.

Quality circles

Quality circles is a system by which those who do the job meet regularly to consider how their own, and others', performance can be improved. The process can be very far reaching, including the abolition of particular areas of work. Good morale and a sense of commitment by the whole of the workforce are essential to successful quality motivation of this sort.

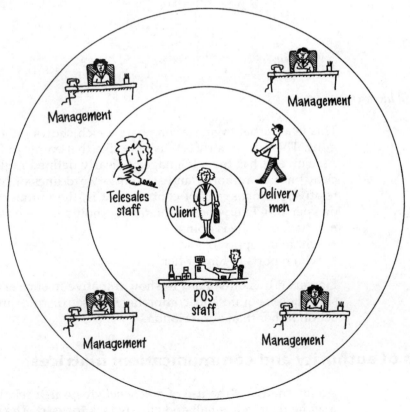

An entire quality circle

Each of John's shops with its regional manager constitutes a *quality circle*. Suggestions for improvement to services, stock holding, new products and replacement products are fed to John via the development manager and regional managers on an across-the-company basis. Where one shop has a strongly held view it is allowed to go ahead but needs to show that the idea is successful and profitable within a certain time period.

Some companies see themselves as an entire quality circle with the client placed at the centre and those who are in touch with the client in the circle closest to the centre. In this system the management occupies the furthest circumference, unless it is called upon to settle a complaint or deal with an emergency.

Please do this 28 ——————————————————————— 2.1.1, 2.1.2

1. Draw an organisation chart for:

    a The school or college in which you are studying.

    b A small local firm with up to about 50 employees.

    c A large company – in excess of 1000 employees – which may be a national or multi-national enterprise (Do an outline only.)

2. Taking one section of the company in **c**, draw it in detail and indicate who reports to whom and who makes decisions about what.

Relationships

Line relationships

Look back at the typical hierarchy shown on page 57. This hierarchy involves relationships between functions and, perhaps even more important, between people. The expression 'line manager' is often heard in businesses and large organisations. This means someone who is responsible for the allocation and monitoring of the work of others. The post can exist at almost any level in the hierarchy, and in any of the functional areas, provided there is someone to manage.

Staff relationships

There is also a 'staff' relationship. This is apparent in the post of personal assistant to the managing director. In this case there is an advisory role which makes the relationship quite different from that of the employee and line manager.

Functional relationships

Functional relationships are those existing between departments across the company. For instance, in a large company there is likely to be a close relationship between the personnel department and the payroll department. One department may advertise a job and make all the arrangements for recruitment, even to the point of settling the salary and conditions. The other may be responsible for paying the employee and making returns of tax and National

Insurance, as well as numerous other tasks. Marketing may be in the business of improving organisational goals, but may well rely on production and distribution departments to carry them out.

Lateral relationships and management ideas

A well-run business has a variety of *lateral relationships*. Thus all the senior managers may meet regularly to consider how they are progressing with the corporate goals and how they can help one another. There may be a less formal meeting of assistant managers where nitty-gritty problems may be dealt with, as well as considering major issues and making proposals to the senior managers.

Informal relations

One of the tests of a successful company, or at least one with all the potential for success, is the quality and number of informal relationships. You will know that some of your acquaintances can be relied on implicitly, whereas others are often unreliable. So it is in businesses. A particular person in another department may be well known to you as one who will invariably try to help out when you need it. You will always reciprocate and the informal relationship is to your mutual advantage.

Another test of success is the extent to which people from different departments and levels are engaged in social activities together, whether these be organised outings, membership of the same church or club, or participation in the works band or sports team. These external activities often pay off substantially, especially when that bit of extra corporate effort is required.

Functions in organisations

We have spent some time looking at structures in organisations. *Functions* are related to the real things that companies do; they have to fit the corporate goals. Whilst an engineering company might expect to have engineering and industrial designers – the former ensuring that products do what they are supposed to whilst the latter make them easier to produce and more attractive to potential purchasers – a large-scale baker is unlikely to have an engineering designer on the staff. However, it may well buy in similar services on a consultancy basis. For example, an industrial designer may have a place in the development of packaging.

Once a product has been designed it has to be produced. This is where the company discovers whether the product has been designed to be easy to manufacture, is as cheap to make as possible, satisfies health and safety laws, has longevity built in and is easy to maintain (if required). The production department of an engineering company will now almost certainly have the acronym CAD/CAM, computer aided design and computer aided manufacture, in its work description.

This is a system for ensuring reliability and, because the design is computerised, you do not have to do the job twice. CNC (computer numerically controlled) lathes, millers, saws and shapers work directly from the original design specification. Although CNC is used principally in engineering, any mass-producer will adopt a CNC approach. For example, big bakers work on mass production lines with all ingredients and processes computer controlled. Standardisation of the quality of ingredients is, of course, essential for success. A small baker, on the other hand, will produce a batch of loaves at a time and then a batch of currant buns. The small baker's specialist confectioner may tend to work on producing a single wedding cake, hand decorated.

In a chemical works production operates 24 hours a day, every day of the year. This is known as *flow production*.

Production planning

Before production can begin, it has to be planned. Raw materials have to be assembled, and some bought in; and finished parts, in appropriate quantities have to be available. Perhaps a just-in-time (JIT) stocking system is operated, where stock arrives from suppliers when it is required rather than being stored in quantity on the premises. The machines which are required and their operators will have to be available and have the necessary skills. If not, they will have to be trained. Training may take three years or 30 seconds, but is essential for success. The length of production time and the timing of the finished article (e.g. for a customer's order to be fulfilled on a specified date), and its packaging also have to be considered.

In addition there will be a partnership between the production planners and the cost accountants in order to determine the total costs and the selling price. Marketing and sales will also have essential parts to play at this stage. There is no point in having a product to manufacture if it cannot be sold.

Please do this 29 2.1.2, 2.1.4

Planning is a complex and difficult process. You are involved in the manufacture of toffee apples. The apples have to be graded after they pass through a wash and rinse bath. The grading is done by a trained human grader who can grade 1000 apples an hour for eight hours a day with less than 0.1 per cent failure rate.

After grading, the apples move on a conveyor belt to dry off and then have a wooden spike inserted through the stalk end. This is another hand operation, but the rate is 500 spikes inserted an hour. Meanwhile, the toffee machine is making hot liquid toffee which it empties into a heated bowl. It takes 30 minutes to get the materials to the correct consistency and each batch of ingredients will supply enough toffee for 250 toffee apples. The dipping of the apples into the bowl is done by hand and the operator can manage 1000 apples an hour. The machine wrapper can manage 2000 apples an hour.

1. Draw a flow chart showing each process and the number of people or machines at each station so that the most economical production is achieved.

2. The maximum production ever needed is 17,500 apples a day. Is there a straightforward method of getting these apples produced without resorting to the employment of more people or investing in more machinery?

Production control

Once production is under way it has to be controlled to make sure that targets are met. In the toffee apple example you might aim at 950 apples an hour by the grader because people need to move about a bit and are entitled to rest periods and time to visit the toilet. Even with stand-by graders on hand the work rate fluctuates during the day, so that it is better to aim at a realistic target in the first place than have to adjust targets constantly.

In a purely machine environment 1000 apples an hour would be essential. Breakdowns would have to be rectified at once and new schedules established to make up for lost time. The faster you work, or the longer the period in a day that you manufacture, the more likely it is that there will be mistakes and a decline in quality. In order to ensure that the consumer does not get a bad apple, or one with no toffee, or a television set with a missing component, manufacturers have quality controllers who assess the product at every stage of its manufacture and particularly when it is complete.

Quality control

At one time quality controllers were people who stood over workers, but much of their function has now been taken over by computers. These can review the product against standards and report on errors and deficiencies. Because specifications are better, raw materials more closely monitored and processes often computerised, quality in mass-produced goods is often much better than it was ten years ago, and in any case is more consistent than it was in the days of hand production.

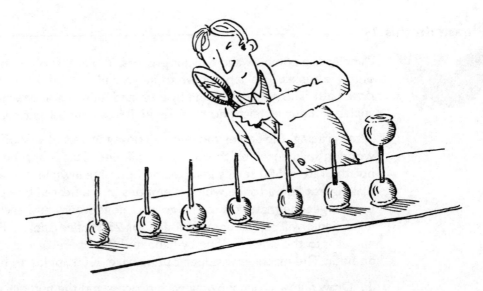

A quality controller in action

Once the robot has been programmed to weld the body work of a car in a particular way, it will do the same thing until it is switched off. The human welder may produce examples of superior welding, but it will be a truly remarkable human being who can be as consistent as a machine both in quality and in length of production run.

Quality assurance

The British Standards Institute (BSI) provides Standards for quality in industry and commerce. The bricks a home is built with, the windows you look out of and the carpets you walk on are all covered by a British Standard establishing fitness for purpose. As far as all businesses are concerned, and that includes educational organisations, the most used single Standard is BS 5750, (International Standards Office (ISO) 9000). This is concerned with guaranteed standards of excellence at every stage of administration and production.

Does the company matter?

Television, either in its advertisements or its scheduled programming, often allows us insights into the factories and works of the companies that manufacture the things that we buy and use. Companies try to establish images in the market place so that you will buy from them and when you are satisfied with their products, you may buy from them again.

The company does matter, but is seen by customers through the eyes of retailers. However, there is one aspect of the company which affects a lot of people who may never buy from the company and never work there – that is the personnel department.

The personnel department

In other parts of this book you are given tips on how to get a job. When you apply to a fair-sized company for a job, you first contact the personnel department. In a sole trader, partnership or small company, the principal owner may well also be the personnel department. In the early days of his business, John planned his manpower, he advertised when he wanted an assistant, he compiled the job specification, he sent out the information and a form to applicants, and he kept records of the person he appointed.

John dealt with the wages and conditions of service. In the event of a disciplinary event he had to take measures; in the event of his assistant having a grievance, he heard it. John provided such welfare activities as he could and ensured that health and safety requirements were satisfied. In the event of an accident, he investigated it and wrote the report on it. He had his own staff appraisal system based on the fact that he was in daily contact with his assistant and could highlight and inform her about good performance, or advise where performance might be improved. He provided training and vetted visitors to the premises, thereby performing a security function.

When his assistant left he rewrote the job description, thought about the best means of filling the vacancy, or whether he should try to do without an assistant, sent out the information and application forms, short-listed the applicants and interviewed and tested those on the shortlist in order to prove abilities and establish the applicants' personal qualities. Once the new assistant had begun work he provided her with plenty of help and guidance, and a prolonged induction programme which indicated that he was willing to make a substantial investment in people.

John knew that whilst the type of shop he was running, its location and the costs associated with running it were all fixed, his assistant was a flexible means of increasing business and deserved careful attention.

Please do this 30 ———————————————————— **2.1.1, 2.1.2, 2.1.3, 2.1.4**

1. Write an induction booklet for a young person of 16+ coming to your school or college for the first time.

2. Write an induction booklet for people who will start on your course in the next session.

John thus performs all the tasks relating to the personnel department of a large company himself. A big company will have a personnel manager, personnel officers and personnel assistants, records clerks, a training officer, security officers, welfare officers, and a canteen supervisor and staff.

Please do this 31 ————————————————————————— **2.1.3**

Fit the jobs which a personnel department has to do to the list of titles which are given in the previous paragraph.

The finance department

A company without a good finance department may founder; a company which is ruled solely by the finance department's words may likewise die. Finance people are rightly cautious; entrepreneurs are justifiably adventurous. The example of John in setting up his first DIY shop is classic because he combined both roles. He wanted to see development and increased profit, but he did not want to overstretch himself. He needed to get additional capital and approached his bank, but he kept a careful tally on all his expenditure and income, constantly comparing the two to see if he was making a profit. He paid wages to his assistant and a salary to himself. With the assistance of a local accountant he prepared his annual accounts. John combined the functions of:

- financial accounting – giving annual profit and loss and balance accounts;
- management accounting – providing guidance for management on the daily, state-of-the-art accounts; and
- cost accounting – working out all the costs of production (or purchases in John's case), establishing selling prices and sorting out *fixed costs* (e.g. rates, machinery, insurance, rent and capital) and the *variable costs* (e.g. raw materials, overtime and fuel).

Please do this 32 ————————————————————————— **2.1.3**

The following are all jobs which you might find in a large finance department. Match the jobs which John does on his own to the posts which are listed:

chief accountant   wages clerks
management accountant   ledger clerks
cost accountant   costing clerks
chief cashier   credit control clerks
credit controller

Sales and marketing

John has a feel for his market. He gets to know most of his customers and asks them their opinions about what he sells directly. In a large organisation this is practically impossible. In reality, John is a salesman and not a marketer. Selling is a part of marketing. Marketing concerns the customer's perceptions of what he or she wants and can be persuaded to acquire.

Marketing people are very keen on catch phrases, even to describe what it is that they really do. One of the more easy to remember of these is the four Ps:
- **product** – the brand name, packaging, quality, after-sales service
- **price** – basic price, credit terms, discounts, comparison with the competition,
- **place** – where it may be bought (e.g. wholesalers, retailers, mail order, agents)
- **promotion** – media used in advertising, promotions, public relations, publicity, selling systems.

The four Ps in action

Market research

So that they get to know exactly what customers want, companies involve themselves in market research either by asking people questions in the street or in their own homes, or enquiring by post or telephone. Completed questionnaires are computer read and analysed. Market research can be carried out at any of the stages of a product's or service's life. It is not just put into operation when a company is thinking of providing something new (the launch stage), though this sort of market research may have the effect of putting a stop to production altogether, or alter the product or service to make it more in line with customer demands.

Whilst the product is growing in the market the company may continue to research the market so that the product continues to fit any changing needs. With major domestic items, like washing machines, every purchaser is invited to contribute to the market research process and to provide evidence for the effectiveness of the marketing programme. The research may go on into the mature phase of the product, after which, unless it is substantially changed, there is a period of decline where the competition moves in on the market, or people no longer wish to buy that product or service, but prefer a redesigned or highly-modified one. For example, there are fewer LP records sold now that CDs are more generally available.

Distribution

Once the product is produced, marketed and launched it needs to be got into the shops or sales points. This is where the distribution department comes in. Stocks to meet anticipated demand have to be built up and warehoused, records kept of stocks held and distributed, documentation made ready for home and export markets, and transport provided to get the product to the right place at the right time.

Please do this 33 ————————————————————————————————— 2.1.3

Think of the jobs which have to be done in the distribution department. List them and try to put a job title next to each one.

The administration department

This is the department which deals with all aspects of administration that are not the direct responsibilities of the functional departments. The company secretary may well head the administration department. This position is a legal requirement in any company, and like all legal requirements there are sanctions against the company and the individual if the work which he or she is required to do is not carried out, or is carried out fraudulently or negligently. The Company Secretary:

- in consultation with the Chairman of the board of directors, arranges meetings of the board,
- prepares agendas,
- keeps the minutes books,
- oversees the administration of the pension scheme and all insurance schemes relating to the company,
- ensures that at all times the company operates legally and communicates with the shareholders about meetings, dividends and other matters concerning the policy, if not the day-to-day conduct, of the company.

The office systems and services, often including computer and reprographic services, the switchboard, reception, word processing, mailroom, filing, secretarial and clerical assistants, will all come under the aegis of the administration department. As you are doing this course you may well end up there yourself!

Please do this 34 ————————————————————————————————— 2.1.2, 2.1.4

Look at the structure of a large company and try to discover as much as you can about the arrangement and functions of the administration department. Consider why the functions are allocated to this department, and think about the cost of the department in relation to the overall cost of the organisation.

Decision making

Almost everything in business is to do with making decisions. Think about John as a sole trader and then as the managing director of a company with a chain of several shops. Did his assistant make decisions when he was in his first shop? Of course she did. But what was the level and nature of the decision? That depended very much on the amount of delegation which John allowed. Certainly, almost all decisions involved in dealing with a particular customer would be made by the assistant. The rules about cheque cards, credit and payment cards would have been immediately familiar to the assistant and reinforced on the first occasion when a mistake was made. Difficulties of a fairly extreme nature can always be referred by the assistant to the owner.

Decisions involve taking a hard look at all the factors you are aware of in a problem, adding a bit of inspiration to ensure that account is taken of the factors you do not know about, and determining what the options are. There will be good and bad points about each option. There will be long-term, medium-term and short-term effects of any decision. Decisions are related to the opportunity to do something. The technical jargon refers to *opportunity costs*. What this means is that if you do one thing, you cannot do the other things that you might have done. The other options are sacrificed in the interests of the option which you have taken.

Imagine the problems which beset Devonport Shipyard and Rosyth in 1991–93 when they were bidding for the building of Trident submarines. Too low a price and the contract could make the yard bankrupt, too high a price and the other contractors get the job. Apart from cost considerations there were major political and social considerations which also had to be taken into account.

Reorganisation and restructuring

When things go wrong in a business, or any organisation – when services or products are no longer wanted, prices are wrong, efficiency and morale are low, or profits are non-existent – there is a tendency to find a solution in reorganisation. This often has the effect of changing structures and procedures without much change in products or services. A fundamental reason for reorganisation is the need to be seen to be doing something in a crisis. One effect may be to turn the crisis into a disaster.

There are other matters such as changes in technology, working practices or consumer habits which affect the organisational structure of companies. For example, those who are very computer-literate in a company may find themselves highly rewarded and promoted to maintain their loyalty and prevent defection to a rival company. Likewise, a national store (like Next) might reduce its branches and perhaps even change its way of selling its products, from outlets which people visit to mail order.

Reorganisation can get rid of perceived dead wood among employees, allows areas of work which are not particularly profitable or may be losing money to be shed, or enables diversification to take place. The process of reorganisation itself can be a means of awarding less beneficial contracts or terms and conditions, or making employees redundant.

Some organisations do little more than move people round. However, this in itself may be sufficient to make people reconsider their positions. The result may be better performance; although it could equally well be low morale.

Strategic reorganisation

Reorganisation may be *strategic* rather than tactical. That is to say it may be part of a long-term analysis of goals. The financial situation may not be worsening, but the example of another competitor may lead management to imitate its style. The reorganisation may be aimed at improving internal communication systems or at introducing total quality management (TQM), or it may be associated with success, as in John's case.

Expansion may be a very good reason to consider reorganisation. That expansion may be within the existing market, or it may be a new product or service.

John may wish to acquire another business in the same line of services as his own. It is not unusual for small businesses with a lot of 'get up and go' to acquire large ones. For example, Sobell Television of Slough acquired GEC which had huge factories everywhere. In the process it had to reorganise both the new and existing businesses to make a successful single business.

Where there are 'ors' in the list of reasons for reorganisation it is often possible to read 'as well as'. A declining market share may lead to a merger with implications for re-engineering the businesses and improving communication whilst imitating some other successful company. The reasons for reorganisation are never as straightforward as the workforce – usually the most affected and most concerned – or the management supposes. Nearly all reorganisations bring unexpected benefits and unexpected problems.

Please do this 35 ——————————————————————————————2.1.5

If you consult the business pages of a number of newspapers you will see references to the reorganisation of companies.

1. Examine carefully the reasons given for the reorganisation and try to follow up during the year the effects of the changes. If these are connected with a public limited company (plc) you can compare the share prices before, immediately after and six months after the reorganisation.

Needless to say there are a lot of other factors which affect changes in share values, and you might want to look at the Financial Times Share Exchange (FTSE) overall values, which are expressed as a number, currently about 3000, in order to see if the company is improving its performance.

An example might be:

Independent Dyers plc

	November Just before reorganistion	**January** Just after reorganisation	**June** Six months later
Share value	231p	234p	224p
FTSE	3024	3176	2786

2. What conclusions can you draw about the effects of reorganisation against the background of FTSE values for the market as a whole?

What you get for what you do

In order to recruit really good quality staff John advertised for the new regional managers and the development manager at a substantial salary with a first-class all-round remuneration package. This consisted of a company car, BUPA (health care insurance), pension, five weeks' holiday a year and a personal assistant.

The package, as advertised, was better than the present regional managers were getting. Charles Hopkinson, one of the managers, decided to ask John two questions;

- Was John not satisfied with their performance, given that 'newcomers' were to be paid more and have better conditions?
- If there was going to be no improvement in their packages, could they apply for the new jobs?

John told Charles to call Kevin, the other regional manager and they would settle the matter at once.

John said, 'I am very keen on recruiting the best quality managers I can, which is why I am offering such a good package. However, I don't see why you should have to apply for jobs in the company, given that you're both successful managers and that the new structure is as much your idea as mine. What I'd like to do is to give you a new package from the first of next month and add to it a profit sharing benefit. After all, we've known each other for a long time and you have helped to build the success of the company, so you should share in it.'

Kevin and Charles left the meeting with smiles on their faces. The relationships of experience, trust and friendship had been well-rewarded.

In practice, the owner of a company now has the right to set whatever pay and conditions he or she thinks fit. Businesses in the UK are neither constrained by the European Community's Social Chapter which guarantees workers' rights, nor are they subject to the Low Pay Unit's minimum levels of pay for particular jobs.

The 'going rate' in most trades and professions has declined in real terms since 1989, partly owing to the recession and partly because there is a large pool of well-qualified people at all levels who are unemployed and looking for employment.

'Permanent', full-time jobs are very hard to find and 'permanent' no longer necessarily means a job for life. What you can get may not reflect what you are worth but will be affected by market force factors.

Summary

What we have tried to do in this chapter is to look at the way businesses are organised, give some examples of the internal functions of organisations and indicate that decision-making is not an easy task. It can be made more difficult:
- if there are many people to consult,
- if there are a number of virtually identically popular options, and
- if psychological and emotional factors influence the quality of communication of ideas and the balance of option choice.

Review questions

Match correct or Match incorrect – these questions require you to match the first statement against the one correct answer in a, b, c and d. This sort of question will be described as *Match correct*. In some questions you may find that you have to pick out the only incorrect answer; these will be referred to as *Match incorrect*.

True/false – these questions require you to look at two statements and decide whether each statement is true or false. You should ring the pair in a, b, c or d which is closest to your opinion of what the statements say. These will be described as *True/false* questions.

Match correct

1. The person in a company who deals with shareholders and makes sure that the company always operates within the law is:

   a The Managing Director

   b The Chief Accountant

   c The Company Secretary

   d The Company Solicitor.

Match correct

2. In the UK a large organisation tends to have:

a A simple structure

b Very few rules and procedures

c A president of the company

d A high level of specialisation of labour.

Match correct

3. Computers are useful for:

a Saving paper

b Providing a lot of employment for data processors

c Storing and handling information

d Finding out confidential information about other companies.

Match correct

4. A hierarchical structure:

a Is likely to be found in small organisations

b Has a small number of levels

c Facilitates informal relationships

d Will have job titles and responsibilities clearly stated.

Match correct

5. Finding out what customers think is conducted by:

a The sales department

b An advertising agency

c The market research department

d The company secretary.

Match correct

6. In a bureaucracy:

a There are narrow spans of control

b Decision making is rapid

c Policy statements are rare

d There are few pre-prepared rules of operation.

Match incorrect

7. The financial department is *not* responsible for:

a Credit control

b Payroll

c Petty cash

d The annual report.

Match correct

8. Organisations are divided into departments so that:

a The manager need not be an expert in a particular area

b Putting together specialised strengths makes the company more effective

c There are fewer opportunities for career development

d Specialist staff can work in a number of departments.

True/false

9. **i** Job production is ideal for manufacturing small numbers of specialised items – from jewellery to aerospace equipment

ii Flow production is utilised in the chemical based industries to produce materials like gas or oil

a i True ii True

b i True ii False

c i False ii False

d i False ii True.

True/false

10. i The personnel department is responsible for staff welfare, recruitment and employment of staff, keeping staff records, health and safety and manpower planning

ii The responsibility of the design department is to create designs which will be cheap, convince customers that the product is as well produced as the design indicates and will cover any deficiencies in the technological production of the item.

a i True ii True

b i True ii False

c i False ii False

d i False ii True.

Assignment 4.1
John diversifies

John has decided to diversify his DIY services by providing an auto-mix paint facility for his customers. This will involve the leasing of a paint mixing machine from the paint manufacturers for a minimum of three years and the purchase of a wide variety of raw materials from the same source. The alternative is to provide a DIY equipment hire service covering small power tools, workbenches, cement mixers, scaffolding towers and ladders, and specialised equipment like mitre boxes, cramps and jacks. Despite his efforts at market research, which have largely been asking the opinions of customers and friends, he is unable to make up his mind which option to go for.

Your tasks

Consider John's problem in relation to Ramstown's needs. Indicate who you would go to for advice. Think of the effects on John's business if a competitor set up in Ramstown to provide DIY services and sales, and either the same additional service that John is contemplating or the one which he decides not to offer at this stage.

Skills achieved

You will certainly be able to claim many of the *Communication skills*, and some of the *Information technology* skills. You may have used a computer package to look at things like payrolls and personnel records. *Application of number* has been tested, particularly with regard to the toffee making assignment.

5 Investigate employee and employer responsibilities and rights

Performance criteria

1. Explain the benefits of employer and employee cooperation;
2. Describe ways to resolve disagreements;
3. Explain employer rights and responsibilities;
4. Explain employee rights and responsibilities to their employers.

Range

- **Benefits of employer and employee co-operation:** survival of the business; improved employee commitment to the business, improved efficiency.
- **Ways to resolve disagreements:** trades union negotiation, legal representation (Advisory, Conciliation and Arbitration Services (ACAS), industrial tribunals, European Court of Justice).
- **Employer rights:** employees' compliance with terms of contract, employees' compliance with health and safety regulations; disciplinary action; legal representation (Advisory, Conciliation and Arbitration Services (ACAS), industrial tribunals, European Court of Justice).
- **Employer responsibilities:** to explain business objectives, to offer and facilitate training, to implement equal opportunities legislation at work (Sex Discrimination Act, Race Relations Act, Equal Pay Act), to comply with health and safety regulations, remuneration (pay, deduction of income tax, payment of National Insurance, pension deductions if in contract).
- **Employee rights:** remuneration, employer compliance with terms of contract, health and safety at work, equal opportunities at work (Sex Discrimination Act, Race Relations Act, Equal Pay Act), legal representation (Advisory, Conciliation and Arbitration Services (ACAS), industrial tribunals, European Court of Justice).
- **Employee responsibilities:** to meet the terms of contract, to meet health and safety regulations, to meet the objectives of the business, to meet customers' needs, to maintain quality standards.

Recruitment

When John Stead decided he needed an assistant he thought hard about what he most needed. Ideally, he required a person with an accounting background, practical engineering and plumbing skills, perhaps some abilities in carpentry and plastic technology, successful sales experience, good communication and personal skills, the ability to strike a bargain with suppliers, look after the stores, be a regular and punctual attender, and work long hours.

Unfortunately, although a variety of skills and a flexible approach are the most desirable characteristics in the majority of jobs, John's ability to reward such a paragon is limited. He writes down a list of everything there is to do in the shop during a week and crosses off the things he likes to do. The remainder will be the main responsibilities of his new assistant.

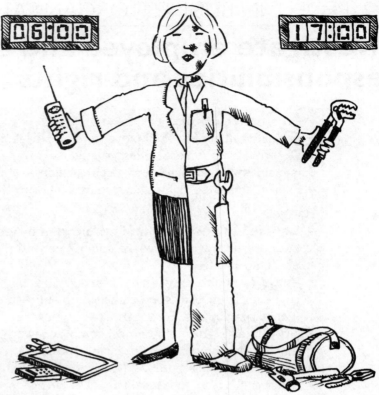

John's ideal assistant

Having made the selection of jobs for the assistant he decides to advertise in the *Ramstown Examiner*. However, he realises that a job advertisement is also a means of advertising his own business, so he constructs a small display advertisement:

John Stead & Co DIY
34 Imperial Road
RAMSTOWN RN21 7DJ
requires a
SALES ASSISTANT
Preferably experienced in DIY equipment and materials
Salary negotiable

He walks round the corner to the newspaper offices and pays to have the advertisement placed in next week's edition.

Please do this 36 ———————————————————————— 2.2.3

1. Look at job advertisements in the local newspaper. With the help of friends draw up a list of things which you would expect to find in a job advertisement.

2. Take 30 advertisements and say whether or not each one satisfies the

criteria which you have proposed. Do any of them exceed what you require and is this helpful? (Using a chart on your computer would be a good way of doing this task.)

3. Rewrite two or three advertisements to make them more complete and eye-catching.

On Friday morning John finds three letters in his letter box, hand delivered, and marks them as such. On Saturday morning he receives five more applications by post and on Monday a further one. Of the nine only three look to John as if they have any potential. He decides to interview each of the three candidates after work on Friday. He writes to each one inviting them to attend for a 40 minute interview at 6 p.m., 7 p.m., and 8 p.m. respectively.

John needs to:
* get together the questions which he wants to ask,
* decide whether some sort of practical test would be helpful, and
* indicate in far more detail what the job entails, as well as discussing likely salary, hours per week and holidays.

He then realises that there are things he as the employer has to comply with legally and he needs to point out the obligations of his chosen employee.

Please do this 37 ———————————————————————— 2.2.2

Look at John's advertisement in the paper.

1. Write a list of questions you would expect him to ask candidates.

2. List the additional information you would expect him to provide at the interview.

3. Add any questions you might expect the candidate to ask.

The contract of employment

The first thing John has to do is to sort out a *contract of employment* with the terms and conditions clearly stated. This will be given to the successful candidate. The contract of employment may well contain clauses about respect for confidentiality – this is to protect the employer's and any clients' businesses. In some cases it may also include a *restrictive covenant* preventing an employee from going to a similar competing company after leaving his or her present employment, either for a specified length of time after leaving, or within a geographical distance. This is to avoid the possibility of transferring trade secrets or taking clients away from the original employer to the new one.

Under the conditions of the Employment Protection (Consolidation) Act 1978 (EPCA) the contractual arrangements must include:
* the job title,
* a written statement of terms and conditions of employment,
* an itemised pay statement,
* a statutory period of notice,
* the right to maternity pay and the opportunity to return to work after having had a child.

There are also rights to redundancy pay and against unfair dismissal.

In formal terms, the contract of employment must include:
- the employer's name and the employee's,
- the date of commencement of work (important because there is greater protection after a certain period of employment),
- the rate of pay and its frequency,
- the hours of work,
- holiday entitlement and payment (if any) during holidays,
- entitlement to sick pay and time off if sick, and
- the length of notice of termination of employment.

Everyone is entitled to equal pay for the same job, the right not to be discriminated against, the right not to be dismissed or otherwise discriminated against because of trade union activities, and (if a woman) time off to have antenatal care.

Within two months of starting work a contract of employment must be forthcoming; after 104 weeks an employee is protected against unfair dismissal, is entitled to maternity pay and the right to return to work after childbirth, and to a redundancy payment if that is necessary.

Notice of termination of employment is not necessary in the first month of employment. Under 104 weeks, one week's notice is to be given and after 104 weeks, one week for each year worked up to a maximum of 12 weeks must be given.

Please do this 38 ————————————————————— **2.2.1, 2.2.2, 2.2.3, 2.2.4**

Draw up a contract of employment for a bus driver who is to be employed by Municipal Mileage plc.

Legislation affecting employment

The Equal Pay Act 1970, The Sex Discrimination Act 1975 and 1986 and the Race Relations Act 1976 all bear heavily on the rights of employees and the responsibilities of employers.

Please do this 39 ————————————————————— **2.2.1, 2.2.2, 2.2.3, 2.2.4**

Have a look at the outline coverage of the four Acts of Parliament referred to above as far as they affect employment. Make notes on the principal requirements which employers and employees must abide by.

Employers' responsibilities

It is not likely that the employee will make an issue out of being a trade union member. John has to make clear his equal opportunities policy so that the assistant cannot feel discriminated against in terms of race or gender (or a wide variety of other matters, including being disabled). John has to indicate such hazards as there are in a DIY shop and guard the new assistant from them. Of course, that works both ways and the employee has to be completely co-operative over the matter of health and safety. Similarly, the terms of the contract of employment, which are taken on quite freely, have to be complied with.

If a candidate does not like the look of what will be in the contract, then it is as well to say so at the earliest possible moment and withdraw as a candidate for the job. If a candidate has, or has had, an illness which would materially affect his or her ability to perform the job it should be reported to the employer. The Rehabilitation of Offenders Act 1974 permits an employee not to reveal to an employer some criminal offences for which he or she has been convicted after a certain period of time has elapsed.

John has difficulty with fixing any sort of salary, but looks carefully in the *Ramstown Examiner* and in several other papers to see what is the going rate. He wants to be fair, but not too generous initially, so that there may be an opportunity for rewarding exceptional service later.

There may be an opportunity for rewarding exceptional service later

Pay and deductions

John will be responsible for the deduction of income tax from the assistant's gross pay and also for the deduction of employee's NI contribution. He has to pay the employer's NI contribution.

Being reasonable

John is a reasonable person and is likely to treat his employee reasonably, and consult over such things as hours to be worked and holidays. Disciplinary matters are unlikely to occur, but some indication of what may happen if things go wrong should also be provided. Of course, if the candidate proves less able, or willing, than the paperwork and the interview indicated, then John has the recourse of dismissal. Although that is generally acknowledged as a statement of failure on both sides, it is usually much more unpleasant for one side than the other. In a larger company there would be a clearly defined disciplinary code.

Disciplinary codes and procedures

Employees are expected to behave reasonably. This involves:
- getting on with the job,
- being polite to supervisors, colleagues, customers and suppliers,
- not staying away from work without a good reason,
- taking care of the employer's property
- keeping confidential the employer's affairs, and
- not being disloyal to the company.

If one of these areas is a reason for complaint by the employer then the disciplinary procedures will be invoked. These are remarkably like what John would do in any case, but formalised.

Whilst John would have explained to his assistant that she should work along with him and follow his lead, the large company is likely to have a formalised and printed rule book to guide employees. This will start with a general statement requiring employees to abide by the rules and procedures.

John, if he is aware of something going wrong, may say to his assistant, 'Hey, it would be better to do . . .', and then see what happens next, and in the future. The large company will have a process which it describes as *informal counselling*. This may be conducted at the work station, where a supervisor may say, 'Hey, Bill, it would be better if you . . .', although generally the employee is taken on one side and the difficulty is discussed in private with him or her.

Usually, this results in an improvement in behaviour. If it does not then the employee will be called to see the supervisor, and may be accompanied by a trade union representative. The meeting will thoroughly investigate the situation, evidence from the employee being as important as that from the management, and a conclusion will be reached. This can either be a *first formal warning* which will be in writing, or a decision to go no further. The warning will remain in the employee's file for a period of six or 12 months, or some other agreed period. This period is important because any further proved transgression during it will result in a further hearing. If proved, the result is likely to be a *final written warning*. One more misbehaviour during the period of validity of the warning, if proved, will result in *dismissal*.

This procedure should be annexed to the contract of employment and explained in detail during the induction process.

Advisory, Conciliation and Arbitration Service (ACAS)

All this sounds very unpleasant, and it is never likely to be pleasant. However, it follows the procedures established by ACAS in its code of practice: *Disciplinary Practice and Procedures in Employment*. If a company does not follow the agreed procedures then it is not likely to win an industrial tribunal hearing, even if the reasons for the dismissal were apparently acceptable.

Gross misconduct

There is a category of offence, *gross misconduct*, which can lead to immediate suspension or dismissal. Such things as being caught stealing, assaulting another member of staff, or virtually any criminal offence are defined as gross misconduct. However, because such activities usually involve calling the police, and may well involve a prosecution, it is more usual to suspend the employee until after the case has come to court and a decision has been reached. Prejudging issues like this can be detrimental to the operation of the justice system and can be dangerous if the employee is found to be not guilty.

The alternative of demotion within the company is also available, as is transfer to another part of the company, or short-term suspension with or without pay. The last is a punishment; the former two are a means of getting a person off the premises whilst there is an investigation, or to give an opportunity for things to cool down.

Grievances

Just because John pays an assistant to come to work and perform a number of jobs, it does not mean that he has absolute rights over her, nor does it mean that he can behave unreasonably towards her. If the assistant is appointed to work in the shop, John would have to negotiate with her if he wished her to start going out to clients' premises and do minor repair jobs. Apart from anything else there would be an insurance requirement, and the original job description and contract of employment would have to be amended. Since she is not a general servant, he cannot force her to wash his car. Although she may be willing to do this in an emergency, it really is a waste of her time and talents.

Even if the job description ends with the words: 'such other tasks as may be required from time to time', this has to be viewed in terms of the principal employment.

Grievance procedures

In a large company the contract of employment refers to the actions an employee should take if he or she feels aggrieved. The first step is usually to take the matter up with the immediate supervisor. If the grievance concerns the type of work being done, or a change from the usual work without warning or consultation, or an apparent error in the payments which are received, it is often the case that this can be settled promptly and successfully. Sometimes the grievance may involve the relationship with the immediate supervisor. In this case, a consultation with the personnel department, or the supervisor's own manager, may be appropriate.

Of course, in the case of a member of a recognised trade union, the trade union will have the right to represent the aggrieved employee to the management. If an entire group is aggrieved, then this is the start of a *collective grievance* which normally the trade union officer will deal with on behalf of those who are aggrieved.

The vast majority of grievances are solved within a few minutes of the management being aware of them. The supervisor who is made aware that the employee has had no training on a particular machine, will do something to ensure that either training is promptly provided, or that the work is reallocated. Where the matter is not so straightforward the grievance will go outside the department in which the employee works. A member of the management will convene a meeting involving those with whom the employee is concerned, and the employee and his or her representative, so that the matter can be thoroughly investigated and settled.

In any case, all the opportunities for solving the problem which led to the grievance must be explored and alternatives put to both the aggrieved employee and whoever it is who has been the source of the grievance. If this does not work it may be possible to introduce an outside organisation, like ACAS, to deal with the grievance.

Please do this 40 ———————————————————— **2.2.1, 2.2.2, 2.2.3, 2.2.4**

1. With some friends, consider how you would go about making a complaint about your teacher. How would you feel about it? What effect do you think such a complaint might have?

2. Has your school/college a disciplinary or grievance procedure which is in writing and available to you? If so, obtain copies and consider how they fit in with the material in this chapter, bearing in mind that you are not employees of the institution.

3. If there are no written procedures, try to make out a case in writing why there should be, and also why there should not.

Trade unions

The trade unions, despite the avalanche of legislation curtailing their normal activities, culminating in the Trades Union Reform and Employment Rights Act 1993, have a substantial part to play in ensuring good relationships between employees and management. The presence of an experienced trade union branch officer may make both disciplinary and grievance hearings more productive. The management may frequently wish to negotiate a change with the trade union, rather than the workers individually.

The trade union and its members have as much interest in the welfare of the business as the management and shareholders have. All of them depend for their livings upon the success of the company, and this is a basic principle which should always be borne in mind in negotiations. Furthermore, the management may benefit considerably from good relations with the trade union because very often good ideas can be channelled to management via the trade union; likewise unacceptable ideas can be dealt with quickly.

If you are an employee you have the right to decide whether you wish to be a union member or not, and if you do join you have the right to take part in union activities. If, in due course, you are elected to a branch office, your employer is required to give you agreed unpaid time off for union activities, such as training and attending meetings. Employers are not allowed to discriminate in any way against union officers in their employ, or harass them because they have the right to take time off for their activities. Almost invariably a company which has good relationships between the management and the trade union is one which is successful in pursuing its goals. Where this is not the case, as in the Timex dispute in Scotland, all parties suffered as a result of the subsequent closure.

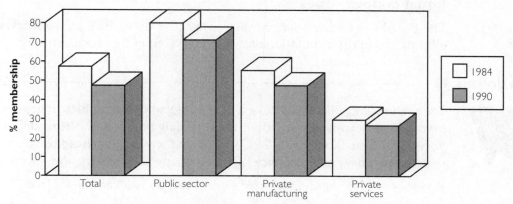

Percentage of employees who belong to a trades union

The changing face of industrial relations in the UK

The first line union officer is the *shop steward*, a term derived from the days of engineering workshops. In a large organisation there may be several shop stewards and a *convenor* who is the person who convenes meetings and chairs them. The convenor will be the principal negotiator with the management. The days of strikes when everyone came out on strike following a show of hands is now long past. Postal ballots have to be held for strike action and the election of paid officials.

Please do this 41 ─────────────────────────────── **2.2.1, 2.2.2, 2.2.4**

In most organisations of any size there is trade union representation.

1. Find out which unions are represented in your school/college and in any other organisation with which you have contact.

2. Talk to two or three members of unions and discover what they think are the principal aims of the union to which they belong. What benefits do they gain from being members?

3. Find out the names and addresses of four or five large unions and see if they publish information booklets for new or intending members. Read any such literature that you can get carefully and see if you can think of other things that unions could do. Are they are now fulfilling their aims successfully? (Remember that evidence in support of your arguments should be given, and you should always analyse the quality of your evidence before putting it forward.)

Discrimination

In itself the ability to discriminate productively is a valuable activity. It enables the apple grader to get rid of the bad apples, discriminating between the good and the bad and treating them suitably. In employment this is a different matter.

Equal opportunities

The Equal Opportunities Commission was set up in 1976 to work towards the elimination of discrimination and to promote equality of opportunity.

Please do this 42 ———————————————————————— **2.2.1, 2.2.3**

Your school or college will have a printed equal opportunities policy document. (In case anyone is in doubt the awarding bodies and National Council for Vocational Qualifications (NCVQ) insist that anyone approved to run a GNVQ course must have such a policy.) Obtain a copy and read it carefully.

1. Does it cover all the forms of discrimination you can think of?

2. Are the categories of those against whom discrimination is not to be practised complete?

3. Does the institution do what it says it will in terms of equality of opportunities?

Disabled employees

There is a distinguished young woman percussion player for whom composers have written work and who is in demand world-wide for her abilities in percussion playing. Several of her CDs are available in the UK and more are to come. She happens to be completely deaf. The lesson from this is to avoid discrimination against people because of your own or other people's prejudices.

The equal opportunities legislation, the Equal Pay Act and, specifically in this case, the Disabled Persons (Employment) Acts 1944 and 1958 give employers who employ over 20 full-time employees the duty to employ a proportion (currently 3 per cent) of registered disabled people. In 1980, it was ruled that every organisation to which the Act applied had to include in its annual report an analysis of how it was complying with the Act, including the number and proportion of registered disabled people employed.

If an employer has not achieved the 3 per cent quota then permission to recruit an able-bodied person to a vacancy must be obtained from the Employment Department.

Please do this 43 ———————————————————————— **2.2.1, 2.2.3**

Find out if your school or college has any disabled people working in it.

1. What is the percentage of the total work force expressed in full-time equivalent (FTE) terms?

2. Are there any disabled students?

3. What is done to make things like access, toilets, classrooms and workshops suitable for them?

4. What more could and should be done?

5. Why is the programme devoted to the handicapped on Radio 4 called 'Does he take sugar?'

Job advertisements and discrimination

John makes sure that his advertisement does not contain any discriminatory matter. Newspapers have a statutory duty to refuse any discriminatory job advertisements, though some very small or specialised enterprises are exempt from the anti-discrimination legislation, certainly as far as gender is concerned. Occasionally, however, something slips through. Have a quick look through several papers to see if you can find a job advertisement which prevents a proportion of the population applying for the job.

It is possible to complain about discrimination to industrial tribunals which deal with most matters concerning employment. If the matter is not resolved at an Industrial Tribunal it is possible to take the case to the Employment Appeal Tribunal.

Race relations

The Race Relations Act 1976 makes it illegal to discriminate on the grounds of colour, race, nationality or ethnic or racial origin. Like the Sex Discrimination Act 1975 and 1980, it indicates categories of discrimination which are forbidden, and includes both *direct* and *indirect* discrimination. An example of direct discrimination is openly saying, 'I won't employ a woman, and never a black woman'. An example of indirect discrimination is wording something so that a black woman could not be considered: 'applicants must have red hair, beards and be over 2 metres in height'. However, if this was for a job modelling clothes or appearing in a film, then the advertiser might just have a case.

Appointing Mary

Late on Friday evening, John makes up his mind to appoint a Chinese woman, Mary Tse (pronounced 'cher'). He has made sure that the rate for the job is what Mary will be paid in a similar situation. Apart from being a charming and hard working person, Mary is also secretary of the local aeromodellers society and a member of the model railway club. She brought to the interview an O gauge model of the railway locomotive 'King George V', complete in detail down to its silver bell. John was very impressed by her craftsmanship, which she learned at Ramstown Technical College.

John offers the job to Mary first thing on Monday morning. Mary is delighted to accept.

Rewarding Mary

Mary soon proves a valuable assistant to John. Apart from her charm and helpfulness, and considerable craft ability, she learns fast, is good at figures, concentrates on what she is doing and is approachable and helpful to customers.

John is pleased with Mary and after a month of increased sales (and profit) and Mary fixing things for customers almost as well as he can, he talks to her about her future. This is a good move because she will, rightly, feel appreciated and that is the beginning of effective human resource management.

It is important to remember that work has satisfactions other than the receipt of wages. At the lowest level of satisfaction we have to survive and the money received from work will help towards that. We need food, clothes and shelter. If that was all there was to it then money would be the only factor we would consider as being important. As it happens, some people will accept low wages for a job they enjoy and/or feel is doing some good. Alys Woodward, for example, receives no wages at all for working in the local Oxfam shop, but she derives a sense of group membership in an organisation with common and socially desirable goals. She contributes to the community and gains acceptance from the group.

The employer's contribution to emotional well-being

Gaining and giving respect, like gaining and giving love, are essential to human emotional well-being. It is as important to feel well thought of in one's job as it is to be well paid for one's efforts. Often this is as much a matter of having a pleasing personality as it is of contributing by very hard work, though hard work will be expected in most jobs. Mary Tse is an interesting person:

- She has the advantage of her Chinese origins which set her slightly apart from the average Lancastrian.
- She can do a lot of things well.
- She is friendly and outward going without being pushy.
- She likes to help people without patronising them.
- She is able to accept help without feeling inadequate.
- She likes to learn new things from John, and from customers and friends.
- She has integrity and good sense.

Health and safety at work

It is up to John to provide a safe and healthy working environment. He is legally required to do so under the terms of the Health and Safety at Work Act 1974 (HASWA). Mary must ensure she obeys the need to be careful and work safely. Deliberately or negligently putting at risk one's self or someone else at work is as likely to lead to legal action as is John's failure to put guards on a machine that requires them. The same applies to an order which John gives Mary. In the normal course of events, Mary must obey the order, but if the order requires her to do something which is illegal or dangerous she may justifiably refuse to do what is asked of her. Even if John is asking her in good faith she must still exercise her judgement in the matter.

If Mary does have an accident at work, John is able to refer the matter to his insurance company as under the Employers' Liability (Compulsory Insurance) Act 1982 he has to be covered against anything which happens to his employee whilst she is working for him.

Please do this 44 ——————————————————————— **2.2.1, 2.2.3, 2.2.4**

Walter Finch works in an engineering workshop with you. He drops a 12 kg piece of metal on his foot. Write down everything you would do as a witness of this accident.

Insurance is essential

Responsibility for employees

John would never discriminate against an employee on grounds of race, colour, gender, religion, age or disability, but he belongs to a minority who do not need the constant reminder of the legislation in order to behave reasonably and sensibly. John works on the principle that he should treat others as he wishes to be treated himself. Not a bad rule, especially as an employer is responsible for the acts of his employees.

John provides such training as Mary needs either personally, or by sending her to Ramstown Technical College. In exchange she works hard and willingly and uses her abilities to help the business prosper.

The personnel department

As we saw in the last chapter, a large employer would have a personnel department which ensures that all the things which John ensures are done for Mary are done for each of the employees. The procedures may not be quite so personal, at least as far as the boss recognising each employee is concerned, but they are effective in protecting each employee. Where there is a problem, the trade union representatives, who are well briefed in the law, as well as local custom and practice, can intervene to help a member who finds him or herself apparently aggrieved.

You will notice the difference between the immediacy of response of the sole trader – who may be able to detect a problem before it is verbalised and formalised, and deal with it at once – and the rather longer processes, which keep employees and their problems at some distance, inherent in the bureaucracy of a large employer. There is the immediacy and personal contact between employee and employer in a small organisation, but this has to be balanced against a possible general lack of knowledge and professionalism.

In a large company one has the distant, but usually wholly professional, view of the personnel department. Personnel officers are trained to deal with a problem unemotionally, tend not to let personal likes or dislikes affect their dealings with employees, and provide reasonably impartial support for all the parties following a dispute or difficulty.

Dismissal of an employee is as much a failure on the part of the management as it is of the employee. Management employs a person for a particular job. Presumably it uses its best judgement about his or her suitability at the time and should have a good record of support for the employee in terms of counselling, advice and training. If these do not work then internal redeployment might well be an option rather than disciplinary procedures for failing to fulfil the terms of the employment contract, or an inability to cope with the job as described. Negotiation is a greater skill than arbitrary decision making.

Job descriptions

Writing job descriptions requires a lot of knowledge and skill, and some very clear guidelines. In the end the only person who really knows what the job entails is the person who is or has been doing it. Asking and employee to write his or her own job description may often be very illuminating.

Henry Walker

An employee of a large engineering firm, Henry Walker, moved from a very large employer which closed to a very small firm. With the big employer he was employed full-time as a fork-lift truck driver in the stores moving raw materials and parts weighing many tons at a time.

Fork-lift trucks are driven sitting down. Although Henry is a big, strong man with tremendous stamina, when he moved to the small firm after 27 years with his previous employer, he was required not only to operate a fork-lift truck, but also to move steel bars by hand. This was not beyond his physical strength by any means. He had to cut up the bars into short lengths for processing on specialised machines.

He became very unhappy as he was unused to handling bar steel and the constant lifting affected his feet. He had reached that time in mid-life when his eyesight changed from 'normal' to long-sighted, so that he had great difficulty in focusing the heavily worn numbers on the dial of the machine cutter. Both these problems were easily solved. First by a visit to the chiropodist and having good quality, well fitting supportive boots. Secondly by having an eye test and glasses which made close, fine work much easier.

Henry found it very difficult to adjust to either of these needs, having always enjoyed good health and perfect vision. He came within an ace of giving up the job because he could not manage it. His job description omitted any reference to standing still for considerable periods, which he was utterly unused to, or the need for a flexible approach to a variety of new tasks, or the need for excellent close range eyesight.

If Henry had written his own job description or person analysis, his employer might have gained a completely different insight into what the job entailed and how it might be readily adapted to make the operation more efficient. Alternatively, Henry could have been redeployed to a more suitable position.

Please do this 45 ———————————————————————— 2.2.3

Try writing a job description for a postal delivery worker *or* a person who delivers milk to the doorstep. Indicate what personal characteristics and abilities are required.

Appraisal

Annual appraisal is the process whereby everyone is appraised by her or his line manager in terms of performance against the job description. It requires tact and sensitivity by the appraiser (the person conducting the appraisal) and a willingness to take criticism and suggestions by the appraisee (the person being appraised). For example, telling someone who is employed as an audio-typist that her output is low, when half her time is spent on filing, which she took over when another employee was declared redundant, is hardly a useful or helpful contribution to employee appraisal, or the effectiveness of the company.

Human beings are the most important part of an enterprise, and the most difficult to deal with. Lack of sensitivity on the part of management or employees; an inability to be flexible or to make the best use of the human resources available; failure to deal successfully with one's colleagues; close adherence to bureaucratic procedures, when a personal intervention at an early stage would have prevented a problem; these are all likely to lead to disputes and lack of efficiency.

It is possible to manage by consensus and by mutual striving for reasonable, achievable and mutually understood corporate goals. On the other hand, it is possible to manage by coercion and fear of losing one's job. The latter is much less difficult, but eventually people rebel, even if only by being less productive than they could be.

Spinning and weaving
Many years ago, spinning and weaving machinery in West Yorkshire was driven by overhead shafting connected to steam engines and by a leather belt from the shafting to the machine. A number of disaffected workers could

gain a break by all dislocating the flat belts from their pulleys at the same time. The curious coincidence in timing and the tight lipped attitude of the 'offenders' to the management meant that the latter could do nothing unless they were prepared to sack the whole shift of weavers. Such an act might have led to further difficulties with the workforce; it would in any case lead to a substantial loss of production.

Review questions

Match correct or Match incorrect – these questions require you to match the first statement against the one correct answer in a, b, c and d. This sort of question will be described as *Match correct*. In some questions you may find that you have to pick out the only incorrect answer; these will be referred to as *Match incorrect*.

True/false – these questions require you to look at two statements and decide whether each statement is true or false. You should ring the pair in a, b, c or d which is closest to your opinion of what the statements say. These will be described as *True/false* questions.

Match incorrect

1. Which of the following is *not* an employee's right?

    a To have a written contract of employment

    b To disobey an order which he or she does not like

    c To be paid

    d To work in an environment which conforms to the requirements of the Health and Safety at Work Act.

True/false

2. **i** An employer accepts responsibility for an employee's actions during the course of employment, but may claim compensation from the employee if he or she breaks the terms of the contract which include using reasonable care and skill

   ii An employer must pay an employee fairly, treat her or him fairly and must not discriminate against the employee on grounds of race or sex

    a i True ii True

    b i True ii False

    c i False ii False

    d i False ii True.

Match incorrect

3. An employer can require a member of staff:

a To do any work which is available

b To wear protective clothing if required

c To wear a company uniform

d To conform to the company image.

True/false

4. **i** An employee must be given a contract of employment within 13 weeks of starting work

   ii A potential employee can be refused a job as a clerk in an office because of her or his race, religion or gender

   a i True ii True

   b i True ii False

   c i False ii False

   d i False ii True.

Match incorrect

5. *One* of these statements is *not* true:

   a After two years full-time continuous employment an employee is protected against unfair dismissal

   b An employee who is no longer required after three years' full-time work is entitled to a redundancy payment

   c A woman who has worked full-time for a company for 18 months is entitled to maternity pay

   d After an employee has been in a job for 13 weeks he or she may not be discriminated against.

True/false

6. **i** An employee may be dismissed if he or she joins a trade union against the wishes of his or her employer

   ii It is always easy to make a complaint to a supervisor about a problem involved with working conditions

   a i True ii True

   b i True ii False

   c i False ii False

   d i False ii True.

Match incorrect

7. One of the following does *not* prevent discrimination against employees:

    a The Disabled Persons (Employment) Acts 1944 and 1958

    b The Equal Pay Act 1970

    c The Health and Safety at Work Act 1986

    d The Sex Discrimination Act 1975.

Match incorrect

8. It is a legal requirement in the UK:

    a To have a worker director in a company

    b To consult an employee before altering her or his conditions of service

    c For an employer to treat employees reasonably

    d To provide a safe and healthy place of work.

Match correct

9. Which of the following is a good reason for instant dismissal:

    a Un-notified absence

    b Swearing

Employee-employer relations

c Clocking or signing in or out for someone else

d Getting drunk at the firm's Christmas party.

Assignment 5.1
The care workers and the union representative

2.2.1, 2.2.2, 2.2.3, 2.2.4

You should now have a good idea of what is required of both employers and employees. In this assignment you will have an opportunity to combine much of the material in this chapter into an original piece of written work.

Jane Cater, Pedro Bianchi, Vladek Lenya and Julius Sykes work as care assistants for a local authority. Up to the present they have each been allocated to an old persons' home or a residential unit for young people. In the interests of efficiency it has been decided to bring them into a central pool with all the other care workers so that they may be allocated on a month-by-month and day-by-day basis to units requiring their services. They consult their union representative, Derick Marshall, who is noted for his good sense and ability to negotiate reasonable agreements, as they are unhappy with the new arrangements. He invites them to write down why they are unhappy and to list the grievances they feel they may have.

Your tasks

1. Imagine you are one of the care workers. Do as Derick suggests. If you are able to work with other people to do this task then do so.

2. Use the list to role play the characters listed above and explain in greater detail to Derick what it is you find difficult about the proposals. (If you are working on your own expand your list into written detail.)

Derick Marshall organises a meeting with the line manager of the care assistants, Terry Sullivan, who is keen on keeping to the management line. She indicates the advantages of the system to both management and employees. The employees indicate that the clients are likely to be less than happy at the arrangement.

3. Write down notes of all the participants' arguments.

Jane is married with two young daughters. She finds that instead of the existing regular 9 a.m. to 4.30 p.m. shift which she works at the old people's home half a mile from home, she may have only one week's notice, or less, of a variable shift pattern involving attendance at any one of the homes in the widespread local authority area. Julius finds himself on a permanent early shift at one of two children's residential homes in the area.

4. What legislation is likely to affect the decisions taken with regard to Jane and Julius?

5. What can be done about these if the local authority persists in its decision?

Vladek Lenya is a very caring person with excellent skills. The whole of his experience has been with old people. He now finds that he will have to work in a home for severely disturbed juveniles. Vladek was injured in a car accident five years ago and has limited use of his right leg and a permanent injury to his back. He is registered disabled. Vladek sees the decision of the local authority as affecting his employability.

6. What legislation might be quoted in his defence?

All the parties meet to thrash out the problem.

7. Write a script (about 1000 words) giving the arguments of both sides.

Skills achieved

Communication and *Information technology* skills are available throughout this chapter.

6 Present results of investigation into job roles

Performance criteria
1. Identify and describe individual's job roles at different levels within organisations.
2. Explain the benefits of team membership in performing job roles.
3. Identify activities performed by individuals at different levels within organisations.
4. Identify tasks in job roles.
5. Present results of investigation into job roles.

Range
- **Job roles:** director, manager, supervisor, production operative, support staff.
- **Levels:** senior, middle and junior.
- **Benefits of team membership:** achievement of objectives and targets, awareness of the needs of team members, improved commitment to job role.
- **Activities:** human resourcing, producing (goods or services), accounting, administration, selling, marketing, distributing, providing customer service, cleaning, security.
- **Tasks:** routine (planning, decision-making, problem solving, setting targets, achieving targets), non-routine (dealing with emergencies or accidents).

Jobs in an organisation

At one time John Stead performed all the roles in his business. In Chapter 5 we saw how he managed to get rid of some of the jobs and shared the work between himself and Mary Tse. Whilst he continued to be capable of doing all the jobs, he no longer had to do them all, and in any case Mary was better at doing some of them than he was. When his company expanded to 40 shops there was a headquarters staff with clearly differentiated roles and John spent most of his time planning the future and keeping an eye on the current progress.

Is a post needed? How do we fill it?

In a large organisation there have to be procedures for considering whether jobs are still needed and if a post falls vacant whether there is someone on the staff who could be appointed to it rather than appointing an external candidate. This is not always a valuable way of going about filling posts. It has the advantage of continuity, but we are living in rapidly changing times, and it could be that bringing in new skills and perspectives would be a better way of going about things.

Why? Who? What? When? How?

In any event, all jobs in an organisation need to be constantly reviewed. Apart from anything else it is necessary to see that there is still a worthwhile job to do. Sometimes people continue to do jobs which, when they have been examined closely, contribute little or nothing to the organisation. It is possible that the person involved is not even aware of this. It is not just 'what' the person does, but 'why' it is done at all. There is also the matter of 'how' it is done, but we'll look at that a little later.

A new job

Purna Karia decided to apply for a job running a small but highly prestigious organisation in a major provincial town. Much to her surprise she was appointed as Chief Executive with a substantial increase in pay and considerably improved conditions of service. She was very convincing at her interview, honestly admitting she knew nothing of the specific activities of the organisation, founded in 1839, but a great deal about how such an organisation should be run. The internal candidate, who was the Deputy Chief Executive, knew exactly what the organisation did, but nothing about how it might be improved. It was clear what the appointing committee had in mind.

First steps as Chief Executive

Purna spent the first three days of her work at the organisation with the Chief Administrative Officer (CAO) and the Chief Finance Officer (CFO). With the former she was introduced to all the members of staff, whilst the latter introduced her to the fact that the current year's activities were likely to lead to a substantial deficit – a fact not mentioned at her appointment.

Analysing the jobs

Purna looked at the job titles, the salary scales and the amount of overtime worked in some areas, and decided to kill two birds with one stone. She would enquire into the total running of the organisation and ask the questions: 'What?', 'Why?' and 'How?'; and see if there were rationalisations and improvements, including diversifications, which could be made.

She discovered that her own role had hitherto been entirely nominal. The previous Chief Executives had left the day-to-day running in the hands of the CAO, though there were professional staff in the Chief Executive's group who were senior to the CAO. Yet the work of the staff members was apparently controlled by the CAO, since the previous Chief Executives had made no attempt to organise their activities.

The Deputy Chief Executive's post appeared to Purna to be one she could do without since in any case the post holder had other interests dominating her life and relatively little interest in the job she was supposed to be doing. Purna was aware that there would be no help forthcoming from this person, so she did what any sensible, efficient manager would do, she sidelined the post and gave the responsibilities to the Assistant CEOs who were well able to perform them.

Redesigning the Chief Executive's role

The first thing that Purna decided to do was tacitly to redefine the Chief Executive's role. It changed from a passive role to being an intervening force in the day-to-day and long-term conduct of the organisation.

She promptly proceeded to write a set of corporate aims for the organisation and tried these on her bright twelve-year-old daughter. Her daughter did not understand two of them so Purna rewrote them. She worked on the principle that they could now be easily understood by all the members of staff.

Having done that, she thought out (on paper) an organisational structure which would give clear lines of responsibility and communication, and would be understandable by everyone. Because she felt that co-ordination and control were the major requirements of the organisation, she decided to use a hierarchical structure with herself at the top of the page. She subsequently altered it to a horizontally drawn hierarchy on an A4 sheet of paper turned 'landscape'.

Purna drafting out her ideas on paper

She put her post on the furthest left of the page. The Assistant Chief Executives (ACEs), were stacked vertically with the CAO and the Chief Finance Officer (CFO). Their roles were to be managerial and professional advisory, with the majority of the professional advice given by the ACEs. The Deputy Chief Executive's post did not feature on the chart and subsequently became the subject of an acrimonious redundancy case.

Differentiation of roles

The management functions were clearly divided with Purna managing the ACEs, CAO and CFO. The ACEs were to spend most of their time preparing client briefs, chairing committees and contributing (or acquiring) good new ideas for business. The CFO was to spend his time getting the accounts and forecasts right, down to the last penny. His responsibility was to give each ACE and the CAO a breakdown of expenditure and income in his or her area over each week, month and year, as well as contributing ideas to produce efficiency and increased income. The CAO would be responsible for the daily running of the organisation. This would include being Company Secretary and having the section heads and their staff reporting to him. These included those who were directly supportive of the ACEs and others who were providers of generalised services like printing and reprographics, filing and security, computer utilisation and the contracts manager.

The Chief Executive and ACEs each had a Personal Assistant (PA) in Purna's revised structure. Each PA also contributed to a general pool of administrative work. Purna was averse to highly-paid executives doing clerical work, hence her provision of opportunities for delegation. The section leaders dealt with specific parts of each contract's operations.

Moving out to move things on

To her surprise Purna discovered that two sections had no current function. One of the section leaders was close to retirement age and Purna offered him an early retirement package. The other, who had been recently appointed, was frustrated because of lack of work, and after discussion, he was happy to be transferred to a new business section. Purna thereby gained a friend and loyal supporter.

Equalising efforts

The sections' staffs were redeployed to areas where overtime at short notice was a common and inconvenient working practice. Among these was the print production area where evening and weekend working was the rule. Purna determined to review the operation. She knew why it existed and what it did; it was the 'how' that concerned her, having seen an abundance of hand work and elderly, inefficient machinery. Desk-top publishing had been introduced by the Computer Manager. Unfortunately the increasing output to be printed had not been matched by any increase in printing equipment or staff.

This was typical of the entire organisation, and many others like it. Good ideas were introduced without thinking through the consequences for the rest of the organisation. Hence Purna's change of the Chief Executive's role from a passive to productive one.

The new structure

With a comprehensible organisation structure and clearly defined roles and responsibilities established through updated job descriptions negotiated with each member of staff, Purna was on her way to having a cohesive enterprise with an opportunity to do away with the deficit and perhaps return to a handsome profit.

Purna's organisation structure looked like this:

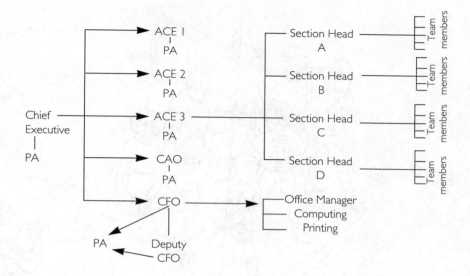

The organisation's services were in demand in any event, but the new arrangements ensured that the role which each person had were sufficiently clearly defined for the Receptionist and the Telephonist to know exactly who was dealing with what and to direct enquirers and clients to the right person first time.

Bureaucracy and the differentiation of jobs

The larger the organisation the narrower and more specific each job description will be. A very large city centre hotel may well have a head doorman and subsidiary doormen working shifts. A small countryside hotel, if it has anything of the sort, will call him or her a porter and will probably require maintenance and cleaning duties as well. Whilst flexibility of activity and attitude is an asset, doing the job as specified has considerable advantages.

Jean is employed as a cleaner. It is better for the company if she does that really well, being conscientious about attendance and cleanliness, than if she answers telephones when they ring. She will need initiative and judgement in knowing what to move whilst she is cleaning and what to put in the black plastic sack she uses to collect rubbish. However, her job is clearly defined as a person who does a limited (but essential) number of things.

Working in teams

Purna divides the staff into teams. She makes clear the roles of the directorate (herself, the ACEs, CAO and CFO). These include:
• co-ordination,
• control, and
• initiatives in the market place.

The next level of managers are the Section Heads who, like the directorate, make decisions, solve problems and set targets, but have a closer connection with achieving them on a day-to-day basis. Their team members will do all these things on a more narrow (but still important) level, particularly as Purna is about to start staff training in order to implement quality circles.

Purna's teams

Because the teams deal with a variety of functions within the organisation they feel themselves to be engaged in major functional areas. Bryan Field is the Chief Administrative Officer. This is a curious title for a man who has co-ordinating, control and personnel functions, but as in so many long-established organisations, job titles are inherited and remain unchanged even when the functions have been modernised, enlarged or modified beyond the recognition of earlier post holders. Purna does not alter it because it is well-recognised and the staff support the pivotal nature of the post and the post holder.

If she had been starting from scratch, Purna would have appointed a Personnel Officer, but seeing how well Bryan does his job, she feels no need to add to the costs of the enterprise.

Curiously enough the organisation has no sales, marketing or distribution divisions, relying on the expert professionalism of the ACEs who have built up and continue to develop a substantial clientele over the years. They are responsible for the design and setting of the manufacturing drawings and specifications for the clients. They discuss each enterprise with Bryan and the section leaders who are likely to be involved in order to establish priorities and times for completion of various aspects of the task and the entire job. They then negotiate with the client as well as establishing a price with the help of Martin Connery, the CFO, and his deputy, Tom Mills.

From the example of Purna's organisation it is possible to make generalisations. We have already looked at the hierarchical arrangement of businesses, and

Purna's organisation chart has only to be turned sideways to reveal its hierarchical nature. Her status as Chief Executive is matched by that of the Managing Director in a business. The latter is normally elected by the other directors.

Responsibilities and functions

The responsibilities of directors

Whilst Purna is busily attaining the targets which she sets, in a company the targets are set by the directors, as are its policies. The directors:
- deal with the longer-term plans of the business;
- make decisions about major expenditure;
- are responsible for ensuring that the company operates within the law;
- appoint senior staff; and
- make agreements about redundancy and dismissal.

Directors have a seat on the board of directors by right, though not all of them will work full-time for the company. (It is not uncommon for a director to hold several different directorships with various companies.) Some of the directors will be *non-executive* directors who are appointed because of their expertise in fields related to the company's interests.

Managers as communicators

A manager works to a director, whose strategy decisions he or she has to put into effect at the operational level. This will require the allocation of tasks in a team or teams and checking that the work is carried out cost-effectively to meet the set targets. Problem-solving and trouble-shooting are a manager's bread and butter. The manager also has a personnel function which involves first line counselling and help, and establishing training opportunities to meet the needs of individuals and the teams.

Acting as a communication channel between the directors and the employees is matched by the communication a manager has to have with the director to keep him or her abreast of progress and difficulties. Managers are supported by assistant managers and supervisors so that the span of command and control is not impossibly wide.

Ways in which job holders work

Being in a team but no team work

Steven, a student on work placement, landed a job with a national organisation. Steven's job was to turn up five minutes before the appointed time and then sit at a computer work station for the next six hours, being replaced by someone else at break times. His work was to receive incoming phone calls regarding queries on various accounts, punch up the information on the screen in front of him and reply or refer to a senior decision maker. He never knowingly met any of the people he dealt with and because of the pressure of work he did not speak to colleagues except at break times; then the subject tended to be football. Despite what looked like very unpromising conditions the service to clients was very good. At the time there appeared to be little opportunity for staff interaction or influence on the way the business was run. Quality circles were, at that time, unheard of but sports and social facilities were excellent.

Steven's situation was remarkable. He had a supervisor, but because he was intelligent, well-trained and conscientious he seldom referred to her. His working day was spent in the company of hundreds of other people but almost entirely isolated by the need to attend to what he was doing. He did not find it boring, he did not feel lonely and the day passed quite quickly. He felt he had helped a good number of people each day, many of whom remembered to say thank you. There was only oral contact with clients and little contact with staff, but limited as it was Steven felt his job was rewarding. His situation was remarkable in that although he was a member of a team he did not do anything like team work.

John Stead's situation in the days of his stall holding was similar in so far as he was literally a sole trader, but he enjoyed the company of fellow stall holders and of his customers. His working life was virtually all personal and direct contact on a one to one basis.

Team working

Most jobs require working in teams. It is unfortunate that the idea of competitiveness, originally meant to be involved with what the whole organisation was doing in the market place, infiltrated the running of many organisations. There is a fundamental weakness in any organisation when people go off on their own tack and ignore the corporate goals in order to gain a competitive advantage for themselves. Anyone can do this, it certainly does not require much more than a desire to 'bust the system'. What is much more difficult, and often undervalued, is the ability to work co-operatively and efficiently as a member of a team whilst progressing the corporate goals and bringing about agreed and effective changes, which in turn are seen to be advantageous.

The usual example of bad teamwork is the football team consisting of stars in each position but without any desire on each person's part to do anything but shine brighter than everyone else. There are not going to be many goals scored by that team in those circumstances. A co-operative team of less talented people will destroy the all stars, despite their individually superior skills.

There are few human activities which are not improved by a bit of teamwork. It is significant that the teachers involved in delivering your GNVQ may be called the GNVQ Intermediate Business team. Each member may belong to other teams as well but for effective delivery and assessment they belong to the team which deals with you and your fellow students. Inevitably, each member has different strengths and the aim of the team is to make these available to you in order to provide the best possible course.

Please do this 46 ———————————————————————— 2.3.1, 2.3.2, 2.3.3

1. List the characteristics of:

a a highly competitive person and

b a highly co-operative person.

c Say whether you think the two sets of characteristics can be combined in one person.

2. Look at a number of job roles which involve working on your own and working in a team. Indicate the differences between the two and the advantages and disadvantages of each to:

a the individuals involved,

b the organisation,

c its clients.

The functions of team members

The team members, who are controlled by supervisors, have to do jobs as specified in their job descriptions, co-operate with other team members and obey reasonable instructions. Team work is not the easiest of activities, since nearly all of the successes depend upon acting and thinking as if the members of the team had exchanged roles. That involves:
- taking account of others' opinions and beliefs,
- offering help and advice when required,
- accepting constructive criticism, and
- being assertive rather than aggressive.

Please do this 47 ————————————————2.3.1, 2.3.2, 2.3.3, 2.3.4, 2.3.5

1. With four friends, using a tube of glue or paste and a block of cheap A4 paper, design and make a bridge to cross a bottomless pit 60 cm wide and capable of supporting a weight of 500 grammes in the middle. You have 75 minutes to perform the design, construction and test. One of the party should take no part in the activity but should sit slightly apart and observe the progress of the undertaking whilst making careful notes of:

a the relationships between members of the group

b how each contributes to the enterprise

c how each is assertive, aggressive or compliant.

2. At the end of the activity each participant should write down how he or she thinks he or she has contributed and how he or she has behaved as a team member.

3. There should then be an opportunity for comparing notes between members of the team and subsequently hearing what a (hopefully) unbiased observer thinks.

Problem solving and decision making

The whole of business is to do with solving problems and making decisions. At the board of directors of Unilever the decisions taken will have huge and far reaching repercussions. The economic futures of some countries may be affected and certainly the economic health of areas and regions will be. At the level which a junior employee of a small provincial motor car repairer operates, then some customer may be inconvenienced if the employee gets it wrong, but for the most part the matter will have a very limited influence and will be forgotten very quickly.

Problems can be solved by:
- going away and thinking about them on one's own,
- considering them with other people, and
- brainstorming solutions and attempting to find the most successful one, given the criteria which you wish to apply.

Problems associated with things are usually relatively easy to solve, but problems with people are almost invariably complex.

The process of decision making is like setting out for school or college. The night before it is necessary to assemble the raw materials for the following day: clothes to wear, money for a meal, a bus pass, pens, pencils, handkerchiefs, keys, books and files.

Please do this 48 ———————————————————————————————————— 2.3.3

1. Consider each stage of getting to school or college on time and how it is achieved. Indicate what could go wrong and what contingency plans you put into operation to cope with substantial difficulties.

2. Whilst it is not a disaster if you arrive late, what could you do about arriving late on a day when there was an important external test which started at 9 a.m.?

3. Consider getting to the station for 7.15 a.m. to catch a train to get to an important interview, *or* consider getting to the nearest airport for 8 a.m. (whichever is the most applicable to your circumstances).

Going about decision making

In doing the above activity you may have put down a list of times which are crucial to getting up, washing, dressing, having breakfast; collecting up books and papers, and checking money, writing equipment and keys; walking to the bus stop, and catching the bus. The final stage of getting from the bus to the ultimate destination should be planned so enough time is provided for settling down to the day without being out of breath or apparently disorganised.

You should also have built in contingency plans in the event that the bus does not arrive, is late or is held up; or the car will not start, etc. All this is exactly what a problem solver and decision maker would do in a business. If you get up late and have no time for breakfast then you have to take more money to get a mid-morning snack. Think about a similar situation in a commercial or business environment – the sums involved are larger and may be crucial. Your timings are the operational targets which you need to reach in order to ensure that the end goal is achieved.

Setting targets

Targets need to be realistic and they need to be the subject of negotiation with those who have to reach them. There is no point in arbitrarily deciding that there will be a daily production of 22,000 widgets if the machines will only produce 17,000 and the employed available are only able to manage the effective supervision of 15,000. Targets which are too high will mean that morale is destroyed; targets that are too low will mean loss of efficiency and thus profitability.

In Chapter 5 we looked at the departments of a business. Each department will have different sorts of targets. Thus in all John's shops the telephone has to be answered before the fourth ring. Likewise, information requests from head office to shops, and vice versa, must be completed and returned within 24 hours. John sets sales targets which are not the same for each shop, and records customer complaints carefully so that each may be learned from. His accounts department has to meet deadlines on processing accounts and must be 100 per cent efficient in paying staff. The distribution network has to get goods to shops on time; failure to do this will lead to a loss in sales and a change of distributor. As you can see, problems and decisions exist constantly for all a company's employees as they do for most us.

Review questions

Match correct or *Match incorrect* – these questions require you to match the first statement against the one correct answer in a, b, c and d. This sort of question will be described as *Match correct*. In some questions you may find that you have to pick out the only incorrect answer; these will be referred to as *Match incorrect*.

True/false – these questions require you to look at two statements and decide whether each statement is true or false. You should ring the pair in a, b, c or d which is closest to your opinion of what the statements say. These will be described as *True/false* questions.

Match correct

1. Which item is true about large organisations in the UK:

  a Job specialisation

  b High salaries for everyone

  c There will be a company president

  d A barrister employed full-time.

Match incorrect

2. The board of directors is responsible for:

  a Establishing policies and priorities for the organisation

  b Making long-term plans

  c Appointing all staff

  d Ensuring that the company acts within the law.

Match incorrect

3. A manager should:

  a Carry out the instructions of the director to whom he or she is responsible

  b Ensure that staff work effectively

  c Delegate all the day to day problem solving

  d Carry out administrative duties relating to his or her area of work.

Match incorrect

4. A manager's responsibilities include:

  a Planning for the future

  b Making decisions

  c Looking after employees' domestic problems

  d Solving problems.

True/False

5. i A manager should consult the staff before setting targets

  ii A manager should frequently monitor the targets that are set

  a i True ii True

b i True ii False

c i False ii False

d i False ii True.

Match incorrect

6. The personnel department deals with:

   a Recruitment of employees

   b Arrangements for interviewing potential employees

   c Issuing reprimands over minor offences

   d Checking staff absences.

Match incorrect

7. The financial manager is responsible for:

   a The payroll system

   b The control of credit

   c Preparing the monthly and annual financial reports

   d Counting the petty cash.

8. The marketing department deals with:

   i Promoting products

   ii Employing public relations staff

   iii Market research

   iv Advising on changes in products.

How many of these statements are true?

   a 1

   b 2

   c 3

   d 4.

Match incorrect

9. A clerk in the administration department of an international company may:

   a Open the correspondence

   b Receive and send faxes

   c Not answer the telephone

   d Operate a photocopier.

Assignment 6.1
Studying a company

You will be accustomed by now to the sort of assignment which concludes each chapter. This one is a bit different since it includes both things to do and advice and information which is relevant to this chapter.

You will need to study a company in some depth, and it is suggested that you make use of your work placement, or your Saturday job if you have one, to ensure that what you are doing is entirely relevant and individual. The ideal size of company to look at has between 50 and 250 employees. If it is larger than 250 you might like to look at the way in which it is organised and some job roles. If very much larger, select a division to examine, preferably the one in which you are situated. You might find that a close study of two or three jobs which are relevant to the GNVQ in Business would be helpful.

In most companies the most approachable people are those in the personnel function. If there is only one personnel officer then things are clear cut and your main problem will be the amount of his or her time which you can reasonably take up. If there is more than one do not choose the Head of Personnel, but instead someone who is in continuous contact with the workforce. Someone in finance is another good bet. Their tasks are normally very clearly defined. Try the person responsible for the payroll, provided you do not try the busiest day, or when there is a particularly difficult problem. Usually the payroll works like clockwork, if only because of the power of the targets set, the hard work of those who have to achieve them and the complaints heaped on people who get things wrong.

A third area which provides interesting jobs is the computer manager's department. The payroll may well be situated there with a finance person providing information and checking entries. A lot of design, records, financial reports and virtually every other part of the company's activities will be using the computing services. You should draw up a check-list of what you want to know. Do not forget the Who?, What?, How?, When? and Why? headings. Purna asked a very simple question, 'Please tell me what you do', and received very complex answers. Decide if the job is cyclical by day, week month or year.

Take the person – Betty Crook – who opens and distributes the incoming mail. She collects it from the Post Office sorting office at 7.30 a.m. and takes it to her offices. She opens it, records items in the incoming post book, allocates them to particular executives and delivers them to desks before the staff arrive. The purple incoming mail folders should receive immediate attention and become purple outgoing mail folders later in the day when they are collected, the letters recorded in the outgoing post file, and the envelopes franked and taken to the Post Office.

Apart from the relatively irregular jobs of purchasing more franking credit and tapes, Betty Crook knows almost exactly what the beginning and end of her day will be like. The only difficult days are when a letter is misallocated (very rare), not answered or the answer not received promptly (not so rare), and she is asked to check the incoming and outgoing mail registers. The CAO considers these to be absolutely accurate records. Betty's work is a daily cycle, the time in between incoming and outgoing mail duties being spent on a variety of 'as needed' administrative and clerical tasks.

For Tom Mills the weekly-paid staff payroll is a weekly cycle and the monthly paid payroll just what it infers. Of course this means that once a month both the weekly and monthly payrolls have to be completed to deadlines, and however well Tom has prepared his ground there are always last minute additions and changes to be made. In addition to these two activities, Tom is involved also in the weekly, monthly, quarterly and annual financial statements, each of which is of increasing complexity. The work for the annual accounts goes on continuously through the year, but is the subject of frenetic activity in the fortnight before it is due at the printers.

In discussing job roles it is interesting to ask to what extent is what is done a matter of individual initiative or involves following carefully laid down guidelines? Personnel functions tend to be a sensitive mixture of the two. Hiring and firing are covered by carefully and closely defined procedures. Dealing with a personal problem will draw on initiative, sympathy and experience. In new product design much of the work will be on professional initiative, but there will be guidelines for the research and development department as there are rules for the handling of petty cash.

How is the job to be done? To whom does the post holder report and who reports to him or her? Can he or she call on support from other people or is he or she always in a supportive role? Who establishes that the work done is cost-effective? Is there an appraisal system and, if so, how does it work and what are its results? Why is it done, or if there is not one, is it a conscious decision (based on what reasoning?), or is it just that nobody has got round to it.

You may find three people involved in a task with two others checking on their progress and efficiency. No one asks whether the job should be done at all, and if it should be done, could it not be done by two people supervised by the team leader.

Most jobs have satisfactions apart from the money received. Betty Crook gets to know just about everyone in the company and exchanges a friendly word with each one every day. Her role substantially affects efficiency and the company's successful bid for BS 5750.

You could make a polite and tactful enquiry about the conditions of service: holidays, working hours, overtime arrangements, amount of stress and pressure, and the suitability of the pay scale (do not ask about specific pay) for the job. These may all give further insights into the job.

Ideally you should go through the entire company asking questions at every level and in each functional area. Time and patience would not stand this, so try two or three people at the most.

Your tasks

1. Draw up a questionnaire and have this approved by your internal assessor.

2. Approach people in the company, once you have established a connection

with it, tentatively and politely. Do take no for an answer and try else-where. If you are on a work placement give a copy of the questionnaire to the person you have picked out a couple of days before the time you want to discuss it with him or her. When people have had a chance to think out answers these are likely to be of better quality than those which are sprung on them. (Remember to ask exactly what the respondent does in each case.)

3. Make a number of copies of the questionnaire with space for your notes, and the answers. If the person you are interviewing does not want to answer a question do not ask why. It is entirely up to them to co-operate and they are doing you a favour by being involved. Always thank the person you have interviewed for the time that has been given to you. When you have all the information you will have a number of insights into the company as a whole and individual job roles as they are perceived by the post holder.

4. Make an organisation chart for the company and indicate where your two or three employees figure on it.

5. Then analyse the responses, indicating on the chart the reporting relation-ships.

6. Write up each job in accordance with the areas of enquiry which are on the questionnaire and the criteria which have been indicated in this assign-ment.

The finished material must be word processed and there should be an oral presentation to a group of four or five of your class, with an opportunity to discuss differences between employees in one company and between com-panies.

Skills achieved

This chapter is not rich in *Application of number* skills, but could be an excel-lent opportunity for word processing and even DTP skill enhancement. In the area of *Communications*, it is difficult to determine where the chapter does not give opportunity for enhancement and practice. Look through the specification and see where you can find evidence to support your claim.

7 Prepare for employment or self-employment

Performance criteria

1. Identify types of employment and self-employment;
2. Identify opportunities for employment or self-employment;
3. Select information from relevant sources which applies to identified employment opportunities;
4. Analyse skills for employment or self-employment;
5. Discuss own strengths and weaknesses in relation to skills for employment or self-employment.

Range

- **Types of employment and self-employment:** paid (private, public sectors), voluntary, own business (family business, business start-up, enterprise scheme, partnership franchise).
- **Opportunities:** local, national, international.
- **Information sources:** Job Centres, media (newspapers, TV, radio), careers office, employment agencies, Federation of Self Employed, banks, Training and Enterprise Councils (TECs), charitable organisations.
- **Analyse:** in terms of: own skills achievement; ways to develop and improve skills.
- **Skills:** working with others, working independently, time management, decision-making, problem-solving, planning, information seeking, evaluating, communication, application of number, information technology, occupational skills.

Introduction

In looking at a portion of John Stead's career we have seen the change from being employed as an engineer through to being employed by a college, which is just a different sort of business, to being self-employed. The aim of this chapter is to consider how to obtain employment and also how to become self-employed.

The great majority of people are employed by other people or organisations, rather than being self-employed. However, there are substantial numbers of people who are self-employed. During 1990–94 more people became unemployed as a result of small businesses closing down than were made redundant by large employers. Large employers take on substantial numbers when times are better for them, whilst small businesses often continue to be constrained by the effort of coping with years of bad trading conditions. Most companies are trying to cut the number of employees in order to reduce costs in an era when input costs – wages and salaries, raw materials, machinery, and energy – are rising whilst output values have so far remained steady or dropped.

How to get a job

You are engaged in a programme of learning and activity which has a specific vocational intention – preparation for entry into the world of business employment. In highly-competitive times you:

- have to be well-qualified, and GNVQ Intermediate is a good start;
- need some experience – work experience or a part-time job help;
- must be a good communicator;
- must be numerate and able to use information technology, hence the importance of the core skills;
- need to be clean and smart in appearance and obviously highly-motivated to succeed.

Finally, politeness and a reasonably warm personality help.

You then have to look for a job. The local newspapers will often prove a useful source of job advertisements, as will the Job Centre and perhaps licensed private employment agencies. Some national newspapers advertise beginners' jobs in business, but you have to take into account the costs of living away from home and the salary offered to cover those costs.

Look at the market carefully. Remember that the salary offered is subject to a number of deductions (tax and National Insurance for a start) and that in London the salary should be 25 per cent more than elsewhere in the UK to account for the additional high cost of living.

For jobs in business, the ability to read and write successfully and accurately is taken for granted. At a Job Centre you complete a form. An answer to an advertisement has to be constructed, usually in terms of a letter. For example, in reply to an advertisement:

- for a clerk with skills in financial transaction recording,
- with William Brown and Co Ltd, Mercury Works, Wood Lane, Hallifield HA3 0PR,
- which requests a written application to be sent to the Personnel Manager,

your letter may be laid out as follows:

```
Personnel Manager                    Your address
William Brown and Co Ltd
Mercury Works                   Your telephone number
Wood Lane
Hallifield HA3 0PR


12th April 1995


Dear Sir/Madam,

        Re: Clerk's post as advertised

Please may I be considered for this post,
advertised in the Hallifield Chronicle on
Thursday 11th April. I enclose a brief CV and
would welcome an opportunity to attend for an
interview.


Yours faithfully,


Sign your name

PRINT YOUR NAME
```

Your curriculum vitae (CV), is even more important. While your letter could be submitted in your (best) handwriting, your CV should be word processed and well laid out. It should include your name, address, age, date of birth, secondary school attended and work experience. You should include in work experience any periods of work during your school life and subsequently, and any part-time jobs which you have had. Insert the dates when these took place.

You should list your qualifications achieved up to 16 and an explanation of your GNVQ. A list of the vocational units and core skills would be helpful. The employer will have been to school, but will certainly not have pursued a GNVQ programme and may not know what you have done. You can add hobbies or exceptional attainments, like being captain of the school hockey/football team or whatever, but remember that your potential employer may have 200 applications to select from so brevity and clarity count.

Do not be put off by advertisements which ask for previous experience, even if they say it is essential. Your part-time job or work experience may be enough to cover this. Everyone has to start somewhere.

Please do this 49 ————————————————————————— 2.4.4, 2.4,5

Answer this advertisement:

> **James Smith and Daughter Ltd**
> **Transport and Warehousing**
> **Gargantua Works**
> **25-51 Rabelais Road**
> **HALLIFIELD HA8 4SP**
>
> There is a vacancy for a Junior Clerk in the Despatch Department. Required at once a well-qualified and experienced clerk with computer and numeracy skills. Salary by negotiation. Apply in writing to Mrs T Walker, Personnel Manager.

There is a lot that this advertisement does not tell you. Mrs Walker has not provided further details, like holidays, hours of work, sick pay, possibility of superannuation and so on. As far as labour of this sort is concerned it is very much a buyer's market. The company has not stated a salary because it wants to try and get the best person for the job at the lowest salary. The idea that you are going to be able to negotiate your salary upwards from an initial offer is probably unrealistic.

Attending for an interview

Your application looks businesslike, even if you have not got everything that the employer is looking for and so you are invited to an interview. Of course everything you wear will be clean, tidy and fairly quiet in appearance. Arrive at least 10 minutes before the time requested on the invitation. Go to reception or the location stated in the invitation and tell them you are there.

In due course you will be invited into a room to talk to representatives of the company. Do not smoke, avoid a cup of tea if it is offered, look straight at whoever is asking questions without going in for fixed stares and keep your answers brief and to the point. When you have finished thank the people for seeing you. They should make it clear to you whether a decision will be made there and then, or whether you will be told the outcome in due course.

The best way to prepare for an interview is to have a simulated interview videoed. Look at your performance with critical friends and an expert teacher. Do not be put off by all their comments, one person's irritating mannerism is another's characterful foible. However, you will soon find out if you do not look at people, mumble or go on too long, and also whether those fluorescent socks and jumper really fit in with your neat grey suit.

Do not try to alter everything about yourself to suit other people's prejudices or advice, but remember to look up, speak up and listen carefully. Do not be worried about being nervous; those interviewing you may also be nervous. In any case, remember that they are also human.

Self-employment

WARNING

If you cannot get a job perhaps you can make one for yourself. But beware:

> UNDER THE AGE OF EIGHTEEN YOU CANNOT LEGALLY ENTER INTO ANY CONTRACT.

What this means is that if you intend to supply goods or services in return for money you must have a guarantor who will honour the contract should you be unable to complete the work. Do *not* pass yourself as over 18 as this is fraud and has substantial legal penalties.

It is not easy to get a job and you may be disillusioned and depressed by the number of rejections or, more likely, the number of complete blanks you get as a result of applying for jobs. Do not get too depressed – just keep trying.

There are four major considerations before venturing into self-employment. You need to ask yourself:
- What can I do?
- What do other people want?
- How do I get the accommodation, equipment and materials to do the job?
- Do I really understand the disadvantages of being self-employed rather than sticking out for a job with someone else.

Obviously, if you are 35 and have a long, interesting and so far successful career behind you, the situation is different from being 17. A 35-year-old might become a management consultant. He or she may have saved enough money to have a sound financial base to set up in business.

Please do this 50 ─── 2.4.2, 2.4.3, 2.4.4

You are young, healthy, determined, patient, hard working and not easily put down. You possess good social skills, so that although you may feel slightly shy, you find it quite possible to engage in reasonable relationships with strangers. You look round the area in which you live. Perhaps it is suburban and people have houses and gardens. Most of them will be working. Looking after the garden or cleaning the house is just one more chore. Could you do that? Suppose you think you could start out in business as:
- a self-employed house cleaner, or
- a self-employed gardener.

You are at once faced by problems.

1. List all the problems you think you would face in either of these occupations as a self-employed person.

2. Against each problem indicate how you would overcome each one.

In either of these two jobs you would be on your own to start with – the classic sole trader. You might want to team up with a trusted friend once you get near to saturation level with work. Do not let the desire to make money lead

115

you to rarely having time off or breaks. Cleaning and gardening may go well with baby sitting and you might find yourself working from 8 a.m. until 1 a.m. the following day. Pace yourself. Remember you need to be able to work tomorrow, and next week, and next year.

Please do this 51 —————————————————————————— 2.4.1, 2.4.2, 2.4.3, 2.4.4, 2.4.5

1. List the different ways in which you can be self-employed. (We have already mentioned sole trader.) Indicate three jobs you think are likely to go with each form of self-employment.

2. What sort of attitudes and skills do you think the self-employed need to be successful?

3. Being self-employed is very different from being employed by someone else. Describe the differences and explain how you would go about coping with them.

Meet yourself

No one knows you better than you do, although you may be surprised to find that others, whose judgement you respect, have a higher opinion of your abilities than you have.

Please do this 52 ——————————————————————— **2.4.4, 2.4.5**

1. Have a think about yourself. Look at the criteria which you think make for success as a self-employed person and indicate if you possess each one.

2. For those criteria which you think you do not possess make a note of what you might do to ensure that you are properly qualified for self-employment.

You are not on your own

Ideally, you should find the names of those organisations which can help you with finding out about self-employment. You will see in the standard for this unit that some are listed. In addition consider the following:

- Chamber of Commerce
- Department of Trade and Industry
- Department of Employment
- Citizens' Advice Bureaux.

You will find the local addresses of all these in the telephone directory.

One very important source of information is the self-employed themselves. Small shop-keepers, your dentist, your solicitor the local vet and possibly the person who delivers the milk are self-employed. But be careful, your dentist may be a person employed by partners in a group practice. He or she may be, along with the receptionist and dental nurses, an employed person.

Tactfully ask any person you think may be self-employed if indeed they are. Then ask them to describe the advantages and disadvantages of self-employment and also how they got started.

What a person who has been through the process of starting up in business on their own can tell you is invaluable. He or she will tell you things you might not have thought of but you need to consider, for example:

- setting-up costs,
- insurance,
- providing for a pension,
- employing an accountant,
- employing other people,
- working on your own or working as a partner in a team,
- getting retraining as skills do not keep up with clients' needs or technology.

Review questions ——————————————————————————

Match correct or Match incorrect – these questions require you to match the first statement against the one correct answer in a, b, c and d. This sort of question will be described as *Match correct*. In some questions you may find that you have to pick out the only incorrect answer; these will be referred to as *Match incorrect*.

Match correct

1. A person of 17 years of age cannot:

    a Enter into a contract for services

    b Start a business for services

    c Enter a partnership

    d Own shares in a public limited company.

Match correct

2. The place to get a job is:

    a Job Centre

    b Newspaper advertisement

    c Employment agency

    d Any of **a** to **c**.

Match correct

3. It is *not* helpful to a self-employed person to have:

    a Skills in decision making

    b Abilities as a communicator

    c No previous experience of being employed

    d An ability to work independently.

Match correct

4. Legal deductions from pay do *not* include:

    a Income tax

    b Pension contributions

    c Rent

    d National Insurance contributions.

Match correct

5. A CV should have

    a Every detail of your past life

    b Complete details of your previous employment

    c Copies of your educational certificates

    d Details of your previous employment and qualifications.

Match incorrect

6. If you are self-employed and you need help, you may approach:

    a A bank

    b Chamber of Commerce

c Department of Education

d Training and Enterprise Council.

Match correct

7. A franchise:

a Cannot be operated by a sole trader

b Requires the franchisee to have no other business interests

c Can be cancelled by the franchisor without notice

d Is a means of engaging in a proved enterprise at the lowest possible cost.

Assignment 7.1
Starting your own business
2.4.1, 2.4.2, 2.4.4, 2.4.5

Earlier in this chapter you looked at a service or supply of goods you could provide as a self-employed person. If you are happy with the example you chose, then apply this assignment to it. If not, make another choice.

You need to consider how to put your choice into operation. This will be a business plan. You will need help to start your business. This can be financial, technical, or most likely both. You should consider the first year of your activities, write your business plan and then try it out on whoever you think may lend you the money to start up.

Your tasks

1. Describe in detail what it is you are going to do. 'Tidy gardens' as a general aim is all right, but you need to detail exactly what it implies, for example, hedge cutting, grass cutting, weeding, providing plants, planting them and so on.

2. Describe how you are going to do the job. What equipment and materials are required? What are you going to do in the winter? What do you need for storage? Do you need any expert help? Indicate the costs in each case.

3. Say how you are going to market your services and the cost of doing so.

4. Indicate how and what you are going to charge for your services and what guarantees of customer satisfaction you will include in your marketing information.

5. State what information you need to run the business and who is likely to provide it.

6. State if you will consider seeking aid from a government scheme. Give your reasons for and against seeking aid.

7. Describe how you will raise start-up finance.

8. Draw up an estimate of income and expenditure for the year. Remember you do have to pay revenue costs as they arise, but you may pay capital costs over a period (usually at a high rate of interest).

9. Indicate exactly how your strengths match the intended activity and where they are not powerful what you propose to do about this.

8 Explain the importance of consumers and customers

Performance criteria

1. Describe the effect of consumers on sales of goods and services;
2. Identify and explain the buying habits of consumers with different characteristics;
3. Identify trends in consumer demand;
4. Produce graphics to illustrate the trends;
5. Explain causes of change in consumer demand for consumer goods and services;
6. Explain and give examples of the importance of customers to business organisations.

Range

- **Effect of consumers:** create demand (weak, strong), cause changes in demand, stimulate supply of goods and services to meet demand.
- **Buying habits of consumers:** types of goods and services, level of buying, frequency of buying.
- **Characteristics:** age, gender, geographical, lifestyle (taste, fashion, preferences).
- **Trends in consumer demand:** past (short-term, long-term), future (short-term, long-term); increasing consumer demand, decreasing consumer demand.
- **Causes of change in consumers' demand:** money to spend (cost of living, earnings); confidence to spend; changing needs, changing wants, advertising.
- **Importance of customers:** to income, to repeat business, to survival of business, for information, to contribute to profit.

Consumers' effect on the market

Redundancy and its effects

Colin Walker had a good job. He worked hard and effectively, but the company he worked for fell victim to 'the recession'. He became redundant but there was nothing in the company funds to pay him a redundancy settlement.

Being unemployed was a new and devastating experience for the 53-year-old. He signed on at the Job Centre and joined the 3 million people seeking work. He could not cope with being at home all day. His life had been his work with breaks for pleasant holidays. His pension, never big, was frozen until he was 65. The mortgage payments on his house, bought in 1988, were so large that he had been unable to save. Now he was unable to keep the payments up despite the 'redundancy insurance' that he had prudently taken out. He became impossible to live with. His wife went to live with her widowed sister. The house was repossessed by the building society.

Colin drifted on to the streets. He had no fixed abode but normally slept under the portico of St Pancras church. Because he had no fixed address he could not claim Social Security or other benefits and resorted to begging. The *Big Issue* tried to rehabilitate him but he was too depressed to do anything but shuffle about and try to avoid thinking.

Colin used to buy a new car every three years and he had a new washing machine every five years. He bought suits, shirts, shoes, wine and food. He employed people to service his car, tidy his garden and clean his house. He paid income tax and community charge and quite large quantities of VAT. He does not do any of that now.

The example in the case study indicates that those with very low incomes exist at the subsistence level. They are unable to have much effect on the market either as purchasers or consumers, except to add to a group which requires nothing in the way of quality and everything in the way of cheapness. This situation applies to a large and increasing section of the community.

Those in work see the effects that redundancy and poverty have on others and it makes them uneasy. Workers worry about the length of time they might hold on to their jobs. The often constant demand for more work for less reward and the state of the employment market makes for further uneasiness. The example of those who bought when the property market was at its highest in 1988 and have lived to become penurious is before them. As a result they do not feel good and try to save for the rainy day which could be just around the corner. Workers do not spend in the market and as a result the economy does not improve by providing more products and employing more people.

We have already seen that the rich–poor gap has widened, but there are relatively few rich people compared with the large numbers of the poor. The rich have the world as their market place and their effect on the market is specialist and small.

People have material needs to survive but in times of hardship these tend to be reduced to the minimum and inessential or so-called 'luxury goods' are purchased by few.

Unless people need or want a product it is destined to fail. If they do not go on wanting it the producers will soon see some substantial drops in sales. The consumer dictates the market, but the consumer can be heavily influenced – primarily by advertising – to prefer some goods and services over others.

Please do this 53 ——————————————————————— 3.1.2, 3.1.5

Consider a purchase which you made during the last week. Why did you make it? Did you have to save up for it? Are you happy with it? What needs or wants does it fulfil? Were there alternatives? If so, why did you choose this particular purchase?

The following text is concerned with individuals as consumers, but businesses and governments are also consumers. When they feel uneasy they do not buy as much: in good times they may well buy more. They are influenced in the same way as individual consumers. They may spend £20 million where we would spend £20 but the motivation and influence remain the same.

Please do this 54 ──────────────────────── 3.1.1, 3.1.3, 3.1.4, 3.1.5

Consider the effect of consumers on the economy and indicate reasons on a national scale for changes in demand.

Consumers

John Stead stands in the rain in Shipton High Street. He smiles at customers he knows and looks encouragingly at other people who might be potential customers. A small child and an elderly lady approach him. As a good salesman he includes them both and is careful not to lose either. The small child is neatly and expensively dressed and proffers £1.50 for three cans of cat food. John gives her the change.

The elderly lady wants to have a chat about her almost equally elderly cat, Twinkle, as well as buying four tins. During the chat a young man in a sweat shirt, jeans and trainers buys six tins and hurries off. Two other men stop. One is obviously wealthy, well turned out and distinguished. He buys nine cans with a £10 note.

In these few minutes we have seen some of the characteristics of consumers. They can be of almost any age, social class, income level or motivation. A consumer can be an individual, a family or an organisation. A consumer buys goods (as in tins of cat food) or services (from a solicitor or an accountant). Whatever is bought satisfies some need or want of the purchaser. It is also common that the need or want will change fairly rapidly, so that this year's highly desired car will be next year's has been.

Please do this 55 ──────────────────────────────────── 3.1.2

Occupations are often associated with social classes and ways of life. Whilst it is possible to bend the occupational class to the social class, 'way of life' is often a myth. Having said all this what considerations do you think each of the following individuals would take into account in each of the following purchases:
- a solicitor, an accountant, a fashion shop sales assistant, a motor mechanic in a large garage, a male veterinary surgeon, a female veterinary surgeon, a fork-lift truck driver, an unemployed bus driver, an old age pensioner, a nurse.
- a refrigerator, lunch, a packet of cigarettes, a railway ticket to a destination 200 miles away, a bet on a horse running at the meeting to be held at Doncaster today.

Give reasons for your views.

Market research

When John Stead owned a market stall he did market research the hard way. He noticed that a certain brand – Pusscateers – did not sell well. It was a bit expensive for a smallish can and cats did not seem to like it. John's market research is based entirely on a sampling of customers' preferences through attempting to sell the products. Of course he does not buy vast quantities of anything so the process is never quite a disaster. However, for the manufacturers of Pusscateers it is a different matter. John can shift the remaining tins at cost price or slightly less, almost using them as a 'loss leader' but the Pusscateers company are in trouble if this trend is nationwide. Pusscateers Ltd is large enough to do other sorts of market research and has its own marketing department. Marketing is defined as:

> *'the anticipation, identification and fulfilment of a consumer need – at a profit'*
> (Chartered Institute of Marketing)

Of course there is one inevitable problem with cat food. People who buy it may like the packaging and perhaps the price, but their cats may not like the contents. A fine balance has to be struck.

Tasty packaging and price, but what about the contents?

Pusscateers Ltd considers the decisions people made before they bought cat food and why they decided on tinned varieties of meat-based foods. Through mailed questionnaires, accompanied by the chance of a cash prize for one of the lucky respondents, and via research assistants questioning customers at super-market shelves, the company discovered that the majority of buyers were women who added the cat food to their weekly groceries. The marketing department found that tinned food made up 85 per cent of the market, with dried food occupying 9 per cent. Consumers mainly bought the cat food at supermarkets with their weekly shopping, though cost-conscious people, or those who disliked or had no easy access to supermarkets, used pet food shops or market stalls. All cat food seems to be bought for cash, except for direct supplies to breeders and kennels/catteries.

John relied on his own views based on the speed at which cans moved. Pusscateers relies on careful market analysis which is reflected, it hopes, in the speed at which pallet loads of boxes of cat food are sold. In John's case the consumers are individuals; in Pusscateers they are generally organisations. John is a retailer; Pusscateers supply wholesalers and are thus one stage further removed from the end consumer.

Please do this 56 ———————————————————— **3.1.3, 3.1.6**

John met Petra Dent who has a small canning factory. She specialises in mushy peas for the North of England market; buying dried peas by the tonne, boiling and then canning them. She does not see much chance of extending her market share since she has already captured 75 per cent of it; the remainder is supplied by a number of major canners for whom this is a tiny proportion of their production. John wonders if there is a case for producing 'own brand' cat food.

What advice would you give him about market research?

Analysing the consumer

John knows many of his consumers personally. He is aware of their economic and cultural backgrounds and their social class. He does not offer the bank manager the cheapest cat food, nor Mrs Wharam, who is a Hindu, cat food made of beef, since this would be offensive to her religious beliefs.

John's geographical area of operation is limited, but larger-scale enterprises have to recognise that there are differences between the UK regions, as there are for example between France as a country and Wales.

Please do this 57 ———————————————————— **3.1.2, 3.1.3, 3.1.5, 3.1.6**

Mary and Harry O'Brien have two children and a gross income of £12,470 a year. They are buying their ex-council home.

1. List essentials which have to be paid for each week or month. Try to put a cost on each of these.

2. List items which have to be bought on a rather longer timescale, for example over a three-month period or a year.

3. Reduce all the items in **2** to a monthly expenditure.

4. Taking into account that gross income is reduced by tax and national insurance by about 20 per cent (accounting for allowances as well), indicate how much the family has 'left over', supposing that it has an insurance policy with monthly instalments of £50.

5. What should it do with its 'disposable income'? Should it contemplate the purchase of a new fitted kitchen at £3500 repayable over three years' interest free?

William and Belinda Warrington also have two children, but their gross income is £27,500 a year.

6. Consider the difference in their life style. What might they think of as essentials?

7. Draw up their budget and see if they should contemplate a new fitted kitchen at £4750 repayable over three years' interest free.

This activity may have given you an insight into what disposable income really means and how people view the consumer durable market.

Marketing in a recession

At present, the UK is emerging very gradually from a five-year recession. The rest of Europe and most of the world, which started into recession much later than the UK, is still struggling with declining production, increasing costs per unit produced and lack of orders for goods and services. In the more affluent parts of Europe, France and Germany, for example, the majority of the population has until recently felt the confidence to buy whatever it wanted, whether for cash or on credit. Once jobs became less permanent and people started worrying about their futures, they lost confidence in buying and the overall market declined rapidly. Thousands of companies have been wound up, not because they do not offer goods and services that people wanted, but because no one felt able to purchase those goods and services. Market research in a time of slump may indicate that the essential is to keep down the price. For a quality product, or to maintain the quality of any sort of product, that may be a disaster.

Please do this 58 ———————————————————— 3.1.3, 3.1.4, 3.1.5, 3.1.6

The Economist Intelligence Unit produces *Business Comparisons – An Analytical and Statistical Survey of Europe and the USA*. A selection of the figures for consumer durable ownership in some European countries, the USA and the UK are given opposite. The figures provided are for 1993 with 1992 (first return) given in brackets.

The figures show some decline in ownership of consumer durables between 1992 and 1993 in Europe. Looking at these figures there is an obvious opportunity to expand markets for some products in some countries and to go into the replacement market in others.

	Belgium	France	W. Germany	Italy	Spain	Sweden	USA	UK
TV	95 (95)	94 (93)	93 (93)	94 (94)	98(99)	90(91)	99(99)	98(97)
Video recorder	13 (16)	10 (17)	30 (38)	9(29)	19(31)	10(20)	−50(53)	
Vacuum cleaner	91 (92)	88 (89)	97 (97)	90(91)	47(47)	99(99)	99(99)	97(96)
Fridge	94 (94)	98 (98)	91 (92)	88(89)	94(96)	96(97)	(100)	98(97)
Washer	86 (86)	87 (87)	91 (91)	91(91)	94(95)	60(61)	73(73)	85(85)
Dish washer	27 (28)	28 (29)	34 (36)	24(27)	13(13)	30(32)	43(45)	9(9)

1. Try to explain which markets are saturated and which can be developed.

2. As a retailer, to which country would you go to sell electrical goods used in the kitchen? Why?

3. If you were retailing in the UK only, which goods would you push in your shops and why?

Marketing and the need for information

Pusscateers was very popular when it was launched, but consumer tastes seem to have changed. Even cats have their changing preferences and producers have to keep up with the changes or go out of business. One of the great differences between the current market place and that of 150 years ago is that for a major producer of almost any goods, the whole country, or the whole world, may be the consumer.

What every producer, wholesaler and retailer needs is *information*. So does each consumer. The information each group gets is likely to be rather different. The consumer sees an advertisement in the newspapers or on the television. These are designed with great care and skill and are very convincing. Often an advertising message lingers in the mind longer than the associated programme. Some people have 'favourite' advertisements even though they do not necessarily buy the products.

The information needed by large-scale producers concerns the social trends, specifically income and spending patterns. The government publishes *Social Trends* in which a wide variety of national and regional data is regularly presented from careful sampling. From the data presented it is possible to see
- how many people are buying houses,
- how many houses are being repossessed,
- how many are in work,
- a fairly well-managed figure for those not employed who would like to be,
- how many people are undergoing hospital treatment,
- how many are getting married,
- how many couples are not married, and
- the disposable incomes of a wide variety of social classes, together with what is being acquired as consumer durables, food and clothing.

The product cycle

In your lifetime the video recorder has gone from being a big specialist piece of equipment used for playing back tapes for scientific, technical or educational purposes, with massive tape width on reels, to a highly-technical piece of equipment at 10 per cent of the cost of the originals. These modern machines use cassette tapes, and are capable of being programmed and operated by remote control and by bar code machines. What required a skilled and trained technician to operate 30 years ago, can now be made to work successfully by a child of ten.

A modern compact video recorder (Source: Philips)

Please do this 59 ———————————————————————————————**3.1.2**

Choice is difficult, especially when you are not an expert in the matter.

1. Where would you enquire about the best buy washing machine?

2. Your house roof leaks. You go to the *Yellow Pages* and look up roofing services. What criteria do you apply to pick out a roofer who will repair your roof?

New equipment or replacement?

During the late 1970s and 1980s video recorders were largely bought for the first time. A small proportion still are, but most are now bought as replacements. From the manufacturers' point of view this illustrates perfectly the product cycle:
- innovation,
- slow market penetration,
- competition,
- full-scale development,
- saturation,
- decline of the product,
- renewed innovation.

Thus we have seen, for video recorders: 5 cm tape for specialists, 2.5 cm tape for educational uses; BETAMAX and VHS competing on almost equal terms; the success of VHS in cassette format; and the introduction of 8 mm cassettes as the renewed innovation.

Happy with what we know and trust or time for something new?

Whilst there is a tendency towards uniformity in things like margarine, washing powder and petrol – with even the names being the same in most countries throughout the world – increased affluence and specific consumer demand has made available quantities of well-designed and manufactured specialist products. The very rich could always have a one-off made of anything that could be designed. What is remarkable is the sale of several thousand specialist mountain bikes each year.

Please do this 60 ─────────────────────────── **3.1.1, 3.1.5, 3.1.6**

1. Consider marketing at each phase of the product cycle. What considerations should be taken into account when thinking of the consumer at each stage?

2. Describe a product for which there has been a change in demand over the last three or four years.

3. Try to indicate why the change has happened.

4. Describe the potential/actual purchasers.

The consumer's wants and needs

In Chapter 1 we looked at the hierarchy of needs. People need to satisfy both needs and wants; the former to survive physically, the latter to survive emotionally and psychologically. The act of purchasing reinforces the consumer's feeling of well-being by involving him or her in making a choice and effecting a purchase.

Satisfied? . . . or not?

Every business organisation wants satisfied customers. Buy a ghetto blaster you like at a good price, and be treated as a valued customer, and you may be back for another one at some point. This *repeat business* is the cheapest way of generating sales. A company's sales and service staff are more effective than any advertising campaign. Besides which, the satisfied customer is inclined, on average, to tell five other people about how pleased he or she is – free and valuable marketing.

The reverse is also true. A dissatisfied customer takes up time, will not come back again and is inclined, on average, to tell 11 people how dissatisfied he or she is. No advertising or marketing campaign is likely to rectify the first-hand evidence of someone who has had a bad experience.

Satisfied customers are profit producers; dissatisfied customers are loss makers.

Please do this 61 ──────────────────────────────── **3.1.5**

The UK government has, so far, managed to opt out of the EC Directive on the brake horsepower (the power production) of motorcycles. However, the remaining EU member states may, in due course, adopt this Directive. Triumph Motorcycles of Hinckley, Leicestershire, may still be able to sell its products in the UK but will not be able to export them to EU countries. Thus, whilst the company has built up a substantial overseas trade, the effects of an unelected, but very powerful legislative body (The Council of Ministers) means that the company will be severely constrained in its opportunities for selling goods. Whilst this situation is regrettable, it is not unusual.

1. Consider carefully some areas in which legislation affects the ability to trade.

    a Examine one in detail and describe why it was thought necessary to introduce legislation, and what the arguments are for and against legislation.

    b State whether it was an ethical or commercial consideration which determined the need for law. (It may be neither of these, in which case try to give as clear as possible an explanation of the reasons behind the law.)

    c Try to explain why there should be legislation to control the power of motorcycles, but none to control the power of cars.

Review questions

Match correct or Match incorrect – these questions require you to match the first statement against the one correct answer in a, b, c and d. This sort of question will be described as *Match correct*. In some questions you may find that you have to pick out the only incorrect answer; these will be referred to as *Match incorrect*.

True/false – these questions require you to look at two statements and decide whether each statement is true or false. You should ring the pair in a, b, c or d which is closest to your opinion of what the statements say. These will be described as *True/false* questions.

True/false

I. **i** High inflation decreases the value of savings

   ii Low inflation means low interest rates which decrease the value of savings

   a i True ii True

   b i True ii False

   c i False ii False

   d i False ii True.

True/false

2. **i** People change as they get older which affects their tastes and the things that they buy

ii The size of income which people enjoy influences the type and quantity of goods they buy

a i True ii True

b i True ii False

c i False ii False

d i False ii True.

3. Market research is concerned with (i) who the customer is, (ii) what affects the number of customers, (iii) how customers think and (iv) the alternative products which are on the market.

How many correct statements are there in this sentence?

a 1

b 2

c 3

d 4.

Match incorrect

4. For marketing purposes, demography is *not* concerned with:

a The number of children born each year

b The number of older people in the population

c Population trends

d The number of people who died last year.

Match correct

5. The principal influence on lifestyle for most people is:

a Personal interests

b A job or lack of one

c A desire to be fashionable

d Memories of parents' lifestyle.

True/false

6. **i** The behaviour of consumers varies considerably between regions of the UK

ii There is relatively little difference in consumers' demand for video recorders throughout the EU

a True ii True

b i True ii False

    c i False ii False

    d i False ii True.

True/false

7.   **i** Nearly everyone has a television set in every country of the EU

    ii Nearly every home in the EU enjoys the benefits of central heating

    a i True ii True

    b i True ii False

    c i False ii False

    d i False ii True.

Match incorrect

8. Trends in consumption are affected by the fact that:

    a People are more health conscious than they were 30 years ago

    b More women are working than men

    c People are less concerned about being in debt than they were 30 years ago

    d Employment is more secure than it was 30 years ago.

True/false

9.   **i** The more people earn, the more they spend

    ii On the whole the lower the price, the more goods are sold

    a i True ii True

    b i True ii False

    c i False ii False

    d i False ii True.

True/false

10.   **i** World events often affect particular purchases

    ii Government legislation can affect purchases

    a i True ii True

    b i True ii False

    c i False ii False

    d i False ii True.

Assignment 8.1
Analysing a product

3.1.1, 3.1.6

If you do this assignment properly it will produce a substantial piece of work.

Your tasks

Either on your own, or with a group of three or four others, consider a product for which you think there has been a substantial market.

1. Describe the product and its market, and the reasons why it might be bought and sold for a profit.

2. State what needs and wants the product seeks to satisfy.

3. Indicate how it was produced and marketed. (You should show how the product developed and the effect of changes in consumer demand, including government legislation, if this is appropriate.) Remember to describe very carefully the consumers for whose needs and wants the product was produced.

4. During this assignment keep a diary of how you approached the project; the problems, difficulties and successes which you had before it was completed; and the contribution (or otherwise) of other people. The diary will be part of the assessment. Your report on the project should be word processed.

Skills achieved

You cannot successfully complete the 'please do this' work in number 57 without understanding percentages, though more direct evidence would be useful. There is plenty of opportunity for written and spoken *Communication* and opportunities for using *Information technology*, both through CD-ROM and for presentation using word-processing packages.

9 Plan, design and produce promotional material

Performance criteria

1. Identify and give examples of **types of promotions** used in marketing goods and services;
2. Describe **constraints** on the content of promotional materials;
3. Plan to produce **promotional materials** to promote particular goods or services;
4. Explain the **purpose** of the planned promotional material;
5. Design and produce promotional materials and use them to promote goods or services;
6. **Evaluate** how successful the promotional materials were in achieving the stated purpose.

Range

- **Types of promotions:** point-of-sale, advertisements (posters, radio, newspaper, magazine), sponsorship, competition.
- **Constraints:** legal (Trades Description Act, Sale of Goods Act, Consumer Protection Act); standards (Trading Standards Office, Advertising Standards Authority).
- **Plan:** time, people, materials, equipment, cost.
- **Promotional materials:** advertisement, sponsorship, competition
- **Purpose:** to communicate a message to an audience, to create sales, to influence customers' perception, to provide information.
- **Evaluate:** effectiveness in communicating to audience, effectiveness in creating sales, influence on customers' perceptions, effectiveness in providing information.

The buy me promotion

When John Stead had a market stall he stood proffering his cat food to the passers by. The tins were labelled with attractive pictures of cats which encouraged cat owners to buy. 'Buy me' they say silently; in some cases the message is quite blatant and often effective. Advertising is no more than what John was doing. He hopes that his sales pitch, which is restrained and honest, will convince buyers to purchase his goods. He succeeded and continues to succeed, but some people promoting their goods are not as successful.

Advertising

Major producers invest in an advertising campaign for the launch and relaunch of each product. Advertising agencies exist to provide this service. The most well-known in this country is probably Saatchi & Saatchi, chosen by Mrs

Thatcher to ensure that she was returned to power at the General Election. Local newspapers tend not to have sophisticated advertising campaigns, but on television, in national newspapers, on the radio, in cinemas and on advertising hoardings, as well as via direct mailing, the effect is often to convince people to buy, sometimes without them noticing.

Please do this 62 ──────────────────────── 3.2.1, 3.2.3, 3.2.4, 3.2.5

1. Consider a variety of companies and organisations (including your school or college) and decide, from an examination of the promotional material each distributes, what the message is that each wishes to give to consumers of its products or services. Choose as many different sectors of business as possible. Do not forget charities, local and central government, and the media themselves.

2. Notice whether there are substantial differences in approach. Are some promotions presented so that the organisation appears old fashioned? If so, why?

3. What does each organisation intend the promotion to achieve?

4. Produce an information sheet on your school, college or a small local company indicating the products or services that it provides. Use your imagination.

The product, the campaign and awareness

The advertising agency starts out with the most difficult part of the job – making the public aware of the existence of the campaign and the product. It

Would you be more careful if it was you that got pregnant?

The advertiser's art (Source: Saatchi & Saatchi)

has to seize the attention not only of those who might have been expected to be interested but also those who are not particularly interested or even totally indifferent. This is the work of the copywriter, the person who provides the words, and the graphic artist or photographer who provides the pictures or photos for still versions of the promotional material.

Gaining interest and changing attitudes

Having gained attention, the campaign has to stir up interest and keep it going. Often it is necessary to change consumer attitudes and make the public want to buy the product being advertised.

Please do this 63 ———————————————————————————3.2.3

Think of an advertising campaign which has *not* been effective; that is one that has resulted in few sales.

1. Examine the product and the reasons why it was not purchased.

2. Compare the product with the promotion.

3. Looking at old newspapers or magazines you may recall some remarkable but unsuccessful attempts at pushing things on the public. Design one aspect of an alternative promotion.

New product problems

You may have noticed that few advertising campaigns deal with an entirely new product, and where they do they may not always be successful. Think of Sir Clive Sinclair's C5 – an electrically driven bicycle with bodywork. Why do you suppose really innovative products are so difficult to promote?

The promotional processes

Advertising in its various forms is generally referred to as the *promotion* of a product. The processes are straightforward.

Creating demand

First demand has to be created for the specific product. It has been known for a wonderful promotion to increase demand for a generic product without much affecting the specific manufacturer's share of the market. For example, getting people to buy more soap powder in general without them buying the specific brand that is being promoted is not exactly profitable to the manufacturer who is paying for the promotion.

There are some pretty hackneyed ways of creating demand, particularly ones giving the impression that buyers will benefit more than non-buyers. The ideas that buyers will be thinner, cleaner, happier, and more socially acceptable are often used. The advertisement may claim special or unique features that are attributed to the product, or it may tempt the greedy with 'special offers'.

If the advertisement does nothing else it may succeed in keeping the product's name before the public. The Guinness advertisements are a good example of this. The TV advertisements tell you nothing about the product and everything about the image of the Guinness name.

Please do this 64 ———————————————————— **3.2.3, 3.2.4, 3.2.5, 3.2.6**

Design the outline of a promotion for a sweat shirt which has a logo on it depicting footwear for young people.

Keeping the satisfied customer

Building up customer loyalty is important. Those who are satisfied once must be encouraged not to change to a competing product. Incipient fear, appeals to snobbery, conservatism, tradition, habit and self-preservation are essential tools in, for example, political advertising.

Knocking copy

Knocking copy – not presenting one's own case but running down the opposition – is used in a variety of advertisements. Car and motorcycle manufacturers, washing-up liquid manufacturers and political organisations freely use such devices. Honda published advertisements for its Gold Wing motorcycle which told the consumer little about the Gold Wing, but relegated the competitor, Harley Davidson, to a place in history. This series of advertisements promoted Honda as the high-tech, efficient, sunrise company; the world leader in technology, assembly, finish and performance. These aspects of the advertisement were intended to give purchasers a good feel about the machines that they bought – the so-called 'feel good factor'. How a set of objectives is achieved depends upon the size of the campaign, which in turn depends upon how much money is available, i.e. the advertising budget.

'Anonymous' advertisements

Cigarette advertising which shows icons, but has no words, not even the name of the manufacturer or the brand name, works on the assumption that the product is so well-known that the advert need only show an image or icon for the public to recognise it instantly.

Please do this 65 ———————————————————————— **3.2.1, 3.2.2**

Find one or more advertisements which do not feature the product, and/or do not mention its name.

1. Describe the product and the way in which it is promoted.

2. Consider and comment on the extent of the risk which the manufacturer takes in not identifying its product clearly.

AIDA

As John has discovered it is essential to create the desire for the product with the intermediary and with the final consumer. His final consumer can only vote with silence and withdrawal. Most consumers are far more vocal and well able to express their preferences. There is an operatic acronym for this process using the initial letters of the following words: **A**ttention, **I**nterest, **D**esire and **A**ction. Remember Verdi's opera Aida.

The company image

Companies develop images. So, for that matter, do individuals. Everything about John indicates integrity, helpfulness and honesty. He has a pleasant appearance and wears quiet sensible clothes. The whole of his image indicates his positive features.

Companies also want to promote a specific image. Their headed notepaper, packaging, delivery vans, brochures, advertisements, the style of correspondence and the general way in which the company communicates internally and externally, all add up to what the company wants people to think of it.

Please do this 66 ———————————————————————— **3.2.1, 3.2.2**

Acquire a number of advertisements which indicate clearly the image of a company. Paste them onto a large sheet of paper and indicate what it is in the advertisement which makes each immediately recognisable as an advertisement from the particular company.

Codes of practice

There are constraints on what advertisers can say about themselves and their products, and about other companies and their products. Codes of practice state that advertisements should be 'legal, decent, honest and truthful'. You will notice in the newspapers the occasional boxed advertisements which tell readers how to complain to the Advertising Standards Authority (ASA) about adverts which do not comply with the code of practice. There are similar regulatory bodies for sales promotion, television and commercial radio.

Enforcing standards

On the legislative side the Trades Descriptions Act 1968 has local Trading Standards Officers to enforce the Act. Companies which make unwarranted claims about their products are forced to withdraw those claims and are prosecuted. The Consumer Protection Act 1987 covers a wide variety of problems from injury received from a toy, to alleged low 'sale' prices which are no lower than usual.

The Medicines Act 1983 regulates claims made about the effects of medicines.

Please do this 67 ————————————————————————————— **3.2.2**

Find the names and addresses of as many regulatory bodies concerned with advertising as you can and indicate which area of the advertising world (or consumers' interests) each seeks to cover and how. A copy of their mission statement or code of practice would be helpful.

Using the media

Magazines

Magazines are kept for some time and may be looked at by several people several times. Specialist magazines can be targeted at particular audiences. Women's magazines are aimed at women and tend to be class and age related, whilst men's magazines are generally subject or hobby related – cars, motorcycles and football being classic examples – although the boundaries between the two sectors are fast blurring. Given the price of magazines, most people who buy them tend to read them quite thoroughly and regard the advertisements as being of almost as much interest as the text and illustrations. Subsequent readers, for example those in doctors' or dentists' waiting rooms, may not be quite so closely involved, but even so these are added opportunities of getting the message across.

Newspapers

National newspapers carry a lot of advertising, nearly all of which is closely aimed at the audience which is targeted by the paper. Not only are advertisements for various products differentiated between one paper and another, but a single product may have different advertising in one paper compared with another.

Please do this 68 ————————————————————————————3.2.1

Look through a number of newspapers, watch television, go to the cinema and look carefully at poster hoardings. See if you can find a product or service which is advertised differently for different media and audiences.

1. Describe the product/service and the differences in the advertisements.

2. Cut out the advertisements in the papers and put them on a large sheet of paper indicating the differences and any reasons you can think of for them.

Television advertising

Television advertising is normally possible only for very large companies because of the huge costs involved in making the advertisement in the first place and then having it screened for a few seconds. Occasionally the advertisements are better made and more interesting than the programmes themselves. It is possible to target regional audiences and even particular sorts of people by inserting advertisements in programmes likely to appeal to those concerned.

On the whole television advertising works on the 'I saw it on TV' principle. Because of the power of moving, speaking, music-supported colourful images exuding glamour and influence people will often follow the television trend in clothes, names, products and services of all kinds.

Product placement
It is becoming common nowadays to see particular product brands being used in actual television programmes. The beer a detective habitually asks for and drinks, the perfume bottle a beautiful woman takes out of her bag, the pre-

ferred designer clothes a hero always wears, are all examples of product placement. In this case, goods (mainly) and services are 'donated' in exchange for their clear usage on screen.

Sponsorship of television

This is another area that is becoming more common. The example most of us will have seen is the weather forecast on television. In the past both Norwich Union and Powergen have 'sponsored' the forecast by paying for their names to appear as sponsors.

Please do this 69 ——————————————————— **3.2.1, 3.2.2**

Compare a cinema advertisement with its television equivalent. Note the differences of length, impact and size. Bear in mind how television is watched in a domestic environment compared to how a film in a cinema is watched.

Teletext, etc.

The alternative for advertisers to network, satellite or cable TV is Teletext, etc. which carries advertisements between information pages.

Commercial radio

Commercial radio is a cheap means of conveying advertisements, and it is possible to direct local radio to quite small areas making it an attractive medium for local companies.

Cinema

Cinema advertising reaches a captive audience who may be less distracted than television viewers. This means that cinema advertisements are often longer versions of television advertisements. Because the majority of cinema audiences are young it is possible to target successfully and at a cost which is audience number related.

Please do this 70 ——————————————————— **3.2.1**

A cinema screen is huge and dominating. How do you think television overcomes the disadvantages that it has compared with the cinema?

Outdoor advertising

There are many advertisements on vast hoardings. Note that these are often very colourful, but usually have no more than seven words on them and often a lot less. Locations can be general or specific to match what is being advertised. Advertisements in bus shelters, on the Underground in London and on transport of different kinds are likely to have a lot more viewing time than those by the side of a main road.

Please do this 71 ── 3.2.3

Look at some advertisements on bus shelters. Make up an advertisement to sell bicycles to bus passengers. Do not forget to lay it out for maximum effect and decide at the beginning whether you are aiming at information, persuasion or both. If possible design this using a graphics package.

Leaflets

When John advertised his local shop he wanted to get over to the consumer as much information as possible. He wanted to mention opening hours, products stocked, special offers, and the services provided. He may have been better off leafleting households in the area, possibly by including a leaflet with the local free paper, distributed to all the households in the town.

Mailshots

Leaflets can go out in mailshots. Many recipients refer to these as 'junk mail', though the technical term is *direct mail*, and many throw them straight in the waste paper basket. However, for every nine people who do that, there may be a tenth who could be a good prospect. You may have seen a code number on much of your mail of this sort. It categorises you by social class, income, age, education and family grouping. These mailing lists are sold (or swapped) from one company to another.

Please do this 72 ──────────────────────────────── 3.2.1, 3.2.3, 3.2.5

1. Examine the junk mail received at your home over a fortnight and try to classify it in terms of:

   a its interest to you or your family,

   b its effectiveness (that is whether it produces a sale),

   c the product or service's cost (if that is revealed),

   d whether or not you received more than one copy of the same promotional literature,

   e whether it was for goods or services, and

   f why you think you, or someone else at your address, were chosen to receive it.

2. Design a mailshot package for a family with two children and a gross income of £16,000 a year, offering private education facilities for each child, to be paid for by instalments over a period of ten years.

Other ways of getting the message across

John stood in the market place and displayed his wares. People bought from him because they liked his prices and, often just as important, because they liked him. Most businesses have to resort to advertising:

- in newspapers and magazines,
- on the radio or television,
- by leafleting via the mail or by hand delivery, or
- by using outdoor advertising such as posters, billboards or the sides of buses.

However there are three other methods that can also be used to get the message across – competitions, sponsorship and promotional events.

Competitions

Running competitions is particularly helpful to magazine proprietors. In the UK only 7 per cent of magazines are bought direct from the publishers by subscription. Although magazines hold surveys to discover the sort of people who buy their product they do not know the names and addresses of those who buy from bookstalls. Getting a provider of goods or services to sponsor a competition is a very good way of obtaining a mailing list, i.e. the names and addresses of consumers.

Crosswords, word squares, choosing best designs, and so on, are all simple ways of getting people to put their names and addresses on the entry form. Someone, somewhere, quite legitimately gets a prize. Everyone who enters is interested in the product and the magazine. The mailing list is quickly built up and can be used relatively easily.

Sponsorship

Lastly, there is sponsorship. This is occasionally not as happy a situation as it might be because the person (or team or animal) sponsored may just not come up with the goods, or may go out of fashion. Coca-Cola rapidly dropped its multi-million dollar sponsorship of Michael Jackson when he gained a good deal of adverse publicity owing to allegations about his private life. What often happens with sponsorship is that a particular famous or up-and-coming person is chosen, always one in whom the media show a continuing interest. The sponsored person's appearances, which may be very frequent and always associated with the name of the sponsor, are recorded on the television and in newspapers thus providing 'free' advertising. Linking Coca-Cola with Michael Jackson presented the most popular entertainer in the USA with the USA's most popular soft drink. Coca-Cola benefited from the glamorous and high-profile image of Michael Jackson and he benefited financially.

Not just individuals but teams and entire events can be sponsored. Motor and motorcycle sport are supported by cigarette manufacturers. Horse racing, cricket and tennis are supported by among others, finance and insurance companies. A really big company will provide all these promotions at once, aimed at different sectors of the market.

Please do this 73 ────────────────────── 3.2.1, 3.2.3, 3.2.4

Choose six products and indicate which means of promotion you would use in each case. Give reasons for your choices and reasons why you discarded the alternatives.

Promotional events

These are usually associated with the launch of a new product. We are all familiar with the star-studded galas involving the launch of a new film. On smaller budgets, promotional events may involve press launches, book signing sessions, appearances on radio or television chat shows, and free tasting sessions at supermarkets.

Planning the promotion

When a company promotes its products, with or without the help of an advertising agency, it has first to plan carefully. If you do not know where you are going, you are not likely to get there. So planning is very carefully undertaken with a statement of aims and the means by which these aims can be achieved.

In a large or medium-sized company it is necessary to indicate:
• which personnel will be involved,
• for how long,
• what each individual has to do, and
• what the deadlines are.

Setting deadlines is very important. People often leave things to the last minute, so a set of deadline stages is useful to check how an overall plan is progressing. Finally it is necessary to know what the budget is and what it covers.

The next stage, possibly left to external professionals, is the creation of the promotional material. This requires a degree of creativity with ideas being translated into physical form and frequent sketches of what is being proposed being rejected or modified.

Please do this 74 ────────────────────────── 3.2.1, 3.2.2

Compare a promotion campaign by a named national or multi-national company and a promotion by a local company, perhaps in the local paper or on commercial radio. Indicate the differences between the two in approach and content.

Evaluation of a campaign

After the campaign has been run, all the promotional events held and the sales estimated, the whole campaign is evaluated. What it cost in real terms is compared with the value of added sales profits. Looking at the results of anything is always a good idea, and it is essential if a lot of money has been spent. Just looking at the end results, however, is not enough; it is vital to see where things have gone right or wrong. Even if the results of a promotion far exceed the promoter's wildest hopes, the promotion itself might still be further improved and there may well be lessons to be learned on how to do it better next time.

Review questions

Match correct or *Match incorrect* – these questions require you to match the first statement against the one correct answer in a, b, c and d. This sort of question will be described as *Match correct*. In some questions you may find that you have to pick out the only incorrect answer; these will be referred to as *Match incorrect*.

True/false – these questions require you to look at two statements and decide whether each statement is true or false. You should ring the pair in a, b, c or d which is closest to your opinion of what the statements say. These will be described as *True/false* questions.

True/false

1. **i** The Advertising Standards Association lays down enforceable rules for all advertisements

    ii The Independent Television Commission has the legal right to punish those who show advertisements which offend

    a i True ii True

    b i True ii False

    c i False ii False

    d i False ii True.

Match incorrect

2. Promotional material aims at:

    a Creating public awareness

    b Capturing the public's attention and gaining interest

    c Changing attitudes

    d Ensuring that the public complies with the promoters' wishes.

Match incorrect

3. Promotions usually can include:

    a Advertising

b Sponsorship

c Editorial coverage in newspapers and magazines

d Government legislation.

Match incorrect

4. Promotions seek to increase demand by:

a Persuasion to buy

b Giving information about products

c Keeping the producer's name before the consumer

d Surveying the market.

True/false

5. i Promotional materials will help sales if they inform people of where and how a product can be obtained

ii Promotional materials will help sales if they persuade potential customers that the product is better value than any other

a i True ii True

b i True ii False

c i False ii False

d False ii True.

Match incorrect

6. One of the following is *not* a promotional material:

a Headed notepaper

b A logo on the product package

c The postmark on out-going letters

d A brochure describing the product.

Match incorrect

7. It is *not* possible to advertise cigarettes in the UK:

a On cinema films

b On TV

c In magazines

d On advertising hoardings.

8. How many correct statements are there in this sentence: Television advertising is more suited to (i) major organisations with large budgets, (ii) raising awareness, (iii) specially selected audiences and (iv) persuasion rather than information.

    a 1

    b 2

    c 3

    d 4.

Match incorrect

  9. Cinema advertising has the advantage of:

    a An entirely captive audience

    b Great impact owing to size and sound quality

    c Covering all parts of the population

    d Providing a reasonably cheap promotion for local traders.

True/false

  10. **i** To have an effective promotional campaign it is necessary to plan, produce, follow up and evaluate

    ii Good copywriting is the basis of all successful promotions

    a i True ii True

    b i True ii False

    c i False ii False

    d False ii True.

Assignment 9.1
Promoting a product or service

3.2.3, 3.2.4, 3.2.5

The different elements of promotion

Having read through this chapter and done the various activities you will experienced a wide range of advertising media and promotional campaigns. You will have gained insights into the planning and targeting processes, the variety of forms of advertising and the effects each one has. Now it is your turn.

Choose your own product or service to promote. There are some examples below, but do try to think of your own and use it:
- a three-wheeled, electrically-powered car;
- the chance to buy or sell a flat or house for £250 inclusive;
- winter underwear made of a very fine and heat-retentive fabric;
- a house paint guaranteed for ten years;
- a television set complete with twin video recorders, radio and CD player;
- a new soap with skin conditioning properties;
- a floppy disc diary which can be used with any computer; and
- a special bath to relieve aching feet.

Your tasks

1. Having chosen your product, consider the appeal that it has for its potential consumers. Indicate what the appeal depends on. What is its likely cost? Who is likely to buy it? Why? How can you get people to buy it? What will the unit cost be? Does it need service back up? If so how will this be arranged and will it be a major part of the sales pitch? What will be the selling price per unit? Can you predict how many you will sell? What will the gross profit per item be? How many are you going to try to sell in this town/area/region/country, and abroad?

2. Plan your campaign with care. Utilise as many means of promoting your product as is possible. Decide what the message will be. Will it be persuasion, or information or both? Will you use a logo or a style of presentation which immediately identifies your company and the product? Lay out the advertisements and write the copy. These should be for a variety of magazines and newspapers as well as advertisement hoardings, leaflets and junk mail packages. If you can make a video you certainly should. Remember to decide on a story line, produce a story board (what each scene will have in it), write the script, and have one or more rehearsals adapting the script and story board if it does not work as well as it should. Video as clean a version as time permits, then view and edit it. In any case you must make a tape suitable for commercial radio. Remember that both tapes must be short and full of impact, and utilise music and/or other sound effects.

3. Keep a note of costs. Keep a diary of all the things that you do, with whom, the problems you encountered and how they were solved. Give reasons for the choice of each of your advertisements. Remember the legal and ethical constraints on advertising and ensure that the costs of the promotion do not overrun the likely benefits.

4. Produce a DTP portfolio of the whole promotion and its evaluation.

Skills achieved

Communication skills are the basis of this element, together with substantial use of *Information technology*. You should claim both. If you have utilised skills in the *Application of number* area, remember to claim this as well.

10 Providing customer service

Performance criteria

1. Identify an organisation's customers and its customer needs;
2. Identify and describe customer service in an organisation;
3. Identify business communications which meets customer needs;
4. Demonstrate business communications which meet customers' needs;
5. Describe procedures in one business organisation for dealing with customer complaints;
6. Identify relevant legislation to protect customers.

Range

- **Customer needs:** wishing to make a purchase, to obtain information, to obtain a refund, to exchange goods, to make a complaint, for special needs, ethical standards.
- **Customer service:** meeting the needs of internal and external customers, providing help or information (for individuals, business organisations).
- **Business communications:** oral (face-to-face, telephone), written (letter, memo), customer/product information (statement of account, prices, guarantees, safety notices).
- **Legislation:** Trades Description, Sale of Goods, Consumer Protection, Health and Safety At Work.

Customer services

It was raining in Shipton High Street, as usual, but this did not stop people crowding the pavements on market day. John Stead stands under the awning of his stall on half a pallet to keep his feet dry and talks to Mrs Sykes.

John:	'It's good cat food; I've sold lots of it. Cats like it and at the price so do their owners. It's mainly beef with some sardine and salmon added and a little bit of cereal, so it's a balanced diet for a cat.'
Mrs Sykes:	'Is there a lot of cereal?'
John:	'No, it's less than 5 per cent, but it's just that necessary bit to keep them healthy.'
Mrs Sykes:	'Can you let me have six dozen tins if we like it?'
John:	'Oh yes, I can deliver that for you.'
Mrs Sykes:	'Do you accept cheques?'
John:	'Certainly, especially if I'm delivering it to your house.'
Mrs Sykes:	'What happens if our cats go off it?'
John:	'Well, we can do an exchange for another variety, though I can assure you I've never had any back.'
Mrs Sykes:	'We've five cats, can you do us a regular delivery service?'
John:	'No trouble. We just have to fix the frequency of delivery and

151

somewhere for me to leave it if you're out, and I'll include an account with each delivery.'

Mrs Sykes:	'That sounds very good news. I'll tell you what. I'll have six tins now. Will you be here on Saturday?'
John:	'Oh yes, Wednesday and Saturday every week.'
Mrs Sykes:	'Good, then I'll come and see you on Saturday and I'll let you know if we want it regularly.'
John:	'Thank you. By the way, the same makers do a variety pack, all of it basically beef with added flavourings so that the cats don't get bored with the same meal all the time. I'll bring you some on Saturday and you can try those too, if you like.'
Mrs Sykes:	'Thanks. Sounds like a good idea.'

She pays for the six tins she's received.

'See you Saturday then. Goodbye.'

John:	'Goodbye and thank you.'

Mrs Sykes is just the sort of customer John needs. A regular supply and opportunity to deliver and run an account. She may tell her cat-owning friends and make it really worthwhile.

Customer services analysed

The scene above exemplifies, in miniature, much of what there is to know about customer needs. Mrs Sykes knows she needs cat food, she has an idea how much, what make it is and how much it costs, how to pay for it and what is in it, and the problem of getting it home on the bus. She discusses these aspects with John, the seller. He provides her with information on the product and she will (he hopes) place an order on Saturday. She is sampling the product with the assurance that a substitute will be offered if her cats (the end consumers) are not happy with it. Dates, times and places for delivery will be established on Saturday. She has warmed to John who has taken a positive interest in her and her cats in order to help her, and has given her a number of useful options with regard to purchase and possible return.

John smiles politely, speaks clearly, is transparently honest and gives customers his full attention. Far from being off-hand, as some sales people are, he is invariably attentive, regarding each of his customers, and even those who are just browsing, as special. Some people have John's qualities naturally; others have to achieve these through training. Good training will make attention to clients' needs appear natural, even if it is not.

The first line of customer services

As a sales person you need to know the products. When John goes to the bank he very seldom sees even an assistant manager; he always sees a cashier. People who work on the counter in direct contact with the public, cashing cheques, dealing with deposits and all the routine daily tasks are usually fairly low down in the banking hierarchy. Yet for most of us they are the bank. They are the people who deal with irate, difficult or disabled customers. They are the first-line question answerers and they need to be thoroughly familiar with bank policy, bank organisation, bank products and who refer to if there is a question which they cannot answer. In their appearance and attitude they represent the bank to the customer and as such have an important role to play.

People who deal with the public need to be able to advise or help at once. They need to know the lines of communication within the company (or branch) and must be fully aware of what to do with a complaint or request which they do not have the authority or experience to deal with.

The receptionist

John used to work in a college. They were lucky to have several receptionists who were highly professional. They always started the conversation with students (or prospective students) with 'good morning/afternoon/evening' and 'How may I help you?' Having written down the enquirer's name, they proceeded to use it. They wore badges with their own names clearly written on them so that the receptionist–enquirer relationship could be established on an equal footing. All enquiries were written down and a note of date, time and solution included.

Listening is a very important skill. Most of us hear what other people are saying, do not always understand what has been said and promptly forget it. Once the receptionist had clearly understood the enquiry then if it could be answered and dealt with immediately, it was. If the answer was not known, the reception desks were in the main offices and the receptionist could turn to another member of staff or quickly phone an expert, explaining to the enquirer what he or she was doing. The result might be that the information or explanation was immediately forthcoming or it could be a while before it was available. If the former was true, the information may need checking for accuracy and currency, and then be explained to the enquirer, with any notes being made on a memo pad. If the latter, the receptionist explained any reason for the delay and then went through the same process. If there was likely to be a substantial delay then name, address and phone number were written down, an apology and reason offered for the delay, and as soon as the information was available it was passed on to the enquirer.

If an enquirer asked for a course which the college did not run, it was recommended that an alternative provider be suggested. The college might lose a student in that year, but being helpful to people makes them remember that organisation in a favourable light. This may lead to additional referrals as satisfied customers pass a name on to others.

The satisfied customer

The best (and possibly the cheapest) advertisement is a satisfied customer. Putting a lot into customer service makes a customer come back and leads to recommendations.

John had, one after another, four cars all of the same make. He was pleased with them all, particularly with their reliability. The dealership from which he bought them changed hands. While John was in the middle of a lot of important long distance journeys, crucial to his business expansion plans, a coolant pipe split on the car. He called into the service department at 4.15 p.m., waited in a queue of account payers and at 4.30 p.m. explained the problem. At 4.43 p.m. the foreman told him that he could not spare anyone to look at it that evening, but if he booked it in for tomorrow . . . John remonstrated, but the foreman was obdurate. John will now never buy that make of car again and has switched his allegiance to another brand.

How better to deal with consumers

Please do this 75 ———————————————————————3.3.4

In order to improve your performance, listen to your voice recorded on a tape recorder. If possible, also watch a video of yourself. Stand by for surprises.

Notice body language when people speak to one another. A finger pointed at another person is a very aggressive signal. An arm round a shoulder when comfort is necessary includes people in a family of feeling. Looking people in the eyes, but not staring, establishes contact. Age, status, gender and nationality all affect the communication of messages. Your tone and vocabulary whilst speaking to a grandparent might well be quite different from that used to a friend of your own age or a toddler, even if the message is exactly the same.

Remember that, in general, people like a bit of social distance when communicating. Apart from the introductory handshake, touching is not usually appropriate. John once worked with a lady who thought she should adjust his tie on a regular basis. He tried to avoid her at all costs. Not a good basis for working together. Try travelling on the Underground in London or standing up in a crowded bus to see how people aim to make space around themselves.

Contact over the telephone

The telephone is most effective if answered clearly and promptly; always keep a pad of paper and a pen to hand. Do not forget to try to smile whilst speaking on the phone. It has a remarkable effect on the voice. Learn how to keep callers on hold whilst transferring them to another extension.

Dealing with those who are handicapped

When John had a market stall he had to deal with any passer-by who wanted to take up his time. He never discriminated on the grounds of disability, age or gender. He was tolerant of sexual, political, and religious orientations that perhaps he did not share. People come with all sorts of personal differences, but John has learned that whatever they are like, people should be valued for themselves and their differences make them more interesting, not less valuable.

One of the best tests of dealing with people with handicaps, or indeed anyone else, is to wonder what you would like others to do if the positions were reversed.

The blind

Some people have inherited or acquired handicaps. In practice, we all have handicaps, it is just that some are more pronounced than others. The courtesy and patience which should be extended to all may be particularly well-deserved by those who are handicapped. The blind may find themselves in unfamiliar, and to them potentially dangerous, surroundings. For a start, try making some sound to alert a blind person to your exact location. Saying 'hello' or 'good morning' is a good start; asking if you can help is another. It is not always apparent that people cannot see and even the signals of the white stick or guide dog may be missing. However, guiding blind people is fairly easy provided that you remember two things:

- Always ask if the blind person wants any help in the first place. You would not readily give up your independence and neither do many blind people.
- The blind person will slip an arm through yours (not the other way round) and will listen carefully to the description of the journey which you provide. It is too late to draw attention to a step when one foot is already on it. A warning given three steps away gives time for adjustment.

People with learning difficulties

People with learning difficulties need time and patience. Just hold on for a moment because they will communicate what is required, much in the same way as people with severe speech impediments. Speak slowly (but do not shout) to people with learning difficulties. Face the deaf, who will normally tell or indicate to you that they are deaf. Whatever else, do not jump to conclusions and do not attempt to hurry things on by completing sentences for other people. This is always an irritating habit, but can be particularly patronising and offensive when applied to people who appear to have handicaps.

The physically handicapped

Those who are using crutches or wheel chairs may appreciate help with heavy doors and will welcome ramps instead of steps.

Problems with English

Those who cannot speak English can communicate in other ways and you should attempt to do the same. Writing down a price, using sign language or speaking simply and clearly are all ways of making communication easier. Again, do not raise your voice – a person will not understand a word if it is shouted any better than if it is clearly said.

Parents and children

Parents and children as a class are not handicapped in the conventional sense of the word, but a man or woman with a buggy that has a hefty infant in it, and another mobile one in tow, is definitely not able to move about very easily or quickly. Again, be helpful and patient. Running a creche is a great selling point if parents need to be on the premises for any length of time. Having a secure pram park, for empty prams, is also helpful.

Small children can be a handicap

Please do this 76 ————————————————————— 3.3.1, 3.3.2

1. Look very carefully at your school, college or a local business and see how it is (or is not) adapted for the convenient use of people with handicaps.

2. Categorise each area of difficulty and how it is (or is not) overcome.

Being snubbed

If you offer help and it is rudely or angrily refused bear in mind that you have done the right thing. Some people are very difficult to help and do not always respond to an offer of help as you might expect. Better to be snubbed ten times than to fail to offer help to someone who really needs it.

Confidential clients

People who need to have special attention include those whose affairs are confidential. The person who has come to discuss marital relationships connected with a child's misbehaviour at school with the headteacher needs to be shown to a private room and should not be asked questions about the exact purpose of the interview. The same goes for people who are enquiring about loans or payments, and people who are making enquiries about their health or other intimate matters. There are some straightforward rules to apply in these matters:

- Never discuss other people's business with colleagues or those outside the company.
- Never examine customer files unless authorised to do so.
- Never discuss financial or other details relating to your job with colleagues or those outside the company except where necessary. This applies especially to those of you who may work in personnel, payroll or financial departments.

The nervous client

The client who lacks confidence, who is hesitant, blushes and avoids eye contact needs careful attention. Be friendly but not pushy. Offer help, speak deliberately, clearly and calmly, and indicate that you have time to deal with them.

Please do this 77 ————————————————————— 3.3.2, 3.3.3

Consider what matters you would like to keep private if you were dealing with a bank or a doctor. Make a list of these and give the related reasons.

The complaining customer – part I

Anita Kapoor shops at Taylors the grocers, and does most of her weekly shop there. Despite the semi-supermarket layout the staff are always about to give help and advice. What is more they allow credit card and Switch payments so that she can avoid carrying cash.

Anita is a heavy credit card and Switch user. Therefore, when her monthly bank statement arrives she has some work to do.

Anita checks her monthly statement of account from the bank against her cheque book, standing orders and Switch withdrawals and finds an entry which she does not understand:

Sundry Debit.........£30

It looks as if someone has removed £30 from her account without a reason and put her close to being overdrawn. At lunch-time she visits her bank and goes to 'Enquiries'. There is a long queue. By the time she gets to the counter half her lunch break is gone and she is irritated. She is normally a sunny and pleasant person but standing and waiting has not helped her already anxious state.

Mary, the young woman on the Enquiries desk is keen on having her lunch. In four minutes her lunch break starts. She hopes that Anita's is a brief enquiry. When Anita hands her the account with the offending item marked and asks for an explanation, Mary realises that this may take some time. So she suggests that rather than keeping Anita waiting any longer she will enquire into the matter with the Assistant Manager and either phone Anita at work in the afternoon or put a letter in the post before the bank closes that day. Either way Anita will know the answer to her enquiry first thing in the morning at the latest. Anita is happy with this arrangement, leaves her work phone number and departs. Mary is relieved by Andrew, who will be on Enquiries while she is at lunch.

Next but one in the queue, now to be dealt with by Andrew, is Fred, a large aggressive person with a loud and complaining voice who has apparently had a potent liquid lunch and is demanding to know from everyone why he cannot get cash from the cheque he has just received. Andrew attempts, as the cashier, to tell him that cheques need clearance which takes time. The aggressive customer becomes the abusive customer. Andrew presses a 'help' bell and refers the matter to a senior member of staff.

Anita is not happy with her account, but she is not yet a dissatisfied customer. She has an apparently unanswerable query but is promised an answer. For most reasonable people this is enough. However, when no phone call transpires and there is no letter the next morning, she begins to think there is a marked lack of service, phones the bank and says so. She gets immediate attention, the explanation she requires and an apology. Good service relationships are re-established.

Fred on the other hand wants a service which cannot be provided. He is very annoyed that he cannot get immediate clearance. He considers the service to be poor. His way of dealing with this is not to be assertive but aggressive and confrontational. If he pushes hard enough he might find that the bank has decided it has had enough of him as a customer and politely but firmly closes his account in the interests of good relationships with the other customers. He will be even more furious, but as a tactical business decision it may be the most appropriate one. Such a decision, however, will not be taken without serious consideration, usually at a fairly senior level, as even customers like Fred have friends who may be affected by his opinions.

Using personal relationship skills in dealing with complaints

Keep your cool when all around are losing theirs

In dealing with any client complaint it may be desirable to use a few personal relationship skills which will defuse the situation even if they do not completely satisfy the customer straight away.

The complaining customer – part 2

Andrew's next enquirer is concerned about her holiday insurance, foreign currency, and travellers' cheques which have not appeared five days before her holiday, despite being ordered well in advance.

Andrew listens to what she has to say and makes a note of what she has said, including her name and address. He does not interrupt until she has finished speaking.

He checks with the customer that there are three items of concern – holiday insurance, foreign currency and travellers' cheques; the date of her holiday; and the date she ordered the, so far, unsupplied, service. He remains polite, friendly and reasonable even when she says it is typical of the bank to mess up her holiday.

Andrew is sympathetic, invites the lady to have a seat, passes the note he has taken to his colleague who deals with foreign currency and attends to the next enquirer.

Within three or four minutes the query is dealt with and the customer goes away happily with an explanation, an apology, her currency, travellers cheques and insurance documents.

This is one example of how to deal correctly with a complaint. The basic rules are:

- Accept the problem, which may seem trivial to you, but is substantial in the customer's mind.
- Deal with it efficiently and always courteously, even when you are being verbally abused.
- Do not put the blame somewhere else, but find someone who can resolve the problem, even if you cannot.
- If there is no apparent action in four or five minutes, chase up whoever you passed the problem on to, again politely.
- Reassure the complainant that the problem is being dealt with and that you have checked its progress.

Whatever you do do not make promises you cannot fulfil. Remember that even if you have solved the problem, the customer may not be happy because the problem should not have arisen in the first place.

Please do this 78 ————————————————————————**3.3.5**

1. With colleagues, friends or family consider a complaint which someone has made and how it was settled. Write down:

   a the nature of the complaint,

   b who made it,

   c to whom it was made,

   d what method was used – phone, letter, fax, face-to-face,

   e what the response was,

   f how it was resolved, if it was.

   What lessons are to be learned from your experience?

Faulty goods

As well as complaints about services it is common to have complaints about goods. In these cases the customer is complaining about goods he or she considers are faulty or do not live up to advertised claims. There is a lot of legislation covering consumer rights. Basically, if a customer picks something from the shelves, looks at it and decides that it will fit a particular purpose, then if it does not do what he or she wants it to do there are two basic reasons for this:

- First, the customer has made the wrong choice. This is generally considered to be the customer's fault and there is no legal redress. However, a customer-centred business may wish to keep the customer in any way it can and may, therefore, exchange the goods or refund money.

- Secondly, the product does not do what it claims to be able to do on the packaging or instruction book, or according to the dealer's advice.

Consumer legislation

Consumer legislation is dealt with in detail in Chapter 11. However, both honesty and health and safety are the main aspects involved. John must not say that his cat food is 100 per cent salmon when it is mainly trimmings from cod with cereal and water. He must not mislead his customers, even if they have no way of checking the real state of affairs. He must not tell them he is offering the tins at 28p each as a 'special offer' implying that they were normally more than that, when in fact they were normally cheaper.

John must not sell goods which are dangerous to the consumer. Almost everything is dangerous and it is possible to get a nasty cut from a tin lid whilst opening it. That would be put down to personal negligence on the part of the purchaser. An exploding glass lemonade bottle, however, would not and many millions of bottles have been withdrawn and destroyed because half a dozen have been faulty.

If John's stall awning falls on a person's head he is liable to pay damages. If his tins are out-of-date and 'blown' customers can seek prompt redress from him and he may be prosecuted by the trading standards officer if someone draws attention to the matter.

If a solicitor fails to attend to a case properly or a surgeon cuts off your leg instead of attending to your broken arm, you can take legal action against the individual for professional negligence.

What companies can do to protect themselves

People can and do have accidents, products can unexpectedly become faulty and professional advice might not be exactly what is required, leading to financial or other losses – so companies take out insurance cover. The most common is *public liability insurance*. This is not insurance against what the public can do to a company but against the costs to the company of what has happened to a customer. This will cover just about everything from catching a hand in the door, or falling on a slippery surface, to death by electrocution. All these have to happen on the company premises or at locations which the company is responsible for, or may be to do with equipment run by the company.

Product liability insurance covers claims against the company made by purchasers, or anyone else who is affected, regarding faulty goods.

Professional indemnity insurance covers claims against the company, partnership or sole trader for professional negligence.

Trade associations have codes of practice to guide members in the way they should conduct their business and they often have mutual indemnity provision. Thus the Association of British Travel Agents (ABTA) indemnifies holiday makers if any of its members go out of business. The product liability is spread over all ABTA's members for the benefit of the customers.

Association of British Travel Agents

The ABTA Travel Agents' Fund

The Travel Agents' Council shall establish and maintain a fund to be known as 'the ABTA Travel Agents' Fund' to which every Travel Agent shall from time to time contribute such amount, not exceeding in any year one half of the amount of his subscription as a member of the Travel Agent's class of the Association, and within such a period as the Travel Agents' Council shall from time to time determine.

The primary purpose of the Fund shall be to indemnify, wholly or in part, members of the travelling public against losses sustained by reason of the default or financial failure of any member who is a Travel Agent; secondarily, the Fund may be used at the discretion of the Committee to indemnify, wholly or in part, members of the Association who are Tour Operators against such losses sustained by them.

Extract from ABTA's code of practice

Please do this 79 ——————————————— 3.3.4, 3.3.5, 3.3.6

Henry visits his dentist for a routine check-up. He has had a bit of toothache and the dentist X-rays his jaw, discovering a very unpleasant state of affairs, which it is explained, will need a prompt extraction of one tooth. Henry takes the advice, and since the dentist has a vacant time in the afternoon, he comes back, is given a general anaesthetic and the tooth is extracted.

Three days later Henry realises that he still has toothache and that the dentist has extracted the wrong tooth. What could Henry do next? How could he pursue any claim against the dentist?

Caveat emptor – let the buyer beware

Consumers are being protected by more and more legislation. This is less an indication that people in business are becoming more dishonest, than a desire to clarify what is good and acceptable practice and to make UK law conform to European Union legislation.

Many years ago an estate agent in London advertised honest, not to say cruel, descriptions of properties he had to sell. What someone else might have described as a 'Bijou Victorian residence, deceptively spacious, in a quiet back-water' he described as a 'small, crumbling, 100-year-old terrace house in an inaccessible location'. People beat a path to his door to buy properties from him and there was no evidence that his prices, or commission, were lower than anyone else's. Nowadays the Property Misdescription Act covers all estate agents who have to be factually accurate in their descriptions of properties.

Please do this 80 ————————————————————— 3.3.4, 3.3.5

You work in a retail shop selling domestic electrical equipment. The range includes just about anything you can find at home except computers. The shop belongs to Mr Haigh and he runs three other shops in the nearby small towns. As you have a good reputation for efficiency and honesty, when Mrs Wallace, who has worked in the shop for 20 years, is unexpectedly taken ill and has to go home for the day, you are left in charge. Mr Haigh rings up and tells you where to find the cash float. As he has an important meeting with a supplier he cannot come to help until later in the day. It is Tuesday, usually the quietest day for retail sales, so he feels you should be able to cope.

Write down what you would do on each of the following occasions:

a At 9.15 a.m. the shop door opens and a customer, who you recognise as Mr Moriarty, comes in. He was promised that his television set would be repaired and returned on Saturday. It was not and he is furious. The repair depot is 12 miles away.

b At 9.25 a.m. a young man with three unruly children who he is ineffectually trying to control, comes into the shop and asks about freezers. You stock three makes in 11 sizes with prices from £180 to £475. His children are running round the shop and you fear than an expensive television set or sound system will be knocked off its stand.

c Mary Smith has had a nasty horse riding accident and is currently confined to a wheel chair. There are two steps up to your shop from the road. Mary gets a passer by to enter the shop and ask you to attend to her. Just as you are speaking to her you hear the telephone ring and a rather scruffy and shifty looking man pushes past you into the unattended shop. It has just started raining and Mary is not wearing a coat.

d At 10.15 a.m. Mrs Alison Mitchell enters the shop shaking her umbrella all over a £700 Nicam Stereo television set and knocking a display of Christmas lights over. She is an overbearing person apparently oblivious to anyone else's presence. It is important that you dry the television case off as water may enter the chassis with disastrous results. Mrs Mitchell has come to complain about a long-life bulb which she bought for her garage three years ago, and nothing will deter her from accusing you of selling her a product which does not live up to her expectations. She also expects you to do something about it. You are behind the counter and Mrs Mitchell is between you and the wet television.

Review questions

Match correct or *Match incorrect* – these questions require you to match the first statement against the one correct answer in a, b, c and d. This sort of question will be described as *Match correct*. In some questions you may find that you have to pick out the only incorrect answer; these will be referred to as *Match incorrect*.

True/false – these questions require you to look at two statements and decide whether each statement is true or false. You should ring the pair in a, b, c or d which is closest to your opinion of what the statements say. These will be described as *True/false* questions.

Match incorrect

1. Customers usually get in touch with an organisation to:

a Obtain information

b Complain

c Gain attention or help

d See if the organisation is helpful.

True/false

2. i Anyone who deals with clients needs to know the products and services offered by the company, who does what in the company, what guarantees are offered and what supporting literature is available.

ii A sales assistant does not need to know the outlines of the Sale of Goods Act and the Trades Description Act.

a i True ii True

b i True ii False

c i False ii False

d i False ii True.

Match incorrect

3. If an organisation goes out of its way to meet customer needs it will have:

a More satisfied customers

b A clear policy on refunds and replacements

c Cheaper goods

d Complaints from shareholders.

Match incorrect

4. To be a good oral communicator it is necessary to have:

a A clear speaking voice

b Constant attention to speed and tone of delivery

c A large vocabulary

d Good listening skills.

Match correct

5. Non-verbal communication depends upon:

a Never speaking

b Hand gestures only

c Using the body to communicate

d Standing close to the other person.

Match correct

6. When dealing with a customer:

a Use his or her name frequently, if you know it

b Be witty and amusing

c Break up the conversation with anecdotes

d Hurry him or her off so that you may deal with the next customer.

7. How many statements in this sentence are correct: An assistant in a toy shop is unlikely to meet customers who are (i) parents, (ii) grand parents, (iii) people in the 18–20 age group, and (iv) children

a 1

b 2

c 3

d 4.

Match correct

8. When dealing with people whose first language is not English:

a Do not patronise them by using simple English

b Say the same thing fairly slowly more than once

c Speak very loudly

d Get someone else to deal with them.

Match incorrect

9. The following matters should be considered as confidential:

a Financial matters

b Marital relationships

c Purchasing a car

d Anything concerned with illness.

Match incorrect

10. Customers should be protected from:

a Faulty and damaged goods

b Running into debt

c Being misled by staff

d Professional negligence.

Assignment 10.1
Analysing an organisation

3.3.1, 3.3.2, 3.3.3, 3.3.4, 3.3.5

Look carefully at the organisation in which you are studying.

Your tasks

1. Is it 'user friendly' to anyone who may wish to visit it and use its facilities? Make a list of the criteria by which it might be judged. Who are its customers? What are their needs?

2. Indicate whether the building, the equipment and the people match these criteria.

3. Where it is necessary, suggest improvements.

4. Using the checklist you made in 1 above – which might well start with street signposting – apply it to three shops in a convenient town. Try to include one that is fairly new, one which is part of a chain and one which is a small business which has been in the same building for some years.

5. Define what 'anyone' means and explain which categories of 'anyone' may have difficulties. Indicate why, and what, if anything, could be done about reducing or removing the difficulties.

6. Look carefully at the sort of letter enquirers receive.

7. Use the telephone to make an enquiry and note the response.

8. Visit the reception area and ask a reasonable question. Note the style and content of the response.

9. Describe in detail how customer service may be improved.

Skills achieved

Communication and *Information technology* skills can be demonstrated throughout this chapter. *Application of number*, however, is difficult to find.

11 Present proposals for improvement to customer service

Performance criteria

1. Explain the importance of customer service in business organisations;
2. Identify how business organisations monitor customer satisfaction;
3. Identify improvements to customer service;
4. Present proposals for improvements to customer services in one organisation.

Range

- **Importance of customer service:** to gain and retain customers, to gain customer satisfaction, customer loyalty, to enhance organisation's image.
- **How businesses monitor customer satisfaction:** numbers of customers, level of sales, feedback (repeat business, complaints), marketing research.
- **Improvements to customer service:** reliability, friendliness, availability of goods or services, speed of delivery, published policy for exchanges or refunds; access to buildings (wheelchairs, pushchairs), care for the environment (rubbish free, clean), customer safety.

Customer services in action

When John Stead had only one shop in Ramstown he used to work in his workshop behind the shop. One day he was very carefully turning a fine thread on a 5 cm diameter 10 swg brass tube. Because he did not do this sort of job very often he was working with exceptional care. The shop door bell rang as someone entered. John did not mutter under his breath. He quickly unwound the die he was using to cut the thread and went at once into the shop.

John: 'Good morning, can I help you?'

Customer: 'Good morning. I'm not sure if you'll have what I'm looking for. It's been very difficult . . .'

The explanation continued for some time, until it became apparent that the matter was to do with plumbing. The customer could not locate a plumber and water was running out of his cold tank overflow. John thought he knew the answer to the problem and asked a number of questions. Could the customer get to the tank? Did he have a pair of pliers and a small screwdriver?

John picked up a cistern ball arm and ball cock from the shelf behind him. He explained how the equipment worked and what was likely to be the problem at home.

John: 'There's a small bung in this end which closes off the water supply when the ball rises. These washers wear out and have to be replaced.'

He explained about turning off the cold water supply, removing the unit and replacing the washer. He sold the customer a packet of four washers for 50p. Since they covered all known sizes, one of them was bound to fit.

The customer departed and John went back to his thread cutting. Just after lunch the customer returned.

Customer: 'It wasn't the washer. I've replaced that. It looks as if the ball has some water in it and isn't returning properly.'

John asked him if he would like a complete unit, or a new ball and arm, or just the ball. The customer took the ball and arm.

The following morning the customer was back.

Customer: 'The arm you sold me doesn't fit, so I put the new ball on the old arm and it all works perfectly, now.' (He has the arm in his hand.) 'By the way I need a carborundum stone for my scythe.'

John suggested that if the customer returned the arm he would knock the price off the cost of the sharpening stone. The customer brightened up at once.

Whilst this negotiation was in progress the phone rang. John excused himself and answered it to find that Mrs Alison Mitchell was complaining about an electric drill her husband had bought from John the previous week.

John: 'Please bring it back and I'll either fix it at once or supply you with another one.'

John took his first customer's money and prepared to make a second nut to go over the brass tube he had been threading in the morning.

From this scenario you can derive all the principal aspects of customer services.

Please do this 81 ————————————————————————————————3.4.1

Examine the above scenario and see how many aspects of customer service you can find in it.

Customer services analysed

Below is a check-list which you can compare with the 'Please do this' above. The examples are drawn from John and his customers' conversations and actions. For 'John' read any member of staff in a company.
* Was John polite?
* Did he know his stock (products/services)?
* Did the customer have to wait to be served?
* If there was a wait, was it reasonable and apologised for?
* Did he listen carefully to what the customer said?
* Was he helpful?
* Did he operate a policy helpful to the customer with regard to faulty goods, or returned goods or repairs?

A customer services check-list

- Did he sell high-quality goods which would do the job they were required for?
- How did he deal with a (telephoned) complaint?

Being consumer-led

You can see that John is quite successful at dealing with customers. He offers a quality service and guarantees of satisfaction. His customers are inclined to come back again once they have experienced the standard of goods and services which he supplies. John's marketing policy is the attitude with which he runs his business. It is *consumer-led*. He aims to keep existing customers, obtain new customers by personal recommendation and thereby increase the size and profitability of his turnover. John is also very much *market-led*. He stocks equipment and materials which his customers have expressed a desire to have. He follows up sales with service. His stock changes to meet the needs of customers and changes in technology and fashion. If he were a manufacturer he would be enquiring via market research what his customers wanted and then making it. The alternative is to make something and then go out and try to sell it, but even with this option you have to have some belief in or indication of consumer interest.

Customer services in the public sector

The advantages of being market or consumer-led in the private sector are obvious. They are perhaps rather less so in the public sector. However, there is now a good deal of competition in most public sector organisations. British Rail (BR) companies have to compete with the private bus companies and with people driving their own cars. At one time BR's information service was something of a joke. It was impossible to get through by phone and there were always long waits at under-staffed counters. That is very far from the case now. BR's information services are a model of their kind. The telephone answering is prompt and the replies helpful, polite and accurate. Long queues seldom occur at the counters, and when they do they are efficiently and quickly dealt with, without any enquirer feeling that an enquiry has been less than fully looked after.

National Health Service (NHS) hospitals have plenty of competition from the private sector hospitals and also from other hospitals within the NHS. If people do not travel on the railways, or choose to go to a particular hospital, the railways and that hospital may close.

Customer service specialisation

When John phoned to book his car in for a service, the receptionist at once punched his name up on a computer VDU and was able to tell him the make and model of the car, its registration number, the nature of the service it required, the length of time it would take and the exact cost. This is an example of specialised customer services at work.

Banks need to know only the account number, or some other form of identification, to deal promptly with complex questions. Such specialised customer care provision ensures that the interface with customers is at as high a level of efficiency as the rest of the company and the quality of the care is as good as the products. In general the disaster of being handed from one person to another, none of whom have recognisable names or posts, has gone.

Please do this 82 ———————————————————— **3.4.2, 3.4.3**

Have a look round a large retail shop in your town. Look for the customer service section. What training do you think those who staff it need to have? What do they need to know? Do you suppose that they have any targets to meet? If so what might these be?

It would be a good idea if several of your fellow students looked at a shop each, and you were able to compare notes after the visits. If one or more of the shops had no customer service section it might be useful to consider why, and whether it would be helpful to have one.

Benefits to the company

A satisfied customer is the best advertisement for a company. Ensuring that customers are satisfied means that repeat orders will follow and that private recommendations will provide more customers. It is difficult to follow this up in the retail trade, especially in huge, impersonal supermarkets, but it is a lot easier in manufacturing and wholesaling, both of which involve issuing invoices to named purchasers.

John Stead dealt with the cash-and-carry wholesaler MARVO. The manager could press a few buttons and immediately have all John's purchases for the last 12 months displayed on his VDU, together with total values month by month and a comparison with the previous year. Retailers have to try to gauge consumers' opinion of their performance by sales figures supplemented by random questionnaires.

Even the dissatisfied customer is a source of valuable information, the goods he or she returns and the complaints about staff will provide useful insights into ways to improve services and products.

Please do this 83 ─────────────────────────── 3.4.3, 3.4.4

1. Think of ways in which a company could improve its services to its customers without cutting its profit margins to the extent that it cannot survive. Take as examples;

   a a chain store dealing with clothing for all ages and both sexes,

   b a shop in a village,

   c a bank, and

   d a bookshop in a city centre.

Where we wish to be

The corporate aims (*mission statements*) of an organisation provide a guide to what it is about and how it is likely to struggle to get there. Knowing what you want to achieve is the first step on the way to achieving it. Your school or college will have a statement of its mission. Mission statements tend to be quite short but encompass wide horizons. For example, ASDA's mission statement reads:

> 'ASDA's mission is to become the UK's leading value for money grocer with an exceptional range of fresh foods together with those clothing, home and leisure products that meet the everyday needs of our target customers.'

Given the clarity of the statement and the obvious will and ability to put it into practice, it seems likely that ASDA will succeed.

Please do this 84 ─────────────────────────────── 3.4.1

1. Obtain a copy of your school or college mission statement (or that of

another organisation if your school or college does not have one) and compare it for effectiveness and clarity with ASDA's.

2. Consider how far the mission statement is put into effect and why it is important.

Buying something

Buying (or purchasing) is a very ordinary process for most of us. Going into a shop for a newspaper or a magazine, or any other purchase, does not present most of us with many problems – yet it is carefully hedged around with the law.

Asking for a packet of chewing gum involves contractual obligations. The purchaser has to make an offer to buy at a stated price, though on most small items, or on things that are clearly marked (nowadays the majority of items), the price is seldom mentioned by the purchaser. The seller then has the right to decide to sell, or not, at the price mentioned or marked. At the point when the seller agrees to sell there is an unalterable contract which is sealed by the *consideration*, that is the money being paid over.

Offers:
- have to be firm and without any ambiguity,
- must be made to the person who is the seller,
- can be written or oral, and
- are sealed by the seller accepting the money or giving the buyer the goods or services.

Contracts of sale

It is not normally possible to enter into a contract of sale if the buyer or seller is a person suffering from a disorder covered by the Mental Health Act 1983, very drunk, or younger than 18 (except in the latter case for necessities like food and clothing).

Contracts of sale have *expressed* or *implied* terms. Buying a television set which turns out to have only adequate sound equipment when it was stated that the quality was good (an expressed term) means that there has been a breach of contract as far as the warranty is concerned. If the television set had no tube, then that would be a breach of the implied terms of the contract as far as a condition of sale is concerned. The difference is that in the former case the set would function to less than the supposed standard and breach the warranty; in the latter case it would not work at all and would breach a fundamental condition involved in the purchase of the set, which is that it should show moving pictures.

The end of a contract of sale is reached when the purchase is made and the buyer goes away with what has been bought. The goods purchased may be returned to the seller and accepted with a refund of the selling price. It may be breached by one side or the other not carrying out the agreement.

Please do this 85 ─────────────────────────────3.3.6

The most usual place to find the details of contractual obligations, usually in very small type, is in holiday brochures. Get hold of a couple of brochures covering areas in which you are interested and compare the contractual information (not the package holidays themselves).

1. Make a list of things which are covered in each brochure and compare what each one says about each criterion. For example what happens if you cancel?

2. Can you draw any conclusions from the comparisons you have made?

Protecting the consumer

There are several major Acts of Parliament which aim to protect the consumer:
- the Trades Description Act 1968
- the Sale of Goods Act 1979 (as amended by the Sale and Supply of Goods Act 1994 and the Supply of Goods and Services Act 1982)
- the Consumer Protection Act 1987.

These Acts apply only to England and Wales. The Office of Fair Trading has publications covering Scotland and Northern Ireland.

The Trades Description Act 1968

This Act deals with the offence of giving a false description of goods in written or spoken words or by graphics of any sort. False statements with regard to quantity (e.g. how many matches in a box), size, means of manufacture and the

False claims contravene the Trades Description Act

ingredients (e.g. a large bottle containing only wild flower perfumes distilled in Grasse, which turns out to be 2.6 ml of a coal tar derivative made in the Wirral).

The Sale of Goods Act 1979

This is the Act which brought to the public the concept of being 'of merchantable quality' and which applied to commercial sales only. Goods not only had to be what they were described as – for example, 'Natural rubber 100 per cent' is not permissible if the product is even 1 per cent synthetic – but they had to do what they were supposed to do and, to be of merchantable quality, they had to go on doing it.

Defects pointed out at the time of sale, or easily noticeable from an inspection which took place at the time of purchase, did not count. Making a reduction in the selling price because the goods are shop soiled, seconds or rejects would imply that the quality was not as good as might be expected of the perfect product.

If things are not what they should be in accordance with this Act's criteria then the purchaser is entitled to a refund.

The Supply of Goods and Services Act 1982

The provisions of the Sale of Goods Act 1979 were strengthened by this Act to include goods which were on hire, on part-exchange or part of a service. It goes one stage further and includes services such as those provided by garages, hairdressers, builders, electricians and others. The services have to be provided within a reasonable time, with care and skill, and for a reasonable charge.

The Sale and Supply of Goods Act 1994

The term 'merchantable quality' used in the 1979 Act has now been replaced with the term 'satisfactory quality'. This term is defined in the Act and by its very wording you can see that it aims to further protect the consumer.

The Consumer Protection Act 1987

It is an offence to pretend that a price is lower than usual if it is not, for example omitting reference to VAT where that is chargeable and has not been included in the offer price. It is also an offence to supply goods which are not reasonably safe. In practice, it is an offence to be a wholesaler of dangerous goods; just having them for the purpose of sale is an offence.

Ombudsmen

This is a system based on a Swedish model. In 1967 the Parliamentary Commissioner for Administration was appointed. His job was to check that government departments dealt fairly with the public. Now there are numerous Ombudsmen covering building societies, the health service, investment, local government, insurance, legal services, pensions, banking and estate agents. The Ombudsmen do not charge for their services and are completely independent of the organisations which they investigate.

The Citizen's Charter 1991

This deals with consumer rights in areas such as health, education, welfare and the privatised utilities like water, telecommunications, electricity and gas. The

The Parent's Charter

organisations involved have to offer specified standards of service to the public. If they can prove that they are coming up to the standards required they can utilise the 'chartermark'.

Seeking help

At the local level

It is not necessary to go far to get some help if you are an aggrieved and dissatisfied consumer. Each local authority employs environmental health officers who, among other responsibilities, are concerned that all premises dealing with food comply with the food hygiene laws. Trading standards officers are also local authority employees and they investigate complaints from consumers about, for example, unfair prices or misleading descriptions of goods.

Citizens' Advice Bureaux give free advice and help with buyer–seller negotiations if there is a problem that the consumer cannot solve.

Please do this 86 ——————————————————————————**3.3.6**

Look in your local paper over a period of weeks and see if you can find any reports concerning environmental health officers and trading standards officers who have had to intervene in areas where there has been a dispute or the consumer has needed their protection. Cut out or copy the reports. Is there any general theme which runs through them? If so indicate what it is. If not, list the specific cases and the areas which they cover.

At the national level

The National Consumer Council is a body which has a liaison function between the consumer, the public and private sectors, and the government. The public sector watchdogs try to look after the consumers in relation to the privatised utilities and some public sector organisations. These bodies all have names starting with 'Office', for example, Office for Telecommunications, and for convenience are described as Oftel (BT), Ofwat (Water companies), Ofgas and so on.

The Office of Fair Trading (OFT):
- can take legal action against offenders,
- supplies information to consumers to alert and advise them on their rights, and
- proposes legislation for the consideration of the government to safeguard consumers.

The Consumers' Association (CA) tests products and services across a wide range of companies. It publishes the results in its magazine *Which*.

John buys an arc welding machine

John decided to buy an arc welding machine to provide further services to his customers. He wanted a reliable machine at a good price, so he read the appropriate trade magazines and used the *Yellow Pages* to contact suppliers in his area and obtain some quotations of costs. He reckoned that 90p on phone calls and half an hour of asking questions was a good investment. Getting a quotation is a very valuable activity: without it he may have had a surprise when he went to buy, or worse still, to pay.

John went to Arcwelders Ltd and talked to the salesman. The deal is a good one, but John is somewhat put off by the salesman's attempt to sell him a piece of equipment which was much bigger and more expensive than he needed or wanted, to say nothing of the request for an advanced payment before delivery. He also noticed that the salesman was trying to put additional items on the invoice. John is not pleased – he believed that he should not have to pay in advance and he certainly did not want added items on the bill. He decided that he is not being treated as he would wish and he politely brought the transaction to an end, deciding to go elsewhere.

At Arcngas Welders the approach was quite different. The motto here seemed to be:

'What you see is what you pay for.'

It also seemed to have an excellent after-sales service.

John carefully checked the appliance which he bought, looked at the computer printed invoice which was on pre-printed fanfold paper, and put it away carefully.

A few days later John was busy doing a bit of very intricate welding when the machine ceased to function. He called to his assistant to look after the shop and took the machine back to Arcngas. He talked to the manager who was apologetic and offered him a replacement. John thought this was a reasonable solution, accepted the replacement and went away mollified, if not completely happy.

If Arcngas had been less helpful than they were John would have written to the head office with a fairly straightforward complaint and a photocopy of the receipt. The company would normally have replied promptly, but if he heard nothing, or nothing satisfactory, there are a number of options open to John:

- He could go to the trading standards officer.
- He could approach the appropriate trade association, if the company is a member.
- He could take his case to the county court where small claims, under £1000, are fairly simply and relatively cheaply dealt with.

The fact that the courts are not overflowing is some indication that dealers, in general, are reasonably honest and prefer to settle matters outside the court and to both parties' satisfaction.

Please do this 87 ——————————————————————— **3.4.1, 3.4.3**

Look at John's experience with his purchase and make a list of the things that any consumer should look out for when undertaking a purchase.

How does an organisation monitor levels of customer satisfaction?

Review questions ———————————————————————————————

Match correct or *Match incorrect* – these questions require you to match the first statement against the one correct answer in a, b, c and d. This sort of question will be described as *Match correct*. In some questions you may find that you have to pick out the only incorrect answer; these will be referred to as *Match incorrect*.

True/false – these questions require you to look at two statements and decide whether each statement is true or false. You should ring the pair in a, b, c or d which is closest to your opinion of what the statements say. These will be described as *True/false* questions.

Match incorrect

1. You may test customer services by:

 a Seeing if you are served promptly

 b The quality of goods sold

 c The uniforms worn by staff

 d The politeness (or otherwise) of staff.

Match incorrect

2. A customer services desk:

 a Gives information and help

177

b Gives advice on after-sales service

c Acts as a deterrent to customers complaining

d May process refunds.

Match incorrect

3. A code of practice for dealing with customers may include:

a Replying to all letters within two days

b Dealing with customers politely

c Dealing with complaints at the most junior level and not bothering a supervisor

d Producing company literature which is simple and easy to read.

Match incorrect

4. Ways of obtaining information about the standard of service in a restaurant include:

a Putting in an employee from elsewhere as a customer

b Staff asking customers if they are satisfied

c Conducting a postal survey in the district

d Setting up a consumer panel with staff and customers on it.

Match incorrect

5. A contract of sale consists of:

a The customer offering to buy at an agreed price

b The seller agreeing to sell at an agreed price

c Guarantees in the case of the death of one party

d The customer paying the seller.

Match incorrect

6. The acceptance of an offer to buy must:

a Be unqualified

b Be firm

c Not introduce new terms

d Be in writing.

Match incorrect

7. A contract of sale concludes:

a By agreement

b By breach

c By performance

d By a counter offer.

Match incorrect

8. Laws which apply to buying and selling are:

a Sale of Goods Act 1979

b Trades Description Act 1968

c Health and Safety at Work Act 1984

d Consumer Protection Act 1987.

Match incorrect

9. The Citizen's Charter:

a Is legally enforceable

b Focuses on consumer rights

c Requires minimum levels of service

d Makes providers aware of the client.

Match incorrect

10. The following help consumers:

a Citizens Advice Bureaux

b The President of the Board of Trade

c Environmental health officers

d The Office of Fair Trading.

Assignment 11.1
Ensuring customer satisfaction 3.4.1, 3.4.2, 3.4.3, 3.4.4

The answers to the following questions should be laid out as a report to John Stead, who is wondering if he is doing enough to ensure consumer satisfaction and wants to compare his performance with others', picking up some ideas at the same time.

Look at a local authority provided service *or* a service for which central government is responsible *or* a local firm, such as solicitors, accountants, estate agents or something of your choice.

1. What services or products does your organisation supply?

2. Are they what people have asked for, or are they supplied because of law or policy rather than consumer need?

3. How does the organisation discover how satisfied its customers are?

4. a Have there been any improvements over the last year which the organisation mentions?

   b Who prompted them?

   c Why were they put into operation?

   d Are there other improvements which have not yet been implemented?

5. Who makes decisions on changes of this sort?

6. What sort of measures can be taken to ensure that consumers get a good deal from the organisation?

7. Is the organisation prompt about rectifying any difficulty which may arise?

8. Are there formalised procedures for dealing with complaints, mistakes or situations in which the customer needs redress for positive and justifiable grievances?

9. What does the organisation do to make sure that its consumers know what their rights are? How does it operate systems for ensuring that consumers are well-treated in this respect?

10. Make your own proposals for improvements in customer service.

Skills achieved

Nearly all the skills which you can claim here are reinforcements of the *Communication* skills which you have gained elsewhere in this work. You should have used *Information technology* equipment, particularly in the presentation of the evidence which you have gathered. There is, however, very little in the way of *Application of number*.

12 Financial transactions

Element 4.1 – Identify and explain financial transactions and documents

Performance criteria:

1. Explain financial transactions which take place regularly in an organisation and explain why records of transactions are kept;
2. Explain and give examples of purchases and purchase documents;
3. Explain and give examples of sales transactions and sales documents;
4. Explain and give examples of payment methods and receipt documents;
5. Explain the importance of security and security checks for receipts and payments.

Range

- **Financial transactions:** outward transactions to pay for costs (wages, materials, overheads), inward transactions to receive income (payments, loans).
- **Records of transactions:** to produce accounts (internal for the business's own use, external to be published annually), to ensure security, to monitor business performance (profit, loss).
- **Purchases:** materials, services, wages.
- **Purchase documents:** orders placed, purchase invoice, credit note, goods received note.
- **Sales transactions:** goods, services, business-to-business, business-to-consumer.
- **Sales documents:** orders received, sales invoice, delivery note, sales credit note, statement of account, remittance advice.
- **Payment methods:** cheque, cash, Banking Automatic Credit Systems (BACS), Electronic data interchange (EDI), credit card, debit card, credit (includes hire purchase).
- **Receipt documents:** receipt, cheque, paying-in slip, bank statement.
- **Importance:** to prevent fraud, to prevent theft, to ensure high standards of honesty.
- **Security checks:** authorisation of orders, invoices checked against orders, invoices checked against goods received notes, cheques signed by authorised signatories.

Element 4.2 – Complete financial documents and explain financial recording

Performance criteria

1. Complete purchase and sales documents clearly and correctly, and calculate totals;
2. Complete payments and receipts documents clearly and correctly and calculate totals;
3. Explain why financial information must be recorded;

4. Identify and give examples of information technology which businesses use to record and monitor financial information.

Range

- **Purchase documents:** orders placed, purchase invoice, credit note, goods received note.
- **Sales documents:** orders received, sales invoice, delivery note, sales credit note, statement of account, remittance advice.
- **Payments documents:** pay slip, cheque, petty cash voucher.
- **Receipt documents:** receipt, cheque, paying-in-slip, bank statement.
- **Financial information:** accounts (internal accounts, external annual accounts), budgets.
- **Recorded:** for security, to monitor income and expenditure, to keep customer accounts up to date, to keep the business accounts up to date, to monitor performance.
- **Information technology:** accounting software, spreadsheets.

Element 4.3 – Produce, evaluate and store business documents

Performance criteria

1. Produce examples and explain the purpose of routine business documents;
2. Evaluate each business document produced;
3. Compare the methods of processing business documents;
4. Reference, correctly file and retrieve business documents;
5. Identify and evaluate ways to send and ways to store business documents.

Range

- **Purpose:** to communicate with customers, to communicate with a colleague, to communicate with other businesses.
- **Business documents:** letters (confirming a meeting, answering an enquiry, dealing with a customer complaint), memo, invitation, notice, message.
- **Evaluate each document:** in terms of appearance (style, format), in terms of language (spelling, grammar).
- **Compare:** in terms of: legibility, cost, time taken to produce, ability to make changes, storage.
- **Methods of processing:** hand-written, typed, word processed, printed, photocopied.
- **Reference:** alphabetically, by subject, number, date.
- **Evaluate ways:** ease of sending and storing; ease of finding and retrieving, cost, safety of documents, security of documents.
- **Ways to send:** special delivery, post, electronic transmission (fax, electronic mail).
- **Ways to store:** paper filing; computer files, computer back-up files.

Why keep financial records?

John Stead could have made more money travelling the world as a consulting engineer. Even his senior position in a college might have been more financially profitable than running his market stall or his subsequent DIY shop. It was not until the business started to expand that he could consider that he had regained his standard of living.

Throughout his self-employed existence John needed to keep records of his financial affairs. Even if he were silly enough to ignore the opportunity to check what his expenditure and income were, he would still have had to keep records because the Inland Revenue wants to know about his profits, and tax them. Likewise, Customs and Excise would have required John to submit VAT returns as he was a VAT registered business.

The banks will not lend money on an unprofitable activity so John has to prove that he is doing all right before he can arrange to do even better. John needs to know if he is making a profit so that he can put some by for his pension, his capital expenditure (a car or a van for a start) and his purchases of stock, as well as his own living expenses – and he might even manage a few savings.

Without adequate records John will never know where he is or what he should do to improve, or even maintain, his position.

John's annual accounts have to go to be audited and are sent to the Inland Revenue. The continuous account-keeping processes ensures that John keeps a careful record of bills which his suppliers send him, and does not pay them twice or pay them the wrong amount.

Good and continuous record-keeping is also a means of insuring himself against theft or errors by staff – potentially expensive mistakes.

Please do this 88 —————————————————————— 4.1.1

1. Enquire about the financial record-keeping procedures in your school or college.

2. Invite the Bursar or Chief Financial Officer to show you examples of the financial documentation and how each document fits into the overall financial procedures of the organisation. Remember that much documentation may be contained on computer discs.

3. If you are currently out on work experience ask if you may have the financial documentation shown and explained to you. Carefully note the explanation given to you and write it up in a brief report. (Do not make reference to any clients or sums of money that you may observe and assure the employer that you will treat the company's affairs as entirely confidential.)

What are financial records?

It is all right knowing that financial records are important, but knowing what they are and how to keep them is essential. Let us deal first with the sort of thing that happens in John's one-shop business and then look at the same activity with regard to a larger organisation using electronic data processing.

Making an order

John has to obtain stock. He goes along to the wholesaler's warehouse and puts a good number of boxes on a trolley. He pushes the trolley to the check out where he gives the cashier his personal wholesaler's card with its number and electronic stripe on it. The cashier runs the card through a slot on her

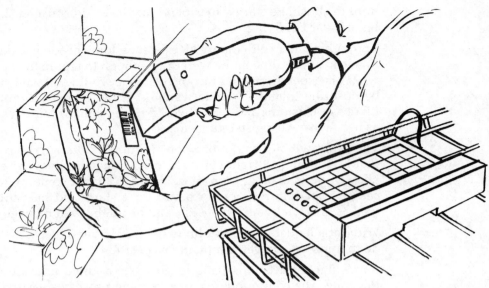

workstation and there is an immediate response from the computer which prints the heading on the account which will follow. The cashier points a registration gun at the bar codes on each box. The gun reads the bar code and transmits the unique numbers for each product to the in-store computer.

The computer starts at once to prepare the bill (invoice) that John is going to have to pay. It also adjusts internal stock records, initiating reorder procedures where necessary. In practice, the in-store computer may well be able to communicate directly with the manufacturer's computer and alert the manufacturer that a delivery will be required at a specified time in the future.

Please do this 89 ————————————————— 4.1.2, 4.2.4

Find two or three organisations which use bar codes. Ask if you may have the system explained to you and gain some insight into its cost effectiveness. Write up what you have learned as a set of notes.

Printing the invoice

Once the cashier has registered all the purchases she asks if that is all, presses a key on the keypad in front of her and the invoice is immediately printed and totalled. This gives details of:
- each package,
- its cost,
- the VAT rate and amount, and
- the totals of costs and VAT.

Please do this 90 ————————————— 4.1.2, 4.1.3, 4.1.4, 4.2.1, 4.2.2

Copy the invoice shown opposite, preferably onto a computer, and complete it for:
- 25kg of potatoes at 35p for 5kg, number 32A465;
- 28lb of Ticco margarine at 50p per half pound pack, number 431G987;
- 24 boxes of Marvo fresh orange juice at 42p plus VAT, number 32C67598;

MARVO						Sales Invoice	

Self-service Wholesalers plc

VAT Registration No. 603 9871 905

Customer   Address   Time   Invoice No.

Cashier

Date

Qty/ weight	Article number	Article description	Unit price	Unit packs	Pack price	VAT code	Goods value

Total: _____

VAT items: _____

Final total: _____

A sales invoice

- 6 dozen pairs of work gloves at 125p a pair, number 433V564.

Alternatively, you can photocopy the invoice and fill in the details by hand.

How to pay

John receives cash for nearly all his sales, which are numerous, but in small quantities. However, when he goes to the wholesaler he has a number methods he could use to pay his bill:
- he can pay cash, and a lot of retailers do,
- he can pay by cheque, though £50 or £100 limits apply to most cheque guarantee cards,
- he can use a credit card, or
- he can use a payment debit card, for example Switch.

Please do this 91 ————————————————————— **4.1.3, 4.1.4, 4.2.2**

Photocopy the blank cheques shown on the opposite page.

1. Complete a copy of one cheque drawn in favour of B&Q for £32.78p. Remember to complete the back of the cheque in accordance with the cheque guarantee card's requirements (in this case assume it is £50).

2. Complete a second copy in favour of Marks & Spencer plc for £74.20p.

Plastic cash

Of the credit cards, Visa, Access, Mastercard, American Express and Diners' Club are the most usual. When John uses the credit card as payment the cashier takes his card and puts it in a machine which reads the magnetic tape on the back. This automatically registers the wholesaler's and John's details and has the amount and date added.

The electronic receipt looks like this:

```
11:33              21/10/94
Auth Code:21445

MARVO
Crosland Hill
Manchester

WELCOME
055476534.6543    5026672314
Staff/Inv. No. 1654365675
VISA
4112343564765487654448793
6527

Thank you
£107.68           Sign below

.....................................
.
```

NATEAST BANK
CIRENCESTER BRANCH
PO BOX 1 CIRENCESTER GLOS

20-03-20

19

PAY ONLY

ACCOUNT PAYEE

£

CALVIN HOBBES ESQ

100415 20 0320 256888714

FOR RETAILER USE ONLY
Card No. Expiry Date
Was cheque signed in front of you Yes/No
IF NO, OBTAIN ANOTHER SIGNATURE HERE
CHECK– SIGNATURE ON CHEQUE AND CARD MATCH
– THE STRIP IS NOT DAMAGED
IF IN DOUBT TELEPHONE NATEAST BANK

NATEAST BANK
CIRENCESTER BRANCH
PO BOX 1 CIRENCESTER GLOS

20-03-20

19

PAY ONLY

ACCOUNT PAYEE

£

CALVIN HOBBES ESQ

100415 20 0320 256888714

FOR RETAILER USE ONLY
Card No. Expiry Date
Was cheque signed in front of you Yes/No
IF NO, OBTAIN ANOTHER SIGNATURE HERE
CHECK– SIGNATURE ON CHEQUE AND CARD MATCH
– THE STRIP IS NOT DAMAGED
IF IN DOUBT TELEPHONE NATEAST BANK

Blank cheques (front and back)

Credit cards

It is possible to use these cards in a manual system in which the card is inserted in a machine and overlaid by a packet of thin pre-printed papers and carbons.

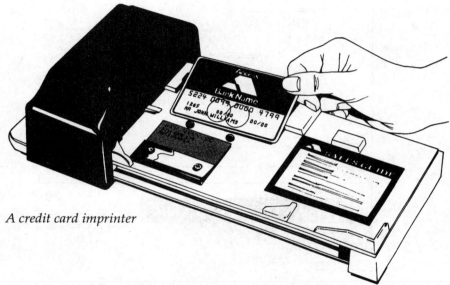

A credit card imprinter

The cashier runs a roller over the packet which is forced against the embossed surface of the card and records all the details of the owner on the sheets in the packet. The details of the purchase, the date and amounts are added in ball-point pen and the purchaser gets a copy.

The manual system looks like this:

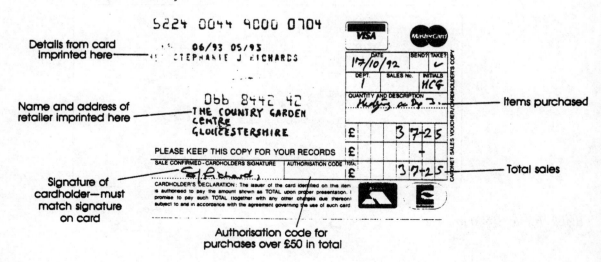

188

Payment debit card

John could have used a payment debit card. That is to say a card which is treated like a credit card but involves the use of Electronic Funds Transfer at Point Of Sale (EFTPOS). Typically, this is a Switch card. As soon as John's card has been inserted in the machine and the amounts typed in, the sum is automatically removed from his account at the bank and transferred to the wholesaler. This is an invisible cash transaction.

A payment debit card looks like this:

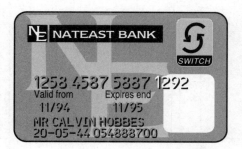 

Recording the transactions

Having completed his transactions at the wholesalers, John returns home with his purchases which he stores in his garage and then goes into his 'office' to record his transaction. He does this in a *day book* (this is a cash book). On the left-hand side he lists all his expenditure. On the right-hand side he lists his income.

For ease of reference each transaction is numbered and dated and the receipts and other documents, like invoices, are numbered to correspond as evidence of the transaction.

Please do this 92 ———————————————————— 4.1.4, 4.2.2

Using the blank day book pages overleaf, which may be photocopied or put on your computer, use the MARVO invoice to complete an entry in the day book. Make others from the cheques for B&Q and Marks & Spencer.

Using the day book

At the end of each page/week/month/quarter/year there must be an addition and reconciliation. Of course this does not take any account of capital assets, or bank or other loans – these are for other records.

When John was a market trader he did not use a till so that there was no record of individual transactions. He put the money he received in a box at the back of the stall and stored the notes in his wallet. He always added up his money before he started out and added it up again when he took down his stall so that he knew what his takings were for the day.

Occasionally, John had a customer who wanted to pay by cheque, usually someone straight from work shortly before the market closed who had not been to the bank. John accepted cheques provided they were covered by a bankers'

Serial	Date	Description	£	p	Serial	Date	Description	£	p
Bfwd					*Bfwd*				

Day book pages

card. These are added separately into the day book and are paid into the bank via the night safe arrangements. This involves John writing a paying-in slip which looks like this:

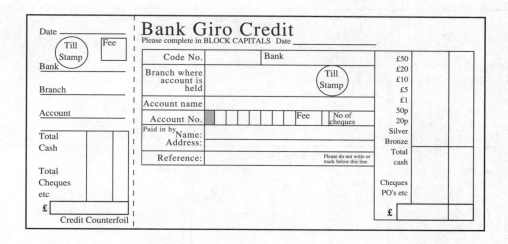

A paying-in slip

Please do this 93 ————————————————————————————————— **4.1.4, 4.2.2**

Complete a paying-in slip dated today for cheques for £53 from Mary Hamilton, £44.40 from Polly Peck plc and £17.95 from the British Rail Pension Fund. There is also £123.56 in cash. You can either get a blank paying-in slip from your bank or photocopy the one above.

The bank statement of account

Each month John receives from the bank a statement of account showing payments in and out. This looks like this:

```
                        NORTH BANK PLC
Bank Statement No.: 61              Branch:  77 High Hill
                                             London N11
Account Number: 44400               Tel:     0171 001 9191
Account Title:  Stagecoach Ltd
                49 White Horse Road
                London N11                  Date: 30 June 1995
```

Date	Details	Withdrawals	Deposits	Balance
1 June	Balance from sheet No. 60			318.20
7 June	00310	41.60		276.60
	00311	22.25		254.35
	Highfield SO	50.00		204.35
11 June	C-C		60.00	264.35
12 June	00313	41.00		223.35
14 June	00315	50.00		173.35
15 June	Bell Insurance DD	42.50		130.85
	TR		25.75	156.60
18 June	00316	32.35		124.25
	C-C		35.30	159.55
21 June	00314	32.80		126.75
	CH	8.55		118.20
22 June	00312	68.40		49.80
28 June	00317	25.50		24.30
30 June	Balance to sheet No. 62			24.30

```
Key: SO Standing order  DV Dividend     C-C Cash &/or Cheques  OD Overdrawn
     CH Bank Charges     DD Direct Debit TR Credit Transfer     AC Automated Cash
```

There are various abbreviations which are used on accounts including:
- CR = Credit,
- D = Debit,
- OD = Overdrawn (he used more money than he had put in),
- Sundry credit = a payment in for which there is no voucher,
- Sundry debit = the same as sundry credit except that money is taken out and there is an explanation elsewhere,
- CH = charges for cashing cheques and performing other transactions.

There may be interest payments on a personal account or interest deductions where the current account is used to service a debt.

Please do this 94 ———————————————————————— 4.1.5, 4.2.3

1. If you can, obtain a bank statement and compare it with the cheques and other records of payments and withdrawals. (Unless you have a bank account of your own, this may be difficult. Either ask to see one of your

family's statements or ask if you can see a statement from the students' association.)

2 Explain why checking the account is important.

A chronology of the purchasing and recording processes

Whether it is John, who is conducting a very small business with little in the way of complications, or a multi-billion pound enterprise, the procedures and documentation are much the same for purchasing and recording.

Stage 1

First there is an official order for goods on a pre-printed form delivered by post, hand or fax (facsimile). The form will probably come as a group of almost identical sheets and will be copied through from the top copy by using NCR (no carbon required) paper. Each sheet relates to the different recipients:

- the customer,
- the supplier,
- the finance department to authorise payment,
- the department checking the goods received against the order, i.e. a goods received note,
- the purchasing department.

John, of course, shops around for the suppliers who will provide the best prices and assured delivery. A larger company might ask for estimates of prices or firm quotations before considering a purchase. In very large contracts, potential suppliers may be asked to *tender* for the opportunity to supply. This is a system by which detailed estimates of costs are provided by each potential supplier, usually in a sealed envelope, and all tenders are opened at the same time. This ensures that all potential suppliers are treated equally in the tender process.

A large company may also be in the position to ask for discounts like those accorded to people in the same trade for:

- minimum guaranteed orders,
- bulk supplies,
- cash, or
- prompt payment.

Please do this 95 ———————————————————————————— **4.1.2, 4.2.1**

1. Photocopy the order form overleaf or copy it onto your computer.

2. Complete an order to be sent to Truesteel DIY Tools Ltd, 23–51 Rothersthorpe Road, Sheffield, S73 9AZ, for:
   - 12 sets of wood turning chisels at £76 a set,
   - six 12.5mm Concorde hammer drills at £55.50 each,
   - one Arundel wood-turning lathe at £240,
   - a dozen each of wood chisels at 1.25cm, 2.5cm and 3.75cm costing £5.25, £6.50 and £7.33 respectively.

   Add VAT to each item and total.

STEADY DIY Ltd
Enterprise House
RAMSTOWN RA1 2LR

Tel: 01777 4521896   VAT Reg. No. 980/567898/987

ORDER

To _____   Date

_____

_____

_____

Order No

Please supply:

Quantity	Code No.	Description	Unit price

Deliver to: _____

Deliver by: _____

Signed _____

An order form

Stage 2

The seller sends the goods with a delivery note and issues an invoice. The *delivery note* is often an invoice without the prices on it. This is another opportunity to use NCR paper and save a lot of duplicated effort.

Please do this 96 ——————————————————————— 4.1.3, 4.2.2, 4.2.3, 4.3.1

1. Complete a copy of the invoice overleaf from the information provided in Steady DIY's order. (The invoice may be photocopied or copied onto your computer.)

2. State why detailed invoices are necessary.

Stage 3

Some of the goods are unsatisfactory and they must be returned. Usually, this is done with the use of a photocopy of the delivery note and a covering explanation. Often there is a telephone call before the goods are returned explaining the difficulty or deficiency.

Please do this 97 ——————————————————————————————— 4.1.2, 4.2.4

The lathe delivered is not an Arundel lathe and is returned. Complete the necessary documentation.

Stage 4

In the event that a replacement for goods is not required by the purchaser the seller has to issue a *credit note,* i.e. a note that records the fact that the purchaser has paid too much and is due either a refund or goods to the equivalent value in compensation. This credit note may be no more than a note on the returned invoice, or an entry on the monthly statement.

Stage 5

There may be several transactions involved with a seller In this case, the seller issues a monthly statement which the purchaser pays in one amount rather than a payment being made for each transaction.

Please do this 98 ———————————————————————— 4.1.3, 4.1.4, 4.2.2, 4.2.4

1. Take a photocopy of the monthly statement on page 197 and complete it with the transactions so far undertaken.

2. Now do the same exercise but on a monthly statement that you have put onto your computer.

3. Explain why the latter method is preferable.

Truesteel DIY Tools Ltd
23–51 Rothersthorpe Rd
SHEFFIELD S73 9AZ

Tel: 01443 77665589   VAT Reg. No. 56667/98

INVOICE

To: _____

Your order number	Invoice date tax point	Invoice	Despatch date

Quantity	Code No.	Description	Unit price	Total price	VAT rate	VAT amount

Delivery charges
Sub total
VAT
Total amount to be paid

Errors and Omissions Excepted

An invoice

Truesteel DIY Tools Ltd
23–51 Rothersthorpe Rd
SHEFFIELD S73 9AZ

Tel: 01443 77665589   VAT Reg. No. 56667/98

STATEMENT

To:

Date: Account No.:

Date	Details	Debit	Credit	Balance

A statement

Sales

Date	Name	Invoice number	£	p

Purchases

Date	Name	Invoice number	£	p

Returns inwards

Date	Name	Invoice number	£	p

Cash book

Receipts				Payments			
Date	Details	Cash	Bank	Date	Details	Cash	Bank

Balance brought fwd: Balance carried fwd:

Day books – example format

Stage 6

Ledgers are kept with transactions processed through *double-entry* book-keeping. This is not as daunting as it sounds. The double-entry system is simply a method of recording transactions so that each is recorded in two places. For example, the purchase of 20 litres of petrol for £10.80 means that there is a credit of the petrol and elsewhere a debit of £10.80. Whatever happens every debit must be matched with a credit and vice versa.

The day books

The prime entry books are the day books:

* the sales day book is based on invoices issued,
* the purchases day book is based on invoices received,
* the returns book is based on credit notes issued and received,
* the cash book records receipts and payments.

The format of these day books is shown opposite.

Every month (or other period) the entries in these books are totalled to give a cumulative total.

The ledgers

There are numerous ledgers as follows:

* the sales ledger contains accounts relating to goods and services provided on credit to people who have not yet paid (*debtors*);
* the purchases ledger contains accounts relating to goods and services acquired from others on credit and which have not yet been paid for (the suppliers in this case are *creditors*);
* the cash book records all receipts and payments;
* the general ledger covers all the other accounts: land, buildings, machinery, capital, loans and so on.

Even John, the small trader, transfers paperwork to his personal computer. His ledgers are stored electronically until he prints out hard copies. At the end of each year John has to produce his annual accounts and balance sheet for the benefit of the tax authorities and to convince the bank he is still a good risk.

Review questions

This unit does not, at the time of writing, have a Unit test set by the awarding body. However, just to keep in practice you might like to try these questions.

Match correct or Match incorrect – these questions require you to match the first statement against the one correct answer in a, b, c and d. This sort of question will be described as *Match correct*. In some questions you may find that you have to pick out the only incorrect answer; these will be referred to as *Match incorrect*.

True/false – these questions require you to look at two statements and decide whether each statement is true or false. You should ring the pair in a, b, c or d which is closest to your opinion of what the statements say. These will be described as *True/false* questions.

Match incorrect

1. Financial transactions are recorded because:

    a Annual accounts can be produced

    b It is traditional to keep records

    c Evidence of the transaction can be produced when required

    d Business performance can be monitored.

Match incorrect

2. Annual accounts:

    a Have to be audited

    b Are necessary for tax purposes

    c Always have to be made public

    d Are the profit and loss account and the balance sheet.

Match correct

3. The difference between the cost price of stock and the selling price is:

    a The net profit

    b The gross profit

    c A liability

    d An asset.

Match correct

4. The money which a business owes its creditors is:

    a A transaction

    b A liability

    c Part of the turnover

    d Not considered for VAT.

Match correct

5. Walker and Woodhouse Ltd have a 1978 16Kb computer which the company does not use. In the accounts it appears as:

    a A liability

    b A raw material

    c An asset

    d Written off against VAT.

Match correct

6. A cheque has to have the amount of money involved written in words and figures:

    a So that the drawer doesn't need to be careful over either of them

    b To ensure a cross check for the sake of absolute accuracy

    c To provide copies for other people

    d In case the bank clerk is illiterate.

Match incorrect

7. There are numerous ways of encouraging companies to place orders. They include giving:

    a A trade discount

    b A cash discount

    c An incentive to buy discount

    d A prompt payment discount.

Match correct

8. The letters E&OE on an invoice refer to:

    a Estimates and omissions expected

    b Errors and omissions excepted

    c Elements and orders excepted

    d Excuses and objections expected.

Match correct

9. A price label on a garment in a shop:

    a Is the price at which the garment must be sold

    b Will not include VAT

    c Is an invitation to trade

    d Is the minimum price which can be charged.

Match correct

10. EFTPOS:

    a Express financial transactions positively observed for security

    b Exceptional funds transfer positively secured

    c Electronic funds transfer at point of sale

    d Executive financial transactions with proof of security.

Assignment 12.1
Keeping financial records   4.1.2, 4.1.3, 4.1.5, 4.2.1, 4.2.2, 4.2.3, 4.2.4

This assignment will provide a set of tasks to prove that you know why financial records are kept and that you can complete them successfully. Remember that financial records are useless unless they are completed promptly, accurately and in full, so check each document to ensure that it is the right one and that you have completed it carefully.

You may photocopy any of the blank documents in this chapter, or you may input them onto your computer and print them out as completed records.

You must attach a piece of paper to each of your documents and state on it why you have used the document, what it is intended to do and how it fits into the flow of financial recording. (Do not forget that when VAT has to be added it is calculated at 17.5 per cent. Take care that you account for VAT on any items below that state 'plus VAT'.)

Your tasks

1. From the information provided below, complete all necessary paperwork.

   Mon Sept. 1

   John buys 60 dozen tins of cat and dog food from the wholesalers Petfoods Unlimited, Bosphorous Industrial Estate, SALFORD, Lancs M29 3QQ. The tins are divided into Purrs 5 dozen; Mouser 10 dozen; Pusscateers 10 dozen; Wooff 5 dozen; Dogs' Breakfast 15 dozen; Cats' Pyjamas 15 dozen. The first three brands are 27p a tin, the latter three are 26p a tin. He will get 7.5% off if he pays within 14 days.

   John sells a friend 24 tins of Purrs, one dozen of Mouser and 2 dozen of Pusscateers, all at 38p a tin. The friend pays by cheque.

   John pays a monthly instalment of £127 on his van. He also buys 7 gallons of petrol at 54.8p a litre so that he can travel to the market. John pays £5.75 for his day's rent of the stall in the market.

   John sells for cash: Purrs 23 tins at 42p, Dogs' Breakfast 107 tins at 44p, Mouser 117 tins at 41p, Pusscateers 135 tins at 42p and Cats' Pyjamas 99 tins at 43p a tin.

   John sends five letters at 25p each to do with orders and payments.

   Tues Sept. 2

   John receives a delivery of tins from the manufacturer – Dog, Cat and Pet Foods Ltd, Boneyard Mill, HALIFAX, W.Yorks HX 12 9RG Tel: 07775 456345, VAT Reg No. 345/9858/675/B – with whom he deals direct.

   Finicky has a unit cost of 25p for quantities over 50 dozen, John buys 60 dozen to sell at 32p a tin plus VAT.

Dogsbreath is a dog biscuit which comes in 2.5 kg bags at £1.44 and sells at £2.00 both plus VAT. He gets 60 bags.

Weds Sept. 3

John goes to Shipton market and sells 430 units of an average cost to him of 33p with a 22 per cent mark-up. Calculate his gross profit for the day as well as filling in the appropriate documents. All payments were in cash.

Thurs Sept. 4

Whilst he was at Shipton market several people approached him to ask if he also sold vitamin supplements for their cats in pill form. John has heard of Kitzyme – a reputable brand of vitamin pills. He phones his wholesaler for advice and possible supplies. He is told that there is an even better (i.e. he has more varied vitamins), more acceptable to cats (cat mint included) and more profitable cat vitamin pill with at least a 50 per cent mark-up, called Cat-a-tonic. This heavy sales pitch makes John think. He knows the excellent qualities of Kitzyme and wonders whether the wholesaler is trying to shift something he's overstocked. John asks if it is on sale or return and rather reluctantly the wholesaler agrees that if he takes two cases and the first case causes him any difficulties he can return the second case for a credit. John orders two cases of 12 dozen packets each at 70p a packet, for which he pays by cheque.

John spends only half the day – very heavy rain sets in at lunch-time – at Rossington Market. Before the rain empties the streets he sells 150 tins of Finicky at 39p a tin, 40 bags of Dogsbreath, 36 tins of Purrs, 52 tins of Mouser, 20 tins of Dogs' Breakfast and 8 of Cats' Pyjamas, all at the usual rates. All transactions are in cash.

Fri Sept. 5

John is at Shipton Market. The weather is better so that he is able to sell all day. He is surprised to find that he has sold exactly double on September 5th compared to what he sold on September 1st, plus 40 boxes of Cat-a-tonic and 32 bags of Dogsbreath. That evening John telephones the wholesalers and orders a complete set of new stock to be delivered on Monday 8th September. He posts official orders on Friday night. The items a

• Purrs 5 dozen, Mouser 20 dozen, Pusscateers 30 dozen, all at 27p a tin.

• Woof 10 dozen, Dogs' Breakfast 25 dozen, Cats' Pyjamas 10 dozen, all at 26p a dozen.

Dogsbreath has sold well so he orders a further 6 dozen bags.

Make out the orders for all these, not forgetting the VAT.

Sat Sept. 6

Saturday is a favourite marketing day in Shipton. John has gathered together nearly all his existing stock which he has stored in his garage and prepares for the best day in the week. John sells, for cash, 43 tins of Mouser, 127 tins of Pusscateers, 90 tins of Purrs, 70 tins of Woof, 115 tins of Dogs' Breakfast and 60 tins of Cats' Pyjamas. He sells out of Dogsbreath (28 bags) and sells 88 tins of Finicky. Calculate the total prices for each brand, not forgetting the VAT and complete the appropriate documents.

Whilst he is selling, several customers complain about Cat-a-tonic. Apparently cats reject it or the results on their digestion appear to be fairly catastrophic for the carpets. John apologises, offers several people their money back and decides to return the second carton.

John likes to finish each week with a total of purchases and sales and see what he has made. Complete the appropriate documents for him. Explain the purpose of all the calculations, documents and entries you have used and made.

2. Write John a letter explaining the advantages of Electronic Data Interchange and what he needs to take part in it.

Skills achieved

In this chapter there has been little chance to exercise the skills of *Communication* listed in the specification. However, there are substantial opportunities for claiming skills in the areas of *Application of number* and *Information technology*. Look at the specification and the work that you have done here and enter the skills that you wish to claim with supporting references to specific activities.

In Chapter 13 there are opportunities to claim all the performance criteria in Element 4.3. You should have completed this material as you went through the programme.

13 Communication

Demonstrating that you possess the skills is an essential part of proving your abilities to claim the whole of the Business Intermediate GNVQ. The material in the following chapters supplements what you should have gained by doing the work in the previous 12 chapters. If you are in doubt about your proof from the preceding chapters the work here will supplement what you have already done and should be included in the documentation for skills.

Speech

Using the spoken word you may persuade, inform, encourage, correct, demand, exhort, etc. However, in general, you do have to be understood and make your message clear. Speech is an immediate process; it is how we communicate. It is less formalised than writing, and reveals the person even more than the written word.

In business dealings it is often a good idea to make a few mental or written notes about what you are going to say, before you say it. This will improve the clarity of your thoughts which in turn will make your communication more accurate.

In day to day speech, words disappear as soon as they are spoken. However, people have selective memories of what has been said to them, and particularly in business it is a good idea to keep your ideas clear and not change your mind too often. Spoken words can often be ambiguous; there is no chance to go over the exact sentence again and hone it to clarity.

Please do this 99

With a small group of friends, consider how the following could be improved. It is a transcript of a not very interesting conversation exactly as it took place.

'How do you, how do you spell accommodation?'

'Wha?'

'I want to, I want to spell accommodation. How do you spell accommodation?'

'I spell it any old how, I can remember a sergeant major telling me off because I'd misspelled it when I was in the army.'

'Well how do you spell it then?'

'I spell it a c c o m m o d a t i o n.'

'Is that right?'

'Well that's how I spell it, right or wrong.'

'I didn't mean that, I meant, is that how it's spelled?'

'I don't know, that's how I spell it and I haven't had too many complaints lately.'

'Oh, thanks. A c c o m o d a t i o n.'

'No, two ms.'

'Two ns?

'Yes, two ms'
'Oh, thanks.'

Making it clear

Not only must the message be clear, but your voice should be clear as well. Suit the volume to the circumstances. Do not mumble, but avoid raising your voice unless there is a very good reason for doing so. Keep a reasonable speed of delivery, though avoid monotones, or talking to quickly or too slowly. Avoid 'er' and catch phrases like 'you know' repeated at the end of sentences to give you thinking time. Likewise, avoid specialist speech, (jargon), unless you are absolutely certain that the other person understands it perfectly. Avoid jargon when there is a third person present who should be taking a part in the conversation but may feel excluded if two people are passing what can only be described as coded messages. This is likely to lead to misunderstandings and resentment.

Please do this 100

During the course of a day listen to several conversations bearing the above in mind. Pick out and write down what it is that could be 'improved'. Then consider your own part in conversations and how this could be improved. Think particularly of conversations with people you know very well and who are a lot older than you are. They may not be able to share, or even understand, your enthusiasm for the latest fashions in clothes or music but consider what you could do to include them in conversations you find interesting.

Body signals

It is possible to say one thing in words and quite another by tone of voice supported by gestures. Saying a formal good morning, but standing well back from the person you are greeting and failing to shake his or her hand, may give two

Contradictory messages

quite different messages. Looking away from someone whilst you are involved in a conversation with them or going so far as to write a letter during a meeting will tell the other person all they need to know. Give the other person your attention. If the other person is standing up, do not sit down without saying something, unless you wish to establish some sort of authority relationship.

Please do this 101

Watch the body signals of people in a variety of situations and work out what their messages might be.

The telephone

All the handbooks tell you to smile when answering people on the telephone and to stand up when making a difficult call. You must come to your own conclusion about this, but generally speaking a laid back attitude with the caller's feet propped up on a desk drawer tends to indicate that the call is informal or personal. When making a telephone call write a couple of notes about what you want to say, and have any supporting papers ready, as well as plenty of paper to write on. When you need to take down an important point from a telephone call then either repeat the message back to the caller or ask him or her to repeat it once more to you.

Listening

It is easy to test whether someone has listened to what you have to say, merely ask them to repeat the important part. If they cannot, it may be that your message was so garbled and unclear that they could not work out which part to take notice of, or they might have been thinking about something else whilst appearing to take notice.

When listening to someone else, make sure that you can hear them and that surrounding noise is not a barrier to communication. It is not a good idea to discuss a sales contract at a disco.
- Do not interrupt the speaker, unless you are asking for a repeat of the point.
- Do not ignore messages that you do not want to hear.
- Do concentrate and show that you are concentrating on the speaker and the message.
- After the message is concluded give some sort of feedback which confirms that you have heard and understood the message, and will, if required, act on it.

The presentation

This is probably a task that few people look forward to unless they are very used to giving presentations and have been well trained in the art. There are a few simple rules which will enable you to be successful:
- **Prepare**. What are you going to talk about? Who is the audience? What do they already know? What do they need to know? What would they like to

know? How long have you got?

- **Make notes of what you are going to say.** Learn the first and last lines off by heart. Rehearse, and not just once. Always have to hand a set of prompt notes that will fit onto a postcard. Read them at quiet moments and fill in the rest of what you are going to say. Do not read verbatim from a script. If you do you will adopt the wrong pace and in any case you might just as well circulate copies of your script rather than standing there and reading it out aloud.

- **Start off with a civil greeting.** 'Good morning, it's nice to be able to speak to you' has merits, even if the main purpose is to get the volume of your voice right. Tell the audience what you are going to tell them. Then tell them, in a well-organised and section by section order. Finally, summarise what it is that you have said, stressing the most important two or three points and then conclude, thanking them for their time and for listening.

- **Smile at the audience and speak clearly.** Speak at rather more slowly than conversational speed, but not at dictation speed unless there is something that you want your audience to write down.

- **Look at the audience.** Making very brief, but not infrequent eye contact. Do not address yourself solely to one person, or the ceiling or the floor. Your rehearsals might have included a video of your presentation which will reveal, and magnify, any irritating mannerisms. On the other hand, standing rigidly and unmoving for five or ten minutes indicates strain.

- **Pause occasionally, particularly after an important point.** If you do dry up do not panic, two deep breaths and a quick look at your notes and you should be able to carry on.

- **Request and answer questions.** If your presentation has led to new material for your audience, you may well have to answer questions. If you really do not know the answer, say so and tell the enquirer you will find out. If you are not sure and want time to collect your thoughts, then ask for a repeat of the question. If you have a point raised that asks for a yes/no answer do not go on at length. It may be useful to ask the people in the audience if they have views on a difficult question.

A check-list

It is possible to draw up a check-list covering the following aspects:
- appearance,
- mannerisms,
- confidence,
- enthusiasm,
- eye contact,
- body language,
- pace of delivery,
- inherent interest of the topic,
- clarity,
- quality of organisation,
- suitability of topic and level for the chosen audience,
- appropriateness of the length of delivery,
- use of notes and visual aids,
- handling of questions,
- pitch of voice and volume.

Did the sound trail away at the end of the sentences or paragraphs? Were pauses significant, or did they just happen because you needed to take a breath or think? Was the tone of the voice and the pace of delivery varied? Was emphasis by word and pace/tone/volume given to important points?

Please do this 102

Convert the points given above into a logically formatted and word-processed or DTP check-list. Give a presentation to your classmates, friends or family and get them to mark your performance on the sheet.

Writing it down

A note

> Bill
> Mr Walker called at 13.30 22 Nov to give you the revised cleaning contract. He has left it with Mary and hopes that you will read it and raise any points with him on 01764 654 768, the 24th, when he'll be in all day.
>
> Jim 22 Nov

A note like this would normally be hand-written and placed with any others relating to events that took place when Bill was out.

A memo

These are often written on pre-printed forms with the company's name and the word MEMORANDUM at the top. They may have a box with pre-printed words to guide the originator. The contents are often written in point form.

> **Steady DIY**
>
> **MEMORANDUM**
>
> To: Bill Smith   From: Jim Giles
> Subject: Revised cleaning contract   Date: 22 Nov 1994
>
> 1. Mr Walker called at 13.30 on 22 November.
> 2. It would be helpful if you could read the contract, which is with Mary, and phone him back on 01764 654 768 on the 24th Nov with any comments.

The memo can be typed or hand written, and may be on NCR paper so that the recipient can write a comment on one side or at the bottom, send back the original sheet and keep a copy of the reply and the original message.

The letter

In businesses, letters are best kept as short as possible. They are usually word-processed on company headed notepaper.

WILSON AND WATSON AUCTIONEERS LTD
23-29 Bishops Gate
YORK YO55 7RGP

Telephone 01777 4235
Fax 01777 4239   Date:

Your Ref:
Our Ref:

Space here for the
addressee's name and address

Dear   (If Sir or Madam then conclude 'Yours faithfully')
        (If Mr/Mrs/Miss/Ms then conclude 'Yours sincerely')

Insert a subject here

Introduce the matter, often referring to previously received correspondence.

Say what you have to add to the matter.

Use the appropriate conclusion, known as a complimentary close.

Leave space for the signature.
Sender's name and job title.

Please do this 103 ───────────────────────────────────── 4.3.1, 4.3.2

Write a reply to each of the following using the appropriate form of communication.

1. Mr Salter has telephoned the office at 14.45 on 17 July asking if it is possible to make an appointment to see the senior partner, Mr Walsh, about a legal matter concerning contracts. He is suggesting that 09.00 on 20 July might be convenient. Unfortunately, Mr Walsh was out when the call came in and had taken his diary with him in case he needed to make a further appointment with the client he was visiting. You are the receptionist, Philip Brierley.

2. You have received the following memo on NCR paper. Reply to it on the right-hand side.

WALSH WILLOUGHBY AND WATSON
Memorandum

To: Philip
From: A W Walsh
Date: 12 March

Subject: Legal Stationery

1. The cupboard in Mr Watson's room
   was left unlocked last night.
   Please ensure that it is always
   locked before you depart.
2. It appears that we have inadequate
   quantities of conveyancing documents.
   Please ensure that we have an immediate
   supply and get in a stock of say, one
   gross. I will sign the order.
3. Please let me have a record of all
   the County Court appearances we have made
   since 1 January.

You also received the following letter.

SHELDON SUMMERLEE AND CHALLENGER
Solicitors and Commissioners for Oaths
Victory Chambers
Royal Way
ACTON W55 7RG

Tel: 0181 432 6577
Fax: 0181 435 65769

Your Ref:
Our Ref: SH/trd/26   15 March 1995

Messrs Walsh Willoughby and Watson
23 Abbey Life House
NORWICH NH6 12PG

Dear Walsh,

Environmental Protection

Your clerk, Mr Brierley, told me that you would be sure to support our
efforts to get the legal profession thoroughly involved in matters concerning
environmental protection. I enclose a leaflet which indicates how we can

---

help with, as you can see, arrangements for low fees for supporting environmentalists in their legal battles with the despoilers. We should also use recycled paper in the offices and for legal documents. The leaflet includes a code of practice for green lawyers.

There is a registration fee of £5 which entitles all those who are complying with the green code of practice to use the Lawyer Friends of the Earth logo.

I do hope that you will be able to support this really worthwhile initiative which is becoming Europe-wide. Our patron is the Mayor of Chernobyl, Mr V I Ulanov.

Yours sincerely

Henry Sheldon
Senior Partner
Sheldon Summerlee and Challenger

Mr Walsh has scribbled on it: ' Philip. Since you've got us into this you can draft a reply and prepare the cheque.'

Whatever you do, always write in the simplest English you can manage. Do not use expressions like 'I am writing this letter.' or 'Referring to your letter...'

Examine what you have written and judge its quality against the criteria in Unit 4.3.

The notice

Have a look at a noticeboard in your school or college, or at the notices in the local newsagents or small local shop's window. You will soon come to a conclusion about which is the most effective notice.

When writing a notice:
- keep it short,
- date it,
- try to find two words which tell everybody what it is about,
- make the message very short,
- try using colour
- make more than one copy of the notice so that it can be repeated at other locations.

Please do this 104 ————————————————————————————4.3.1

1. Compose a notice telling everyone on your course that the annual bring and buy sale for textbooks, equipment and clothes will be held shortly.

2. Judge the quality of your notice.

The report

The report is usually the most complex of the written documents in a company. It should be word processed or desk-top published. It should be written in the third person, unless you are instructed to write it differently. For example, not 'I have watched the photocopier break down on 22 occasions' but 'The photocopier was observed to break down on 22 occasions . . .'

Here are some basic rules:
- Start off by giving the report a title which summarises its contents. (This is not an opportunity for coining eye-catching phrases, but for being absolutely clear.)
- Then put down who the report is for or is aimed at. This may be the person who asked you to write it.
- Date it.
- Put in the terms of reference, i.e. the reason why you are writing the report.
- Put in any recommendations. There are reports which are simply accounts of events and do not require any conclusions or recommendations to be made; for example, an accident report where both conclusions and recommendations, other than from an authorised source, would be unhelpful and might be misleading.
- The main body of the report then follows. This is usually concerned with observations and tests.
- From these there is a section entitled conclusions. These should not be mixed with recommendations. Very often people do not read the whole report but look at the conclusions and recommendations. If these are not what they expect, they may be inclined to read the rest of the report to see if the evidence supports the important points that they have read.
- Reports should have headings and sub-headings.
- Paragraphs should preferably be numbered with a major section having a number (e.g. 5), and the sub-units or paragraphs being numbered within (e.g. 5.1, 5.2). If necessary a further sub-unit can be used (e.g. 5.2.1).

Please do this 105 ———————————————————————— **4.3.1, 4.3.2, 4.3.4**

1. Write a brief report on how you think this book could be improved. The main body of the report should concern itself with the book's content, layout and presentation, style, number and type of exercises, etc. You should draw conclusions from what you have read and done, and make recommendations. (Do not forget to send the author a copy, care of the publishers.)

2. Get hold of an accident report form used in your school or college, or in a local company. Mrs Walker, a visitor, tripped over a curled up carpet tile, has a suspected broken arm and an ambulance was called to take her to hospital. Fill in the remaining details.

Alternative ways of conveying the message – graphics

Instead of a lot of words a simple graphic, usually computer generated, can help people understand something clearly. Figures can be put into a line graph, a bar chart, a pie chart or as pictograms.

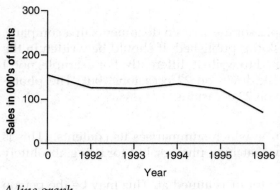

A line graph

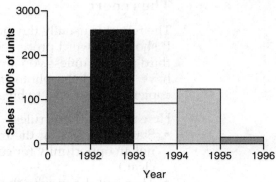

A bar chart

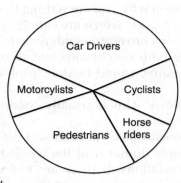

A pie chart

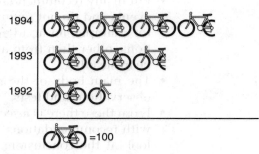

A pictogram

Spelling

You have had at least ten or 11 years of full-time education and you have probably been reading longer than that. However, if you cannot spell, it may affect your job prospects or career progression.

Here are a few tips:

- Buy a small pocket dictionary and keep it with you. Use it to check spellings you may not be sure about.
- Know the difference between words that sound alike; practise (a verb) but practice a noun; devise and device (the rule here is the same for all the –ise, –ice words).
- Think about words such as almighty, already, always, altogether (derived from 'all'), and full + fill = fulfil, will + full = wilful, skill + full = skilful.
- But remember beautiful + ly = Beautifully; thoughtful + ly = thoughtfully.
- Remember separate.
- If in doubt about words ending -ise or -ize use -ise, which is more common in English. Alternatively, look the word up.
- Frequent errors:
  - there (in there) their (belongs to them)
  - whose (book is that?), who's (that you were speaking to, an abridgement of who is)
  - affect (the new law will affect me), effect (this law will put the government's policy into effect)

– principle (an ethical decision), principal (main thing or head of a college)
– 'to' as a preposition; use it with a verb, for instance 'give it to me';
– 'too' as a comparison with a standard – too big, too few; the number two.

Business words often misspelt

abridgement, accelerate, accept, accommodation, acquaintance, acquire, adjacent, advantageous, allowed, alter, appalling, ascent, assent, benefit (bene-fited), Caribbean, commemorate, committee, develop(ment), discreet, discrete, dividend, exaggerate, except, extreme, feasible, foreign, government, independence, irrelevant, judgement (but a legal judgment), livelihood, minute, necessary, occurrence, possess, precede, privilege, relevant, rigour, satellite, seize, seizure, success, withhold, woollen.

Punctuation

- **Full stop** – ends a sentence and can be used within the letters of an abbreviation such as R.S.P.C.A.
- **Question mark** – and exclamation mark – also used to end a sentence.
- **Comma** – breaks up phrases in a sentence, or is used between words in a list.
- **Apostrophe** – shows there is a letter missing, (eg shows there's a . . .); also used to show ownership (Tim's = belongs to Tim).
- **Quotation marks** 'Bother,' he said (these can be 'single' or "double").
- **Capital letters**, at the beginning of a sentence, at the beginning of a person's or place's name (eg John, Aberdeen).

Please do this 106 ———————————————————————4.3.1, 4.3.2, 4.3.3, 4.3.4, 4.3.5

1. Make arrangements to visit your school/college or work placement office. Write a report, addressed to your assessor, on the ways in which business information is processed, produced and sent to the individuals concerned, and copies filed.

2. Obtain an explanation of the filing system and how it is edited.

3. Take several documents and provide proposed filing destinations.

4. Check with the office supervisor that you have got them in the right places.

5. Retrieve five documents for the person in charge of the filing system. Indicate in your report your evaluation of the most cost-effective means of sending and storing information, and what precautions should be taken to ensure safety and security.

   Refer particularly to electronic document transfer (EDT).

Formal meetings

Business meetings, like every other formalised meeting, are held to make one or more decisions, usually about some existing or impending problem and to

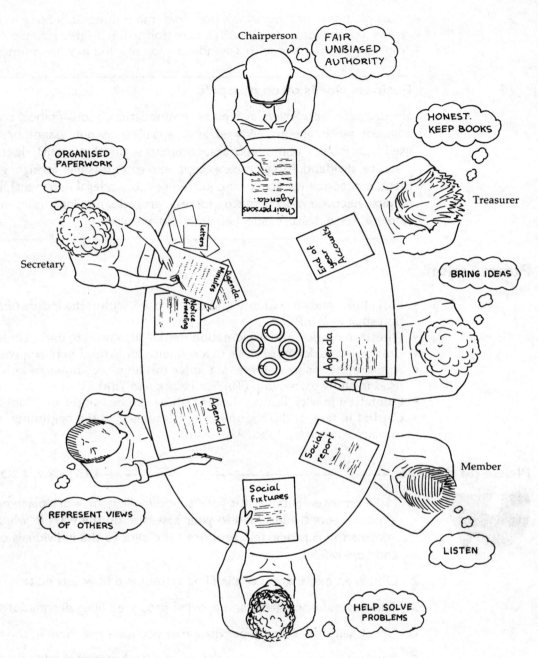

The committee

agree some sort of plan of action to deal with the problem and put the solution into effect. At its most informal, friends may meet in the week, to decide what to do at the weekend. Between you, you decide when to meet, how to get there and have some idea of how and when you will get back. Because no two people have exactly the same constraints on their time and their finances there may have to be a bit of negotiation, for example a bus there and a taxi back may be the solution. In this case you do not need to write down exactly what it is you have to discuss, or the conclusion reached, you can easily remember these details.

The agenda

To avoid lapses in members' memories and to ensure that what has to be considered is attended to, people who run formal business meetings issue, usually in advance, an *agenda*. This is a list of items to be discussed and an agenda is usually set out quite formally.

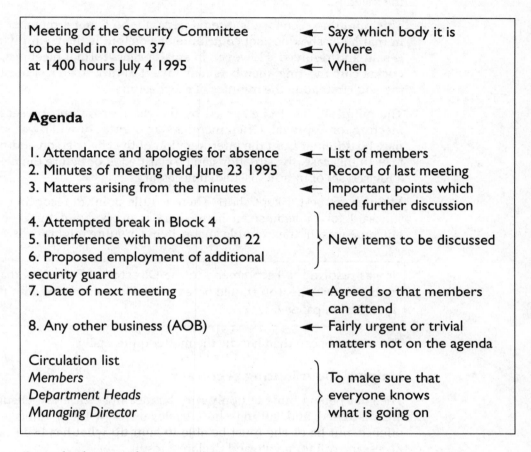

Meeting of the Security Committee — Says which body it is
to be held in room 37 — Where
at 1400 hours July 4 1995 — When

Agenda

1. Attendance and apologies for absence — List of members
2. Minutes of meeting held June 23 1995 — Record of last meeting
3. Matters arising from the minutes — Important points which need further discussion

4. Attempted break in Block 4
5. Interference with modem room 22 } New items to be discussed
6. Proposed employment of additional security guard
7. Date of next meeting — Agreed so that members can attend

8. Any other business (AOB) — Fairly urgent or trivial matters not on the agenda

Circulation list
Members
Department Heads } To make sure that everyone knows
Managing Director what is going on

Example of an agenda

The role of the chairperson

Business meetings are often timed to start and finish at specified times. This practice helps the chairperson to organise the running of the meeting so that each item gets satisfactory treatment.

The agenda may have items contributed by members or other interested parties as well as the chairperson and the secretary, but it is the chairperson who decides, after item 3 (1, 2, and 3 are always the same) the order in which items appear.

Apart from arranging the order of items on the agenda with their supporting papers, the chairperson is responsible for the conduct of the meeting. In the example, item 6 would certainly have supporting papers. Items 4 and 5 may be the subject of oral reports, perhaps by the Chief Security Officer or someone else with first-hand knowledge of events.

The minuting secretary

With the printed agenda and its accompanying papers issued in advance of the meeting, there is also usually an account of the previous meeting, described as the *minutes of the meeting*. It is usually a secretary who takes notes (minutes) of what is said and the outcome of each item on the agenda during the progress of the meeting.

This minuting secretary is often a person who is not a member of the meeting in that he or she does not contribute or vote but is there simply to record what is said and resolved. However, in small or less formal meetings, for example a cricket club meeting, members may take it in turn to be responsible for producing and circulating the minutes of the meetings.

The minutes have to be agreed by the chairperson and presented to the next meeting for approval. Often members' memories of what was said or resolved may be different from the interpretation of the chairperson and minuting secretary. In this case, the situation can be clarified at or before the next meeting and a revised set of minutes issued, if necessary.

Minutes are best if kept short. There is little point in recording what each person said for or against an item; there is every point in recording what the outcome was. In the example above, item 6 minute might read:

> It was resolved to recommend to the Director of Personnel that an additional security person should be employed in accordance with the terms indicated in paper 6.1.

The secretary can then handle the matter quite easily.

Helping the minuting secretary

The chairperson must not only run the meeting efficiently, ensuring that items are discussed and cutting short irrelevancies without unnecessarily causing offence, but he or she must be able to sum up what has been said and, where necessary, call for a vote and declare a result.

Votes have to be about something and thus members (usually) put their intentions into a proposition which to gain a discussion will need a *seconder*, that is another person on the committee who agrees with it. The *proposition* is a form of words which indicates, for example, that the committee recommends that another security person is employed. Another member may feel that this is not good enough and asks for an *amendment* along the lines of:

> The committee recommends the appointment of two additional security people.

The amendment is voted on first. If it is passed then the original proposition is ignored and the amendment is recorded in the minutes as a resolution of the committee. If the amendment fails to secure enough votes to pass then the original proposal is voted on. It, too, may have insufficient support, in which case it is noted that the proposition was defeated and the committee moves on to the next item. If it succeeds then it becomes a *resolution* of the committee.

Handling this part of the business of the meeting can be quite difficult and the secretary and the chairperson often work together in mutual support.

Keeping order and structure

Should the meeting become rowdy the chairperson will call for order and if this is not forthcoming will close the meeting. That very seldom occurs in business meetings, though you might wonder how the Speaker (Chairperson) of the House of Commons manages to keep order!

In all cases, the person who is speaking must address the chairperson. This ensures that private conversations or meetings do not start between members and that there is far less chance of scoring personal points rather than attending to the debate.

Dealing with any other business (AOB)

The chairperson has to suspend the progress of the meeting if a member wishes to make a point of order. A *point of order* may be about the way in which the chairperson is conducting the meeting. For example, he or she may have omitted to call someone to speak who wishes to contribute, or about something another member has said or proposed.

The final item on the agenda is *any other business (AOB)*. This may allow for raising important and very recent matters or even bring the date of the next meeting forward.

The minutes

What the committee has decided is listed in the minutes of the meeting. Like the agenda, there is a formal layout for this (see overleaf).

Minutes are subsequently distributed to those on the circulation list.

Please do this 107 ————————————————————————— **4.3.1, 4.3.4, 4.3.5**

With four or five other students, convene a meeting of the Student Facilities Committee, whose aim is to improve facilities for students.

1. Each person should independently produce an agenda.

The first meeting will be concerned with the election of a chairperson.

2. Describe the skills required by a chairperson.

The aim of the meeting will be to put forward a single agenda and indicate which items require supporting papers.

3. Each member, including the chairperson, should produce one item.

4. All members, including the chairperson, should write their own set of minutes of the meeting. At the end of the meeting the chairperson relinquishes the post and becomes minuting secretary for the next meeting, which should be held within ten days. At the second meeting a chairperson is elected. Each member's minutes are circulated.

Minutes of the meeting of the Security Committee ◄— Which Body
held at 1400 hours July 3 1995 ◄— When

1. Present
Mrs K Strike, Mr J Wallace, Ms T Weller, ◄— A record of
Miss P Wilson (Chair), Mr K Young who was there
  Apologies
Mrs K Able, Mr T Flint, Mr E Cambell ◄— And who was not

2. The minutes of the meeting held ◄— Chair signs
on 23 June1995 were signed as a these and they
correct record. are kept in a
minute book

3. Matters arising from the minutes
3.1 Item 5 Security cameras block C ◄— Refers to
These have now been fitted. incomplete dis-
3.2 Item 7 Prosecution of J Mather cussion at the
Found guilty, 6 months imprisonment. previous
meeting

4. Attempted break-in Block 4 ◄— 4,5 and 6 are
An oral report was received from the current issues
Chief Security Officer. The attempt was foiled which form the
by the use of the new security cameras and majority of the
the prompt action of security staff. Mrs Joanne business of the
Lee and Mr William Sykes were commended by the meeting
committee. Offender is in police custody.

7. Date of the next meeting
July 15 at 13.00 in room 32 ◄— Warning for
all those who
should attend

8. Any other business
8.1 Use of smart card ID deferred ◄— Item for
8.2 Construction of internal security July 15
locking system. Chair indicated that this
was underway and meeting agreed dates

9. Meeting closed at 15.05 ◄— Included to
indicate extent
of meeting

Example of minutes

5. Each person should make a note of differences in style, emphasis and content of the other member's minutes. The committee then considers each item before it.

6. The minuting secretary must prepare a set of minutes which are circulated to the members for comment.

14 Application of Number

The four rules

Addition

Adding two or more numbers together. You should be able to add 73 to 239 and make 312. An addition looks like this: 73 + 239 = 312.

Subtraction

Finding the difference between two numbers. Subtract the smaller number from the larger. You should be able to subtract 73 from 312 and make 239. A subtraction looks like this: 312 − 73 = 239.

Multiplication

Finding the product of multiplying two numbers one by the other. You should be able to multiply 312 by 73 and make 22,776. A multiplication looks like this $312 \times 73 = 22,776$.

Division

Dividing one number by another. It is not necessary for the number being divided to be larger than the divider. You should be able to divide 239 by 73 and make 3.274, and divide 73 by 239 and make 0.305. Divisions look like this: 239 ÷ 73 = 3.274, 73 ÷ 239 = 0.305

Some important terms

The decimal point

The decimal point indicates that the numbers before it are whole numbers, whilst those after it are tenths, hundredths, thousandths etc. (moving from left to right). We will come back to decimals later.

The square and square root

The square of a number is that number multiplied by itself. $6 \times 6 = 36$, so 6 squared is 36. This is written 6^2. The square root of a number is exactly the opposite; it is the number which has to be multiplied by itself to produce that number. The square root of 36 is 6. This is written $\sqrt{36}$.

Fractions

These are generally fairly straightforward. We tend to deal in easy quantities, usually fewer than you might find in the slices of a cake, and relegate the other proportions to decimals or percentages.

Half of something is written: $\frac{1}{2}$. Half of a half is a quarter: $\frac{1}{4}$. The other common fraction is a third. There are three of these in one whole. Halves, quarters and thirds are easy to visualise as fractions. After that it is usually better to use decimals.

Fractions on their own do not cause much difficulty. However, it is often necessary to add fractions together. You have a pretty good idea of what half a cup of tea looks like and a third must be a bit less, but how do you add $\frac{1}{2}$ to $\frac{1}{3}$, and what about $2\frac{1}{2} + 3\frac{1}{3}$? Easy, do the whole numbers first and then make sure that the denominators are all the same. A fraction has a top and a bottom part, the top part is called the *numerator* and the bottom part is called the *denominator*. Cancel down the fractions. You do this by dividing the numerator and denominator by a number which will go into both.

If, for example, we want to add $\frac{1}{2} + \frac{9}{12} + \frac{12}{48}$, start by making each fraction have the same denominator.

Our line of figures is now $\frac{24}{48} + \frac{36}{48} + \frac{12}{48}$. This adds up to $\frac{72}{48}$ which is represented as $1\frac{24}{48}$ or $1\frac{1}{2}$.

Subtraction also involves finding a common denominator and subtracting the smaller from the larger denominator. If the fraction you are left with after dealing with the whole numbers is smaller than the one which is going to be subtracted from it, then put back 1 as a fraction into the small one making an *improper fraction*, so $9\frac{1}{4}$ becomes $8\frac{5}{4}$.

Multiplying fractions is done by multiplying all the numerators together, then multiplying all the denominators together and then cancelling down if you can:

$\frac{3}{5} \times \frac{5}{6} \times \frac{4}{7} = \frac{60}{210} = \frac{6}{20} = \frac{3}{10}$.

Dividing fractions is done by turning the second one upside down and multiplying:

$\frac{5}{7} \div \frac{1}{3}$ becomes $\frac{5}{7} \times \frac{3}{1} = \frac{15}{7}$ (which is represented as $2\frac{1}{7}$).

Fractions can be converted to decimals by dividing the numerator by the denominator and into percentages by multiplying by 100. For example $\frac{11}{64} = 0.172$ or 17.2%.

Decimals

Decimals express numbers in tenths, hundredths and thousandths: 0.1 is one tenth, 0.11 is one tenth and one hundredth or eleven hundredths. Decimals are useful for expressing lengths in kilometres and metres, as there are 1000 metres in one kilometre: for example, 2 km 876 metres can be expressed as 2.876 km or 2876 m. They are also used for money: £5 and 23p can be £5.23 or 523p. For the purposes of money transactions only two places after the decimal point are required. For example, seven men do a job for which the contract says they will be paid £1500. £1500 divided by 7 is £214.28571. What we have to do is round up the decimals from the right. Any decimal under 5 is ignored. 7 is rounded up then added to the 5 making it 6. The 6 is rounded up and added to the 8 to make it 9. Each man receives £214.29p. When the £1500 is divided the amount distributed is 2.8p more than it should be.

Percentages

1 per cent means, literally, one in a hundred, hence its link with decimals. For example 1 per cent of £36.50 is 36.5p. It is always possible to work out, say, 15

per cent of £36.50 by finding 1 per cent and multiplying by 15. 36.5p × 15 = £5.475 (£5.48 when we round up to two decimal places). This is not a particularly efficient method, but it works. A better way to work is to remember that 15 per cent is $\frac{15}{100}$ and lay out the sum like this:

$\frac{15}{100}$ × £36.50 = $\frac{5475}{100}$ = £5.475 = £5.48

If you have a calculator enter the two numbers as a multiplication and press the % key.

The other thing that you can do with percentages is to find what percentage one number is of another. To take an easy example: 100 is half (50%) of 200. This is laid out like this:

$\frac{100}{200}$ × 100 = 50.

Another example:

$\frac{24}{220}$ × 100 = 10.90909.

Doing business

Value added tax

Value added tax (VAT) is calculated as a percentage of the total selling price. The current rate is 17.5 per cent. If a bicycle's selling price is £165 plus VAT the amount of VAT payable is: £165 × 17.5 = £28.88. So the total selling price is: £165 + £28.88 = £193.88.

225

Borrowing money

When you borrow money to buy a capital item, such as a car or a video recorder, you normally have to pay interest. This is calculated as the *annual percentage rate (APR)*. If, for example, you borrowed £1000 at an APR of 20 per cent over one year you would pay back £1200. Look carefully at the APR since it is calculated on the original capital sum borrowed, not on the balance which declines as you pay back the capital.

Discounts

Most traders give discounts for prompt payments, for being 'in the trade' and for bulk purchases. A 5 per cent discount is quite usual. A purchase worth £640 might well attract this sort of discount. To find out what the discount would be, find 5 per cent of £640, which is £32. There is a quick way of doing this in your head:

£640 ÷ 10 = 64 divide by 2 (to bring it to 5 per cent) = 32.

Please do this 108

John Stead has been working hard all day at the market, and now he is back home doing his paper work. He is sure that one of his suppliers has got his figures wrong on an invoice and he is using his calculator, a pencil and paper to work out the figures. He feels that the wholesaler has added in a figure or made some other expensive error. There are only four items, but he is having some difficulty in finding the error.

These are the items that appear on the invoice:
- 288 tins of Wuffer at 23p a tin
- 96 bags of Catbix at £1.25 a bag
- 144 tins of Special Katz at 26p a tin
- 30 kg of Dogbones at 88p a kg.

He is entitled to a discount of 5 per cent for quantity and VAT is payable on all the items at 17.5 per cent.

The wholesaler's figure is £303.56. John thinks it should be £277.78.

1. Work out the figures, showing your working at each stage, and explaining in writing what you are doing. Say who you think has got the figures right.

After that, John feels that nothing much more could go wrong, but he is in for a shock. When he inspects the bags of Catbix, he discovers that a third of them are torn and the contents are spilling out.

2. Work out how many complete bags he has.

His bank statement has arrived covering the previous month. He sees that the account includes a debit for the interest payment of a loan which he has taken out. This payment is £36. The APR is 24 per cent.

3. Calculate the size of the loan. Show your working at every stage and explain what you are doing.

Probability

All business is a risk. People might not want to buy the service which you are providing, despite it being cheap and top quality. What successful business persons have to do is to work out the probability that their venture will (or will not) succeed.

A gambler knows that a coin tossed in the air will come down heads and tails an equal number of times if it is thrown often enough. The probability of it coming down heads at any one throw is 0.5, or, expressed as a ratio, 50:50.

Probabilities are sometimes used in manufacturing industry to predict faulty components. The probability of a fault occurring is often very small. We could take as an example exploding lemonade bottles. Normally there is less than one failure in 100,000, sometimes less than one in a million. If the figure rises above four in 100,000 the manufacturer of the lemonade may have to withdraw 250,000 bottles of lemonade in order to safeguard people against 12 faulty bottles. The chances of there being a defective bottle are usually less than 0.00001 *or* 0.001 per cent *or* 1:100,000.

Please do this 109 ─────────────────

Probabilities are most used in business by insurance companies. A life insurance company will look at your life and decide that it expects you to live to be 73, because that is the average age that people live to. However, if you have lived in the tropics a lot that cuts your life expectancy by 10 per cent; if you smoke 20 cigarettes a day it is cut by another 7.5 per cent; if you are not married that is another 8 per cent cut.

1. What is their estimate of your age at death?

2. What is the probability, according to them, that you will live to be 55?

Show all your workings and explain what you are doing at each stage.

Using a formula

A formula is a way of going about a calculation which can be used again and again to come to an accurate result, even if all the figures are changed.

If, for example, you want to know the percentage of VAT in a bill which just gives an inclusive total figure, you can use a formula:

$$\frac{\text{Rate of VAT}}{\text{VAT rate} + 100} \times \text{Amount spent}$$

Try it on a bill for clothes of £264

$$\frac{17.5}{17.5 + 100} \times £264 = \frac{17.5}{117.5} \times £264 = £39.319 \ (£39.32)$$

Please do this 110

1. Use the formula for calculating the VAT exclusive price of paper worth £276 where the VAT rate is 17.5 per cent

2 Calculate the exclusive price for a ton of lemonade at £190 where the VAT rate is 8 per cent.

There are formulae for calculating many things, including area. The area of a regular quadrangle (a shape in which all the lines are straight and all the angles are right angles) can be calculated using the following formula:

Length × Width = Area

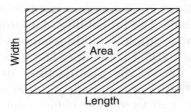

Metric measurements and conversions

At one time about a quarter of the world used the imperial system of measurement and money. Measurement of length was in inches, feet, yards and miles. A metre is roughly equivalent to a yard, and a kilometre is about 0.6 of a mile. Volume used to be measured in cubic inches, feet and yards; money in farthings, halfpennies, pennies, shillings and pounds. In the late 1960s the government decided to 'go metric'. All measurements were converted to the metric system which we use now. This is very much easier to handle.

In practice, there are still a few areas where the imperial system is used. Milk and beer still come in pints and people generally still talk about how many miles a car will do to the gallon. Cars, motorcycles and other vehicles are still equipped with mileometers, but their fuel tanks are rated in litres. You will find conversion tables in your diary. You may need to use them in what follows.

Please do this 111

You work as a clerk in the offices of Snuffling, Snodgrass and Snuffling, solicitors. The present senior partner, who is 78, is the great-grandson of the founder of the business which has been in the same premises since it was started in the mid-nineteenth century. Mr Snuffling asks you to take three parcels and a packet to the post office. They weigh 6lbs 4ozs (ounces), 4lbs 12ozs, 7lbs 15ozs and 12ozs respectively. Post office scales weigh in grams and kilograms.

1. Convert the imperial measurements to metric ones.

The plans of the office say that the senior partner's office is 18 feet by 15 feet.

2. How many square metres of plain carpet tiles will be required to cover it?

Mr Snodgrass boasts that when he took his Rolls Royce to France, he drove from Dunkirk to Nice in a day and used only 36 gallons of petrol. His car does 21 miles per gallon.

3. How far is it from Dunkirk to Nice in kilometres?

Mr Snuffling junior, says that he can drink 3 litres of lager during an evening without any adverse effects.

4. How many pints is that?

The senior clerk, Mr Pickwick, says that the senior partner's office would be much improved by the provision of a semi-circular rug in front of the desk. The desk is 9 feet 10 inches wide. You are told to get the closest fit metric sized rug, but before you buy it, Mr Pickwick wants an estimate of its cost. This is calculated at £34 for each square metre of material. You look blank but he tells you that you may calculate the area of a circle by using the formula $\pi \times r^2$, where π (pronouced pi) = 3.14, r = the radius of the circle, which is half the diameter. The diameter is a straight line touching the circumference at both ends and going through the centre point.

Area = $\pi \times r^2$

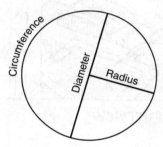

You get out your pencil and paper, draw the carpet, add the dimensions and do the calculations. You think it will cost £240.29.

5 Explain in detail how you got to this figure, (or any other you may calculate) showing all your calculations.

Conducting a survey

Several times during the work you have been asked to do in this book there have been references to surveys. Often these are used to obtain information about the potential of a product in the market place. Before conducting a survey you should make sure that you know exactly what it is you want to know.

Door-to-door interviews

Face-to-face interviews in the street

Telephone interviews

Group interviews

Interviewing is a method of surveying

Surveying a drop-in study centre

The information collected about the use of a drop-in study centre over two weeks enabled a college to close the centre for half the time it had been open and thereby save on staffing. This survey of student use was based simply on how many people were present every 5 minutes throughout the day. A sheet was designed with one column for the time to be entered every five minutes and another one next to it for the number of people present to be entered. This was followed up by a questionnaire given to all users asking whether they would be inconvenienced if the centre was closed at times when there were only two or three people in it.

Please do this 112 ————————————————————————

1. Design an observation sheet for Monday covering the times from 8.45 a.m. to 12.00 p.m.

2. What sort of question would you ask students coming out of the centre about proposed changes to the opening hours? Word the question so that you get a 'yes' or 'no' answer.

One of the reasons why the study centre is not popular is that it is not user-friendly. It has been staffed by part-time teachers who are paid £2 an hour. It might be that the furniture, computers, reference books, lighting or temperature could be improved.

3. Design a questionnaire including open-ended questions like 'What would you improve first in the study centre?' Keep the questions brief and use as few as you can. Normally such a questionnaire would be tried out on a few people first to see if it yielded the information required.

4. Adapt what you have learned to a situation in your school or college where it would be desirable to consult the users. Convert your analysis of the responses to statistics using the graphics which were included in Chapter 13.

Averages

When surveys are conducted and the results analysed they often come up with results which no one recognises. This is because the results are reduced to *averages* or *means*. An average is calculated by adding the numbers in a set of cases together and dividing the result by the number of cases. For example:

Four people are weighed and their weights are recorded as 48 kg, 81 kg, 63 kg, and 71 kg. The four weights are added together and the result is divided by the number of people to find the average: $263 \div 4 = 65.75$ kg.

Another way of doing this, particularly with very large samples of numbers, or if you are in a hurry is to establish the *range*, that is the highest and lowest figure, add them together and divide by two: $\dfrac{48 + 81}{2} = 64.5$. Try this for yourself with people's ages or heights.

15 Information technology

Health, safety and efficient computer use

In the first 12 chapters of this book there have been numerous opportunities for using a computer:
- to present text and graphics,
- to create files,
- to save files,
- to edit and print, and
- to retrieve files that you have created earlier.

Nowadays, computers are present in every educational institution, most businesses and a fair proportion of homes, so it is important that you should be reasonably competent with the keyboard and understand how to use the machine.

The very first thing to do is to make sure that all the equipment you use is properly wired and that the wires do not trail over the floor where people may trip over them. All the plugs must be properly inserted before the electric current is turned on. The machine needs to be mounted on a solidly built table or trolley with a paper store underneath it and a space for a printer. Whatever else happens, the computer must never get wet, nor must it be dropped or pulled by its cables. Computers should never be placed near powerful magnets (like those in loud speakers), nor must they be allowed to become dusty or dirty.

When using a computer you should not normally sit in front of it for more than 40 minutes at a time. You should then take a break and walk about and rest your eyes. These simple precautions can prevent eyestrain and repetitive strain injury (RSI). Avoid carrying a computer any distance unless you have reconnoitred the way first and are accompanied by someone else who can open any doors for you.

If a computer or its printer is not functioning as it should consult the instruction book. If appropriate, switch off the machine and isolate it from the electricity supply. If the problem is not something you can sort out yourself refer it to an expert for help. In a school or college refer the matter to a tutor or a technician. Normally, there is a helpline available; look in the tutorial installed on the hard disk. *Never* use a screwdriver or any other tool on a computer.

If the computer which you are using goes wrong warn other people not to use it. If it is linked into a network which might be disrupted by its malfunction, make sure that it is isolated as quickly as possible. Leave a message taped on the VDU indicating that the machine must not be used before the problem is sorted out.

Do not sit with the keyboard at an uncomfortable angle or height. Make sure that the screen and the keyboard are neither over-lit nor over-reflective. It is equally important that they are not in a place where the lighting is poor, the keyboard inconveniently shaded or the screen too bright. Adjust the level of brightness to suit yourself and your surroundings.

Label each floppy disk clearly and store them in the correct file or box.

Whilst using the computer save your work frequently to ensure that text is not irrevocably damaged or lost. Keep back-up copies of all important material.

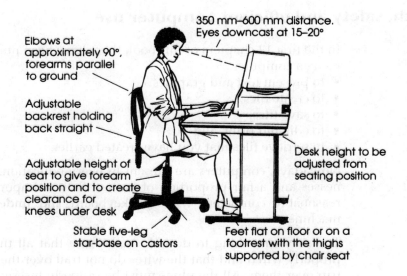

350 mm–600 mm distance.
Eyes downcast at 15–20°

Elbows at approximately 90°, forearms parallel to ground

Adjustable backrest holding back straight

Adjustable height of seat to give forearm position and to create clearance for knees under desk

Stable five-leg star-base on castors

Desk height to be adjusted from seating position

Feet flat on floor or on a footrest with the thighs supported by chair seat

Please do this 113

1. With the assistance of other people in your class, produce a word-processed or DTP check-list of exactly what to watch out for when using a computer from the operational and health and safety points of view. After you have decided what you are going to include do not spend more than 30 minutes on producing your list.

2. Mount the check-list on card and, if possible, cover it with a sheet of laminate.

The stand alone system

This consists of a keyboard and a separate visual display unit (VDU), or screen. Everything which is input via the keyboard goes through the central processing unit (CPU) which contains the disk drive and supplies the information to the printer. The whole set-up is referred to as a *work station*. In lap-top systems it is completely portable. Any stand alone system may be linked to other systems nearby to produce a local area network (LAN), or to systems further away to create a wide area network (WAN). To use a network you have to log on and log off using a personal identification code to get into the system.

Please do this 114

1. Write down as many reasons as you can think of why you should need to log on and off when using a network.

Mainframes

These are the original computers that today's stand alone systems developed from. All that the user sees of a mainframe, which might be 100 or more miles away is a terminal, a VDU and a keyboard. Mainframe computers have a colossal capacity and are capable of processing at lightning speed. However, they cost millions of pounds and it is essential to use the equipment 24 hours a day every day. This means that shift working is usually necessary.

What the words mean

As in the case of every new science or technology there are many acronyms used in the IT industry. Here is a selection of the most important which are in general use with some idea of what they mean and how they are used:

Memory: the number of characters, or bytes, that the computer can store at any one time. This determines the amount of data that can be stored.

Bytes: an average desk-top system will have between 1 and 4 mega bytes of memory: mega means million. A mainframe's capacity may be measured in giga-bytes, giga means 100,000,000.

RAM: random access memory. This is the working memory of the computer which you may access and change at any moment. As it is temporary it must be stored somewhere, usually on the hard disk.

ROM: read only memory. As the name implies this is the memory which can be read, but which cannot be changed. Windows and DOS (disk operating system) are software packages which tell the computer how to operate; they are stored here.

Hard disk: this is contained inside the computer, and you should never need to see it.

Floppy disk: there are two sorts of floppy disk; $5\frac{1}{4}$ inch and $3\frac{1}{2}$ inch. Both of them can be *write protected*. This means that they can be treated to prevent any over-writing of material already on the disk. This is done by moving a plastic plug on the smaller disk and by covering the write protected slot with a piece of paper on the bigger disk.

Format: before using a floppy disk it has to be formatted. This means that a code has to be put on to the disk so that the processor will recognise it. You can buy pre-formatted disks or format your own on your terminal.

Optical disks: these look like CDs. A *CD ROM* can contain an enormous database, up to 250,000 pages, which can be accessed but not altered. Write once read many times, *CD WORM*, are unalterable files. Erasable disks are just like floppies but more expensive.

Peripherals: 'extras' that can be bought and added on to your computer. The most usual one is a *mouse* which is a box with a ball in it which moves the cursor. A *scanner* reads documents and puts the text straight into the computer. A *bar code reader* and a *light pen* are used with bar codes and to put graphics straight on to a computer screen. *Touch sensitive screens* can be used to input data and are often found in hospitals. A *digitiser* converts drawings or photographs into bytes which can be stored.

Looking after disks

Label each one clearly, keep them in a box away from magnetic sources, heat and wet and never touch the recording surface.

Please do this 115 ────────────────────────────────

Try to find and use each of the peripherals mentioned above. Word process an account of what you did with them and present the material which they helped you to create.

Output devices

Once you have put the data into the central processor and on to a disk, you will need to be able to get at it again. If it is on a hard disk, a floppy disk or a CD ROM it can be accessed by bringing the text or graphics on to the VDU. However, only a limited amount of material can be put on the screen at any one time and reading things off a VDU is not ideal.

Data can be output in the form of hard copy using an impact printer. There are several types of printer:
- Dot matrix printers, which make each character up out of a set of dots.
- Daisy wheel printers, which have a wheel with petals, each of which carries one or more characters. Numerous type styles are available and the quality is as good as a good typewriter. The text is better quality than that produced by a dot matrix printer.
- Bubble jet or ink jet printers, which are very high quality and can print text or graphics onto almost any surface. The ink cartridges are very expensive and even refillable ones may mean that a page of type can cost 5p in ink alone.
- Laser printers – these produce the best quality text of all. They work on the same principle as a Xerox machine, transferring an image to a drum which then transfers it to paper. They are very expensive, but office laser printers are one of the best investments that a company can make. They are ideal for text or graphics.

Using a printer

Knowing how to start a printer is one thing, but it is even more important to know how to stop it. This may be via the computer keyboard, or it may entail using the on/off switch on the printer. Unless there is a major crisis always turn ink/bubble jet and laser printers off at the machine and not by turning the electricity supply off at the socket. In the case of bubble jet printers, turning the machine on and off at the machine initiates a cartridge head cleaning routine which ensures perfect printing.

Here are some general rules for using a printer:
- Keep the paper within the guidelines shown on the machine.
- Make sure that it is the weight and quality specified in the maker's instructions.
- If nothing happens make sure the printer is on line.

- Printers should be kept shut at all times and must not be tampered with, even when not connected to the electricity supply.
- If you cannot solve your problem by looking at the instruction manual call for expert help. You may electrocute yourself or destroy an expensive piece of equipment if you do not know what you are doing.

Please do this 116

1. Read the printer instruction book and the part of the computer manual where it talks about printers.

2. Compile a single page A4 checklist on operating the printer safely and efficiently.

3. Print the list out on a printer.

Getting started

The best possible thing that you can do before you use a computer seriously is to have some lessons from an expert. Failing that, read the tutorial material which is included on the computer's hard disk and the tutorial booklet which accompanies the computer. Do not worry if you cannot remember how to use every single function on the computer. Make sure you are comfortable with straightforward operations first, and then build on your existing expertise as you need to.

Please do this 117

By pressing each key and using the instruction handbook, try to identify what every key on the keyboard does. Start at the top left corner and compile a handbook of uses for each key. Leave the 'Control' key to the last as it has so many functions.

Word-processing

This is by far the most common use for computing equipment nowadays. Word-processing packages are all different, but perform more or less the same functions.

Please do this 118

1. Word process a document which tells the reader exactly how to go about the following:

   a Putting a letter from you to your aunt about your summer holiday, on the screen, and printing it.

   b Taking out a block of the type and transferring it to a letter which you are writing to your friend in New Zealand.

   c Removing a block of type from the text altogether.

d Underlining words and making them bold.

e Checking the spelling of a piece of text.

f Finding a word or symbol in the text.

g Retrieving a file from the memory and then deleting it.

h Converting a block of type from lower case to CAPITALS.

Business packages

Your computer will probably have;
- a word-processing package,
- a database, for keeping records of people like customers and suppliers,
- a graphics package for creating art work for posters and desk-top publishing, and
- a spreadsheet package which enables all the financial variables in a situation to interact.

Please do this 119

Look through all the packages which are installed on your computer and produce printouts from each showing that you understand how to use them.

Proof-reading

Before you print you should check the data on the screen for accuracy of spelling and grammar. One of the easiest ways of checking your spelling is to run a spell check. Of course the computer will hesitate at proper names etc. but you can by-pass these. It is important to remember that a spell check does not invariably pick up every mistake and you must always proof-read your work as well. Whenever possible get someone else to read it for you afterwards.

The law

Every piece of data which is kept in a computer or on a disk is subject to the Data Protection Act 1984. A company which stores data about anyone in a computer must register with the Data Protection Registrar. No personal data may be disclosed to others unless it is for a use which is compatible with the original (legal) acquisition and use. The information must be the minimum required to fulfil the purpose for which it is designed. It must be kept secure and should be erased when no longer of use. It is possible to find out what is held on any company's files by looking them up on the Data Protection Register (available in public libraries) and writing to the data holder to ask what information is held on you. There are exceptions to this; MI5, MI6, the Inland Revenue, the Department of Social Security and the Social Services Department are not obliged to disclose what is on their files. Whilst the holder may not withhold information there is often a charge for supplying it.

Glossary

Below are some terms that you may find useful to have defined before you begin to look at the chapters. You can come back to these as and when you need to clarify something. The terms relate both to the GNVQ syllabus structure and to the content of the GNVQ Intermediate Business.

Acronym A name made up from the first letters of a series of words, thus the North Atlantic Treaty Organisation is better known as NATO. Some are clever and have hidden meanings; for example, the assistant chief executives are not called ACEs for nothing.

Assessor Probably your teacher, but could be another expert in a particular part of the programme. She or he provides correction and guidance for you.

BS 5750 A British Standards Institute Standard which is aimed at ensuring and proving that at every stage in a business there are mechanisms in place for ensuring efficiency and good communication.

Bureaucracy As an organisation grows there is differentiation of labour and a consequent need for improved internal communications and the standardisation of procedures. At its worst this may rely on vast quantities of form filling.

Chief executive The senior manager in an organisation who may also be a member of the board of directors and have a title like managing director. In a school it is the headteacher; in a college it is the principal.

Corporate aims Also called mission statements. What the organisation wishes to do, but not, usually, how it is going to go about doing it.

Economies of scale The bigger the better. A very large company still has only one managing director and it can afford effective marketing apparatus within its own hierarchy. For example, it can buy in bulk at considerable savings and therefore sell on more cheaply than its competitors (in theory anyway).

Element A part of a unit. Rather like a chapter in a book, and treated like that here.

External verifier A person who visits your teachers on behalf of the awarding body (BTEC, CGLI, RSA) to ensure that quality control mechanisms to guarantee standards are in place and working effectively.

Hidden agenda The 'hidden' purpose behind an activity which ostensibly has another aim. Making you write a report has the principal aim of putting down information, drawing conclusions and making recommendations. It also checks your ability to spell, to think constructively and to write clearly.

Hierarchy, hierarchical A system for differentiating by layers the importance of people's status within an organisation, and perhaps also the lines of authority and even communication.

Internal verifier The person who is responsible for seeing that all the assessments of your (and other people's) work are at the right level.

Limited company An enterprise owned by a number of people who have shares in the company. Their liability, and also their income, is determined by the proportion of the shares that they own. Ltd after a company name means that it is a private limited company and whilst it may be possible to buy shares these are not generally traded for the benefit of the public. Many limited companies remain family firms.

Mandatory If something is mandatory you have to do it.

Market force economics An idea based on the assumption that what people want is the best guide to the provision of services or goods.

Monopoly An organisation which has more than 25 per cent of the market share. Some notable monopolies include the water and electricity companies, British Telecom and the gas industry. The problem for the consumer is that the monopolist has a strangle hold on supply and can dictate prices and quality. The problem for the monopolist is that the organisation has little motivation to improve until someone else is able to move in on it when it may quickly collapse.

Multi-media A term usually used in connection with the promotion of goods and services. Refers to newspapers, periodicals, radio, television, posters, cinemas and mail shots. Also used to refer to products, such as CD ROMs, which combine various media (text, sound, video) within one format.

Multi-national companies Companies with subsidiaries all over the world. DuPont is an example: DuPont plc in the UK, DuPont SA (societe anonyme) in France; DuPont Inc in the USA and so on throughout the world.

National insurance A compulsory levy from all wage earners and salaried staff guaranteeing them access to benefits, the principal among which is the state pension.

Partnership A group of people, usually less than 20, who own a business, not always in totally equal shares.

Performance criterion What you have to be able to do, and prove that you can do, as an essential part of an element.

Plc Public limited company. The limitation on shareholders' liabilities remains, but the shares are traded on the stock exchange and are generally available to anyone who wishes to buy them.

Portfolio The collection of your work, each part of it indicating which unit, element and performance criterion it covers, carefully filed, and having been assessed. Kept ready for the internal and external verifiers.

Profit The difference between the costs of providing goods and services and the income received. Not always easy to achieve.

Quality circles A system by which those who do jobs meet and discuss how, why and often when, and make recommendations on the improvement of their activities for the benefit of the company.

Range The background against which each performance criterion is set.

Redundant A person becomes redundant when his or her employer considers there is no longer a job for him or her owing to changes in the market or practices within the company.

Skills These are the same for any area of study, but to be successful in demonstrating that you have achieved them they have to be provided with a setting which is relevant to your programme (in this case Business).

Sole trader A person who owns and is totally responsible for a business. He or she may employ many people, but it is the responsibility and ownership which is important.

Stock exchange A place where shares in businesses may be bought and sold.

Turnover What a company makes in money by its activities, usually during a year.

Unit A part of a qualification which may be certificated separately.

Unit 1 test: Business organisations and employment

Try to do this test in one hour without any distractions or interruptions. The practice will stand you in good stead for the external tests.

Business organisations

1. The letters plc after a company name indicate that the company:

    a is owned by a multi-national

    b has its shares sold on the stock exchange

    c directors must own 60 per cent of the shares

    d shareholders have unlimited liability.

2. The maximum number of partners there can be in a trading partnership is:

    a five

    b fifteen

    c twenty

    d no limit.

3. A limited company is owned by:

    a the directors

    b debenture holders

    c shareholders

    d stockbrokers.

4. A sole trader:

    a does not employ anyone else

    b is liable for all debts

    c can open the business for trading at any time

    d can sell shares to anyone.

5. The principal objective of a public sector organisation is to:

    a provide dividends for shareholders

    b provide employment

    c provide a service for the public

    d make a profit.

6. A public sector organisation:

   a must lose money

   b is owned by the government

   c has registered shareholders

   d can operate only in England.

Industrial sectors

7. Someone employed in the primary sector of industry would work:

   a in a dock

   b at an airport

   c in a quarry

   d in a supermarket.

8. Which organisation is in the primary sector of industry:

   a Ford Motor Company

   b British Coal

   c Lloyds Bank plc

   d National Health Service.

9. The secondary sector provides:

   a coal, iron and steel

   b services to industry

   c life assurance

   d manufactured goods.

10. A tertiary sector organisation's role is to provide:

   a roofing slates

   b property insurance

   c car parts for manufacturers

   d equipment for the armed forces.

Business locations

11. A multi-national company:

   a has to have foreigners on its board of directors

   b has branches or factories in several countries

   c must issue shares in every country in which it trades

d has a monopoly in its area of operation.

12. Japanese motorcycle manufacturers have the major market share in the UK.

    Market share is measured by:

    a the quality of the products

    b the number of motorcycles sold

    c the number of employees

    d the low prices of the products.

Questions 13–15 share answer options **a** to **d**.

William and Mary want to start up a hotel. They consider the following sites:

 a city centre

 b seaside resort

 c a green field close to a motorway junction

 d a rural village.

Which site would best suit the following?

13. Bed and breakfast

14. Conference accommodation

15. Commercial representatives

16. Rudge Whitworth Ltd manufactures car and motorcycle parts. The company is looking for a new location. The company has limited resources and employs about 250 production workers.

    Which of the following locations would be most suitable for the company:

    a one with a low unemployment rate where the local industry is distilling whisky

    b a seaside resort with high seasonal unemployment

    c one with a high unemployment rate and government incentives for industries new to the area

    d a rural site 20 miles from the nearest large town.

17. Which business is not tied to a certain type of location?

    a a dairy farmer

    b a slate quarry

    c a mail order clothing supplier

    d a tuna fisherman.

Products

18. A travel agent sells a lot of cut-price holidays abroad. Which nearby shop may sell more products as a result?

    a furniture supplier

    b stationers

    c leisure wear

    d jeweller.

19. Which of the following is a manufactured product?

    a potatoes

    b domestic gas

    c whisky

    d life insurance.

20. JKX Garments manufactures clothes. A new product takes three months to reach the shops.

Which product should JKX start developing in July?

    a swimwear

    b spring fashions

    c thermal underwear

    d tennis clothes.

Employment

21. Net wages are:

    a extra pay earned as commission

    b bonuses

    c total earnings less deductions

    d total amount earned.

22. The PAYE system:

    a enables employers to deduct tax from wages

    b applies to all those receiving money

    c enables employees to save money

    d does not differentiate between the low-paid and the high-paid.

23. Which of the following is a fringe benefit of a job?

    a National insurance

b overtime pay

c superannuation

d a free work place creche.

Questions 24 – 26 share answer options **a** to **d**.

Mary and Fred make leather sports clothes. They have usually supplied retailers but propose to supply direct through mail order and from stalls at shows. They employ Charles and Susan on a commission basis to travel to shows as they occur. Abbie and Peter are fully employed running the office and packing the mail orders.

The following are types of employment:

    a self-employed

    b full-time

    c part-time

    d temporary.

Which type of employment applies to:

24. Mary

25. Susan

26. Alice

Technology and employment

Questions 27 and 28 relate to the same company.

When Imperial Producers Ltd introduced personal computers into their finance department

27. Some staff were likely to be unhappy about this because:

    a efficiency was reduced

    b costs were increased

    c they feared that there would be job losses

    d on-the-job training was reduced.

28. Following the introduction of the new computer network, staff immediately needed:

    a to transfer to another department

    b retraining

    c information on financial procedures

    d an explanation from the personnel director.

29. More people now work from home, rather than in an office.

For those working from home the principal benefit of telecommunications is:

a lack of interruptions by colleagues

b no one knows if they are working or not

c they can communicate instantly with their office whenever they need to

d phone bills are paid by the employers.

30. After using a computer for long periods staff may suffer from repetitive strain injury. What helps to prevent this?

a safety lights

b change of keyboard

c pre-programmed breaks

d air conditioning.

Unit 2 test: People in business organisations

Try to do this test in one hour without any distractions or interruptions. The practice will stand you in good stead for the external tests.

Organisation structures

1. In a flat organisation structure:

    a everyone knows what everyone else is doing

    b there are easy to use lines of communication

    c there are few rules

    d there is little opportunity for promotion.

2. In a hierarchical structure, there are:

    a poorly defined lines of authority

    b very few line managers

    c clearly defined lines of communication

    d no subordinates.

3. An organisation chart shows:

    a the conditions of employment

    b the pay scales of employees

    c reporting relationships

    d which offices employees occupy.

4. A successful manager working in a large organisation with a hierarchical structure is most likely to have:

    a a substantial knowledge of one business function

    b a wide range of skills and knowledge

    c worked in the same company all his career

    d a large number of assistant managers.

5. Hierarchical organisations have:

    a high levels of specialisation

    b easy access to the management

    c small salary differentials

    d democratic decision making built in.

Functions in business organisations

6. In order to create the right product the design team needs information from:

    a the personnel department

    b the production department

    c the administration department

    d the marketing department.

Questions 7–9 share answer options **a** to **d**.

A company has the following departments within its organisation:

    a finance

    b research and development

    c personnel

    d production.

Which of the above would carry out the following functions?

7. Paying suppliers

8. Manufacturing goods

9. Recruiting and training staff.

Job roles/functions

Questions 10–12 share answer options **a** to **d**.

The following are roles in a business organisation:

    a manager

    b director

    c team member

    d administrator.

Which of the above would carry out the following?

10. Supervise the activities of one section of the organisation

11. Be most closely involved with the products

12. Oversee the running of the organisation.

13. The personnel department:

    a pays staff

   b helps with product research and development

   c recruits staff

   d enforces rules and regulations within the company.

14. The finance department:

   a sets financial targets

   b establishes product prices

   c prepares monthly income and expenditure statements

   d audits the company accounts.

15. The research and development department:

   a advertises new products

   b makes staff redundant

   c explores the scientific background of new products

   d designs new products.

Job roles/tasks

16. A good team leader should:

   a take over team decisions

   b have no part in team decisions

   c make decisions for the team

   d include members of the team in making decisions.

17. Quality assurance is wholly the responsibility of:

   a the production manager

   b the research and development manager

   c everyone in the organisation

   d the senior management.

Questions 18–20 share answer options **a** to **d**.

The following roles exist in many companies:

   a company accountant

   b production manager

   c personnel director

   d marketing manager.

Which of the above would have responsibility for:

18. Setting quality targets for the products

19. Sealing with a redundancy problem

20. Ensuring there is an effective sales team.

21. It is the responsibility of the manager of a distribution department to ensure that:

    a sales targets are met

    b items purchased by the company are available when needed

    c customers receive goods they have ordered on time

    d goods are available throughout the world.

Legislation

22. The principal advantage of a contract of employment is that it:

    a has the employer's signature on it

    b is not subject to any changes

    c clearly describes the employee's rights and responsibilities

    d prevents dismissal.

23. If you are subject to a disciplinary hearing you must:

    a be given 24 hours notice of the meeting

    b not involve any other employee

    c have written details of the reason for attendance

    d do exactly what you are told.

24. An employer may impose an effective ban on smoking in the workplace because:

    a he objects to the tax on tobacco

    b he is a non-smoker

    c smoking wastes time and the cleaners complain about the ash

    d he is required to provide a healthy working environment.

25. A VDU operator must have:

    a special training

    b protective spectacles

    c an increase in pay

    d regular breaks away from the work station.

26. Your colleague comes from Bengal. Which of these organisations is concerned to see that she is not discriminated against:

   a the local authority ombudsman

   b an industrial tribunal

   c the Health and Safety Executive

   d the Equal Opportunities Commission.

27. Which of these safety measures must be provided in a public building?

   a floodlights

   b secondary lighting

   c reflective glass VDU screens

   d alarm buttons.

Rights and responsibilities of employees

28. Any employee has the right to:

   a belong to a trade union

   b have another job in his or her spare time

   c leave an employment at any time

   d receive a contract of employment.

29. An employee starts work for the first time at 7.30 a.m. on Tuesday and is at once required to mix cement using a shovel. The employee has no protective clothing. Who is responsible under the Health and Safety at Work Act:

   a the employee and supervisor

   b the employer and supervisor

   c the employer

   d the employer and employee.

30. Employees have a legal right to know:

   a their basic rate of pay

   b their basic rate of pay and frequency of payment

   c their basic rate of pay, bonuses and overtime rate

   d their basic rate of pay and place of work.

31. An employee may be dismissed on the spot for one of the following:

   a late arrival at work

   b clocking in for another employee

c swearing at a colleague

d sexually harassing a colleague.

Rights and responsibilities of employers

32. An employer must provide statutory sick pay if an employee is away from work sick for:

    a any three days in one week

    b more than three consecutive days

    c more than four consecutive days

    d two days.

33. Health and safety at work legislation requires an employer in a large organisation to provide:

    a private health insurance

    b qualified medical personnel on the premises

    c first aid facilities

    d regular medical check-ups.

34. An employer who wishes to alter an employees conditions of work may do so if:

    a it is necessary to improve profitability

    b it is necessary to reduce the number of employees

    c the employee agrees

    d it is necessary to increase productivity.

35. An employer may legally:

    a dismiss an employee without warning if he or she wishes

    b reduce an employee's pay without notice if profitability is low

    c dismiss an employee if his or her contract is ended

    d dismiss an employee if the employee has attended a union meeting.

36. An employer must ensure that:

    a all absences are recorded

    b all accidents at work are recorded

    c the next of kin of all employees are listed

    d no one under the age of 16 is employed.

37. Disciplinary procedures may:

a always indicate that the employee was in the wrong

b require oral and written warnings before dismissal

c inevitably lead to dismissal

d necessarily result in a reduction of wages.

Unit 3 test: Consumers and customers

Try to do this test in one hour without any distractions or interruptions. The practice will stand you in good stead for the external tests.

Characteristics of consumers

1. Which of these is most likely to cause an increased demand for video recorders?

   a a rise in the VAT rate

   b a rise in the cost of living

   c a rise in average incomes

   d a rise in interest rates.

2. Consultants are advising on the site for a new hypermarket. What information would be most useful?

   a cost of living

   b average incomes

   c size of population

   d rate of unemployment.

3. What information about the population of an area would be most useful to a new sports centre?

   a nationality

   b religion

   c lifestyle

   d gender.

4. Which factor is likely to have most influence on the demand for houses:

   a rising mortgage rates

   b labour costs

   c population growth

   d price of land.

5. Which of the following is most likely to go on a six month world package tour:

   a a student immediately before going to university

   b a recently retired solicitor

    c a retail sales manager

    d a single parent with two children under five years.

6. Which of these is a definition of gross income?

    a the amount of money left after paying income tax

    b the amount of money which can be spent on consumer goods

    c the amount of money people earn

    d the amount of money left after paying living expenses.

Promotional methods and resources

7. Sales and profits are declining. Should you:

    a cut the advertising budget

    b close the marketing department

    c increase the amount spent on advertising

    d wait for an up-turn in the economy?

8. Which of these is responsible for regulating advertising on television?

    a local authorities

    b central government

    c Advertising Standards Authority

    d Independent Television Commission.

9. Having just perfected his electric roller skates which he is going to produce in a small factory, Harry wishes to choose the most cost effective way to promote sales. Should he choose to:

    a advertise in a magazine for young people

    b distribute hand bills door-to-door in the town

    c advertise in newspapers

    d produce a video tape.

10. Which of the following would bring most effective attention to a new T-shirt design?

    a a local poster campaign

    b local cinema advertising

    c a one day exhibition

    d advertising on national television.

11. The illustration in an advertisement is usually the responsibility of a:

    a campaign manager

    b copywriter

    c sales representative

    d graphic designer.

12. Sponsorship of a leading athlete would be good method of promoting branded sportswear because:

    a the sponsor can guarantee success

    b it will be cheap

    c the company image is improved if the athlete is successful

    d it is always cost effective.

Objectives and constraints for promotional material

13. A sales promotion:

    a is a short-term offer to increase sales

    b creates a demand for a new product

    c builds the image of the company name

    d is a means of employing more staff in the sales department.

14. A complaint under the Trade Descriptions Act would be investigated by:

    a the police

    b a private enquiry agent

    c consumer standards officers

    d the Director of Fair Trading.

15. A multi-national chemical company uses television advertisements to show its range of activities, including its concern for the environment.

    The most likely aim of the campaign is to:

    a give vital information to chemical consumers

    b create more awareness of the environment

    c promote sales of a specific chemical

    d create a favourable company image.

16. Torens Trusty Insurance is falsely claiming, during its summer promotion, that all its policies have a 25 per cent reduction on normal prices.

    The promotion is:

    a perfectly legal and widely used in the UK

b legal because the company is foreign owned

c illegal under the Consumer Protection Act

d illegal under the Sale of Goods Act.

17. Which type of advertisement is most suitable for a local hardware shop to promote a special offer?

   a a trade magazine

   b nationwide television

   c a mail shot

   d a neighbourhood newspaper.

Provide customer service

18. Which would be used by a major chain of grocers to promote special offers?

   a door-to-door leaflets

   b advertising in local newspapers

   c advertising on television

   d sponsoring local events.

19. Retail shops improve services to customers in order to:

   a improve security

   b win competitions

   c increase sales by a more helpful image

   d reduce loss of stock.

20. Which would be most likely to promote the image of a national company?

   a local commercial radio advertising

   b money-off coupons

   c local newspaper advertising

   d sports sponsorship.

21. You work on your company enquiry line. A customer rings with a detailed problem when most of the staff are out of the office. You cannot answer the enquiry. What is the best thing to do?

   a find some sales literature and read the details over the phone

   b tell the customer that the company no longer stocks that product

   c ask the caller to hold the line while you try to find someone to answer the question

d write down the customer's details and get a salesperson to call them back.

22. Customers may prefer to use a large supermarket rather than a smaller local shop because of:

    a personal service

    b own brand products

    c involves a journey

    d lower prices?

Investigating customer services

23. Which of the following organisations does not work to a Citizen's Charter?

    a Intercity East Coast

    b Co-operative Wholesale Society

    c Bedford Hospital Trust

    d British Airways.

24. Which of the following services is usually provided by a public sector organisation?

    a life assurance

    b domestic mortgages

    c education

    d commercial banking.

25. A car manufacturer works closely with its main customers, the fleet car buyers, when designing and producing new cars.

    The main advantage for the car company is that they:

    a reduce the cost of customer relations

    b invest more in customer relations

    c increase customer satisfaction with new cars

    d increase the cost of producing new cars.

26. In order to improve the quality of its service to its customers a motor-cycle dealer can provide:

    a free refreshments in the sales area

    b better advertising of the machines

    c friendly staff

    d after sales checks on the machines.

27. Customer satisfaction leads to:

    a increased sales

    b lower prices

    c higher prices

    d rapid changes in products.

28. Which of these objectives aimed at improving customer satisfaction can be measured accurately?

    a training staff

    b decrease in prices of 10 per cent

    c decrease in complaints of 10 per cent

    d improving the quality of the product.

Customer protection

29. In which of the following circumstances can the purchaser of a pair of wellington boots demand a refund?

    a colour not liked

    b not waterproof

    c style not liked

    d now being sold at a lower price.

30. To which of the following would you complain if you had received poor treatment from your local council?

    a The Department of the Environment

    b the local government ombudsman

    c The Citizen's Advice Bureau

    d The Audit Office.

31. The Citizen's Charter exists to:

    a provide a complaints procedure for MPs

    b set a standard of service for public sector organisations

    c explain how the community should treat the individual

    d provide opportunities to complain about MPs.

32. A company which sold goods which had undisclosed faults in them would be in breach of:

    a rules established by the Consumers Association

    b health and safety legislation

    c Citizen's Charter rules

    d consumer protection legislation.

33. Mrs Smith's hair dryer did not work when she got it home. What are her legal rights?

    a to receive her money back

    b to return it to the manufacturer for a free repair

    c to get the retailer to return it to the manufacturer for repair

    d to get the retailer to pay for the repair.

Answers to review questions

Chapter 1	Chapter 2	Chapter 3	Chapter 4
1 a	**1** b	**1** c	**1** c
2 c	**2** c	**2** c	**2** d
3 a	**3** c	**3** c	**3** c
4 b	**4** c	**4** b	**4** d
5 c	**5** b	**5** b	**5** c
6 a	**6** d	**6** c	**6** a
7 d	**7** c	**7** c	**7** d
8 c	**8** d	**8** b	**8** b
9 c	**9** c	**9** c	**9** a
10 a	**10** c	**10** c	**10** b

Chapter 5	Chapter 6	Chapter 7	Chapter 8
1 b	**1** a	**1** a	**1** d
2 a	**2** c	**2** d	**2** d
3 a	**3** c	**3** d	**3** d
4 b	**4** c	**4** c	**4** d
5 d	**5** a	**5** d	**5** a
6 c	**6** c	**6** c	**6** a
7 c	**7** d	**7** d	**7** b
8 a	**8** d		**8** c
9 c	**9** c		**9** c
			10 a

Chapter 9	Chapter 10	Chapter 11	Chapter 12
1 d	**1** c	**1** b	**1** a
2 b	**2** c	**2** c	**2** a
3 a	**3** c	**3** b	**3** d
4 a	**4** c	**4** b	**4** d
5 c	**5** d	**5** c	**5** b
6 a	**6** d	**6** b	**6** c
7 c	**7** d	**7** b	**7** b
8 b	**8** c	**8** b	**8** d
9 c	**9** a	**9** c	**9** d
10 b	**10** b	**10** c	**10** a

Index